Minding *the* *South*

Minding the South

John Shelton Reed

Transaction Publishers

New Brunswick (U.S.A.) and London (U.K.)

Published in 2014 by Transaction Publishers, New Brunswick, New Jersey. Originally published in 2003 by University of Missouri Press. Copyright © 2003 by The Curators of the University of Missouri.

This book is printed on acid-free paper that meets the American National Standard for Permanence of Paper for Printed Library Materials.

Library of Congress Catalog Number: 2013003505
ISBN: 978-1-4128-5252-4
Printed in the United States of America

Library of Congress Cataloging-in-Publication Data

Reed, John Shelton.
Minding the South / John Shelton Reed; with a new introduction by the author.
    pages cm
    "Originally published in 2003 by the University of Missouri Press"--Title page verso.
    Includes bibliographical references.
    ISBN 978-1-4128-5252-4 (acid-free paper)
        1.   Southern States--Civilization. 2.   Southern States--Social life and customs. 3.   Southern States--History. 4.   Southern States--Historiography.
    I. Title.
F209.R435 2013
975--dc23
                                                                    2013003505

In memory of
Eugene D. Genovese (1930–2012),
C. Vann Woodward (1908–1999),
and M. E. Bradford (1934–1993)

Contents

Introduction to the Transaction Edition   1

Preface   5

The Three Souths   9

I. The Journalistic Eye   23

     The Mind of the South and Southern Distinctiveness   25

     The *Times* Looks at Dixie   37

     Among the Believers   45

     The Secret History of Civil Rights   49

     The Smoke Never Clears   55

     One Tough Lady   59

     A South That Never Was   63

II. History and Historians   67

     American Weed   69

     Slaves View Slavery   71

     Slipshod Totalitarianism   77

     Southern Intellect   81

     Southern Studies Abroad   89

III. Friends and Masters   91

    C. Vann Woodward   93

    Eugene D. Genovese   97

    M. E. Bradford   101

IV. What They Say about Dixie   105

    Of Collard Greens and Kings   107

    Red and Yellow, Black and White   111

    Telling about the South   115

    The Imagined South   119

V. Six Southerners   123

    Lady Propagandist of the Old South   125

    The Man from New Orleans   131

    The World's Best-Selling Novelist   137

    Mover and Shaker   141

    Hardy Perennial   149

    The Southern Elvis   155

    The End of Elvis   169

VI. Southern Culture, High and Low   175

    Southern Laughter   177

    A Cokelorist at Work   185

    The National Magazine of the South   191

    Carolina Couch Crime   195

VII. Southern Lit (and One Movie)   199

    Taking a Stand   201

    Portrait of Atlanta   205

    Nebbish from Mississippi   211

    Hollywood Chain Gangs   215

VIII. Reflections   219

    The Banner That Won't Stay Furled   221

    The Most Southern State?   239

    Brits and Grits   245

    Missing   249

    He's Baaack   253

    If at First You Don't Secede . . .   257

    Party Down   263

    Our Kind of Yankee   267

IX. But Let's Talk about Me   273

    Mixing in the Mountains   275

    Among the Baptists   285

    Choosing the South   297

Sources   307

Introduction to the Transaction Edition

Some authors finish their books and don't look back. But others would constantly revise them if they could, and I fall in that camp. From time to time, I take up one of my old books and find that the ratio of "Hey, this is all right" to "Good Lord, did I really write that?" is changing inexorably for the worse. If the words weren't irrevocably in print, I'd still be editing books from the 1970s. (E-books may make that possible, which I'm not sure is a wholly good thing.)

As I said in this book's original preface, when I collected these essays and reviews, I tinkered with them a bit. Now I have yet another opportunity, but this time I haven't really seized it. I fear that if I started fiddling with things, Transaction Publishers might change its mind about the new edition before I stopped. So I've just corrected a couple of trivial errors and changed the book's dedication to reflect the fact that Eugene Genovese has now uncharacteristically joined the majority (a sad fact for his friends, though not, I think, for him). Otherwise I've pretty much let stand what I published a decade ago. Many passages I'd like to reword, sentences and paragraphs I'd like to rearrange, but . . . *stet*. There are only a few really substantive changes I'd make if I were starting over, and I'll just use this introduction to mention a few of them.

Some would be occasioned by what I've learned since 2003. For instance, my review of some books about William Spratling didn't mention that he was the model for a character in William Faulkner's novel *Mosquitoes* because I didn't know that. Since then, though, I've learned that and a great deal more about Spratling and his New Orleans friends—so much, in fact, that I've written a book about them. (You can read *Dixie Bohemia: A French Quarter Circle in the 1920s* if you care.)

1

I've also learned where Tom Wolfe got his title for *A Man in Full*. My review mentions Wolfe's penchant for slipping sly little jokes into his books, like a character named Ulrich B. "Eubie" Honeyshuck, whose name alludes to an eminent historian of the Old South. "If you didn't catch it don't worry," I wrote. "Lord knows what *I* missed." Well, one thing I missed was a bawdy folk song that Zora Neale Hurston collected for the WPA in the 1930s. It's about Uncle Bud, "a man in full, [whose] nuts hung down like a Georgia bull." (Miss Hurston sang it for a Library of Congress recording that can be heard on the Internet.) I wish I'd known about that earlier.

Similarly, discussing Senator Strom Thurmond's reputation as a lothario, I mentioned that "there are these *stories* about him." Sure enough, shortly after he died in 2003—and shortly after *Minding the South* went to press—his illegitimate, mixed-race daughter, Essie Mae Washington-Williams, broke her seventy-year silence about her paternity. That was one of the stories. Thurmond had stayed in communication with his daughter and helped her and her family financially; his staff and, it seems, his white family knew of the relationship; but he never publicly acknowledged her. Few would have predicted the denouement, in which Ms. Washington-Williams met with her half-siblings, the South Carolina General Assembly added her name to those of the senator's four other children on the base of his statue, and after her death in 2013 the South Carolina Senate unanimously approved a request by her half-brother, Republican State Senator Paul Thurmond, that it adjourn in her memory.

As that suggests, recent years have also seen a great many changes not just in the extent of my ignorance but in the South itself. Of course, some things haven't changed at all: Richard Ford and Florence King still do what they do, the Confederate battle flag is still provocative, Louisa McCord is still unknown, Elvis is still dead. And it's true that some changes have simply been reversions to historical norms. (Today's bitter red state-blue state division, for example, is nothing new; the post 9/11 interlude of national unity that one of these essays discusses is what was unusual.) But, gracious, a lot of what we're now seeing is completely unprecedented. That's the second reason I'd like to have made a few additions to some of these pieces: to slip something into them that would let me pretend that I saw this stuff coming.

In my review of *Life at Southern Living* I quoted that magazine's editor, who characterized his product as "simple, square, and straightforward." I called it "anodyne," and I'd argue that it still is studiedly uncontroversial and goes to great lengths not to upset its readers. Which makes it interesting that these days those readers are apparently not startled by recipes for Kwanzaa and an article about a couple of young men who share a house and a fabulous Christmas ornament collection.

Another magazine, *Garden & Gun*, is even more strikingly new. Like *Southern Living*, it is unapologetically Southern, but with a deliberately provocative name and content that runs to seventy-dollar secateurs, high-toned locavore chefs, Billy Reid clothing, and Purdey shotguns—all that, and writing good enough to win a 2011 Award for General Excellence from the American Society of Magazine Editors. Founded in 2007, it exemplifies and serves an emerging South still unfamiliar to many Southerners, still unrecognized by most non-Southerners, and unimaginable by anyone fifty years ago. My review of Peter Applebome's *Dixie Rising* commends Applebome for observing that the country-music group BR-549 took its name from a Junior Samples routine on "Hee Haw," and asks, "How's *that* for a postmodern lick?" Well, try this one: *Garden & Gun* got its name from a gay bar in Charleston.

All this buzz and whirl makes me dizzy, and I suspect I'm not alone. That's one reason I seem to be writing more and more about the South's history. It's not true that history doesn't change, but it changes *slowly*.

Of the future—well, as Junior Samples used to say, "I don't know nothing, but I suspect a lot." (I suspect, for example, that fifty years from now our cookbooks will be treating cilantro as an Old Southern foodstuff.) But I wrote once that if I were any good at prophecy, I'd be living off my investments somewhere. In one of these essays I've quoted W. J. Cash, writing in *The Mind of the South*: "Of the future I shall venture no definite prophecies." And I called Cash wise.

Preface

The essays and reviews collected here reflect the variety of publications and occasions for which they were written, but they are all about "minding" the South, in one sense of the word or another. If you think of minding as a process, for instance, like (say) salting or seeding—spreading minds around—well, here is a sprinkling of minds. The South has produced or attracted a great many interesting ones, but many are not well known as they should be. I hope readers of this book will encounter at least one or two thinkers that they will be glad to have met.

And "minding" has other, more familiar, meanings. Many of those thinkers have themselves minded the South, in the sense of watching it, even tending it—and a few have minded it in yet another way: they have been distressed by it. The South-minders in this book (as outside it, no doubt) are mostly Southerners themselves, but some come from elsewhere, from all over the United States and Europe, as well as Trinidad and Korea. Surely I am not the only Southerner who wants to know whether they got it right.

In short, most of these chapters look at people looking at the South. A couple of them, in the section "What They Say about Dixie," even look at people looking at people looking at the South, which is getting pretty rarified. But the South is not the only thing Southerners think about. A few chapters here examine Southerners who have devoted their minds and talents to different subjects altogether, from politics to soft drinks, rock and roll to the design of silver jewelry.

In addition, minding the South—in the watching sense—is something I have been up to for thirty-odd years myself. In fact I have been accused of having no unpublished thoughts on the subject, but some of these chapters contain observations that at least haven't been published in a book before. In any case, my sales figures suggest that not many people will recognize any repetition and at least I have tried to say it differently. And there do always seem to be new things to say about the South. New issues and problems keep arising; if nothing else, some of what I said thirty years ago needs (not so much retraction as) qualification.

Finally, a word about the last three entries: They are the most explicitly autobiographical part of this book—indeed, of any of my books. In the essays I confess something of my embarrassment at this immodesty, and I reiterate it here. But I have included them in this collection because I hope a few selected aspects of my life will illustrate or direct attention to more general themes, of greater interest.

That many of these pieces are about history, or historians, may seem odd given the fact that I never studied Southern history, if that means taking courses in it. Indeed, I could probably serve as a sort of Southern history poster child: "Study Southern history or you'll end up like this." "You can teach him Southern history, or you can turn the page." My interest has always been less in the South's history itself than in Southerners' present-day culture and consciousness. But I study the South historically because that's the only way it makes sense. Rupert Vance, my predecessor in the sociology department at Chapel Hill and a dab hand at writing Southern history himself, once observed that the very existence of the South is a triumph of history over geography and economics. What holds the South together in the face of the centrifugal forces that are always trying to tear it into smaller subregions, and what holds it apart from the larger US society with its great leveling, assimilative power, is the South's distinctive history—that, and the distinctive culture that history has produced and reflected.

Anyway, Southerners have never been much impressed by mere credentials, and they have kindly not held my lack of them against me. Certainly, I have *read* a lot of Southern history and in that sense I've studied it, with mixed pleasure and dismay, but almost always with profit. Some of what I've read is discussed in this book.

I thought about subtitling this book "Essays and Reviews, 1973–2003." That has a nice magisterial ring to it, but in truth only three of these pieces date from before 1985, and more than half were written after 1993. Most were written in response to the ordinary duties and opportunities of late-twentieth-century academic life. Nearly all have been published before, and I thank the publishers for permission to reprint them and for publishing them in the first place. A list of sources is appended to the book, but when it seemed possibly interesting or amusing I have provided information about the provenance, circumstances, or afterlife of particular chapters in headnotes. I have touched up a few of these pieces, edited some for clarity, added a bit of new material here and there, and tried to impose what consistency and to remove what repetition I could without damaging individual essays. I have omitted citations and other notes as (in this context) needless clutter, but anyone who cares can find them in the original versions, citied in the list of sources.

A great many people share the responsibility for these chapters, having solicited them, provoked them, commented on them, or otherwise made them what they are. Although I am in their debt, I will leave most of them nameless here, counting on their understanding and perhaps even their gratitude. But I must thank the Center for Advanced Study in the Behavioral Sciences and the University of London's Institute of United States Studies, both of which gave me the freedom and facilities to write some of these pieces and to prepare their collection. Bob Scott at CASBS and Gary McDowell at IUSS made those visits possible, and I want them to know how much I appreciate their hospitality. I am also grateful to Beverly Jarrett, director of the University of Missouri Press, who encouraged me to undertake this; Bruce Clayton and Jim Cobb, who read and criticized the ensemble; Gary Kass, who copyedited it; and my wife (and, recently, coauthor), Dale Volberg Reed, who gave me the benefit of her editing skills and critical intelligence when these pieces were first written, and has just done it again. None of these folks shares all my opinions, not even Dale—but many things are more important than opinions.

The Three Souths

This essay was written for the "Official Souvenir Program" of the 1996 Centennial Olympic Games in Atlanta to introduce foreign visitors to the South, but may it serve to introduce readers to this book.

You're in the American South now, a proud region with a distinctive history and culture.

A place that echoes with names like Thomas Jefferson and Robert E. Lee, Scarlett O'Hara and Uncle Remus, Martin Luther King and William Faulkner, Billy Graham, Mahalia Jackson, Muhammad Ali, Elvis Presley. Home of the country blues and country music, bluegrass and Dixieland jazz, gospel music and rock and roll. Where menus offer both down-home biscuits and gravy and uptown shrimp and grits. Where churches preach against "cigarettes, whiskey, and wild, wild women" (all Southern products) and American football is a religion.

You're in the region that leads the nation in job creation, the most industrialized part of the country, a place of shining skyscrapers, sprawling suburbs, and boundless optimism. You're in a region where problems of rural poverty still defy easy solution, where many still live in the shadow of the plantation.

You're in the only part of America that ever fought the Stars and Stripes, the only one to suffer military defeat and occupation. You're in the region that now supplies the biggest proportionate share of America's soldiers and wears its American patriotism most conspicuously.

You're in the part of America where slavery lasted longest and died hardest, where a system of virtual apartheid prevailed for decades, where only yesterday "white supremacy" was preached as a positive good. You're in a region that is now attracting black migrants by the hundreds of thousands, where schools are less segregated and more blacks hold public office than anywhere else in the country.

You're in what used to be called "the Solid South"—solid in support of the Democratic Party and opposition to the party of Lincoln, the Union, and Reconstruction. You're in a region that cast most of its votes in 1992 against a Democratic ticket from Arkansas and Tennessee, and now dominates the leadership of the national Republican Party.

You're in a region renowned for Southern hospitality, for its ladies and gentlemen, for its courtesy and gracious living; a region with the nation's highest rate of church membership—and its highest homicide rate. A place whose name has evoked moonlight and magnolias, pellagra and poll taxes, now home to the Cable News Network and Compaq Computers.

You're below the Mason-Dixon Line. In the Cotton Kingdom, the Old Confederacy, Dixie. In the Bible Belt, the Sahara of Bozart. In the New South, the Sunbelt, the Southeast. In "Uncle Sam's other province." You're in a land of contradictions.

Welcome to the South. Confusing, ain't it?

*   *   *

One source of confusion is that the phrase "the South" refers to at least three different regions. They overlap one another and all sometimes go by that same name, but their origins, their defining features, their prospects, and even their boundaries are quite distinct.

The old South—call it "Dixie"—came into being with the spread of cotton agriculture and slavery in the early 1800s. This South was an agricultural region, and after 1865 it was a *poor* agricultural region, with unique racial and economic problems. It lasted well into this century and some aspects of it still survive here and there, but it's less of a reality each decade, and in most respects it will soon be of interest only to historians.

Emerging as we watch, however, is a quite different South that we can call (for reasons we will get to) the "Southeast." This is a vibrant, dynamic, industrial region, a magnet for migration and investment from other parts of the nation and increasingly from abroad. It is a metropolitan region, its cities linked by innumerable ties of commerce and communication. It is in fact a *nation* in every sense but the political.

At the same time, there is an enduring *cultural* South, set off from the rest of the United States by its people's distinctive ways of doing things. This South is defined by things like religion, cuisine, family life, manners, musical styles, sports and recreation—all of the idioms and imponderables that make a population a people—and this is the South that evokes the pride and enlists the loyalties of Southerners.

In Atlanta, you're in all three of these Souths at once. Let's try to sort them out.

*   *   *

"Let us begin by discussing the weather," wrote the distinguished historian Ulrich B. Phillips in 1929, "for that has been the chief agency in making the South distinctive." You have undoubtedly noticed that the South can be hot and humid. Some vegetable life loves that—a fact with fateful consequences.

In particular, much of the South is suited for the cultivation of cotton, and for nearly a century Southerners grew that crop everywhere they *could* grow it: everywhere with two hundred or more frost-free days, annual precipitation of twenty-three inches or more, and soil that wasn't swamp. This created a peculiar region, defined in the early 1800s by plantation agriculture and slavery and distinguished ever since by the consequences of those institutions.

This is Dixie, the land of cotton, where (as Abe Lincoln's favorite Confederate song observed) old times are not forgotten. Even today a band of rural counties with substantial black populations trace the old cotton belt in a long arc from southeastern Virginia down and across to eastern Texas, with arms reaching north and south through the bottomlands along the Mississippi River. The cotton South is the *Deep* South: many "Southern" characteristics and phenomena have been concentrated here; some have been found *only* here.

Alabama calls itself "the heart of Dixie," but the real core of the Cotton Kingdom is probably the Mississippi Delta south of Memphis, "the most Southern place on earth"—if what you mean by Southern has to do with plantations, the blues, and the civil rights movement.

For decades this was seen as what the South was all about, and rightly so.

This was the South that went to war in 1861, when South Carolina, "the cradle of secession," left the Union, joined by six other Deep South states that shared its commitment to the future of plantation agriculture and slavery. (Only later, and with some reluctance, did the states of the upper South add their stars to the Confederate flag.)

This was the South celebrated at Atlanta's great Cotton States and International Exposition of 1895. That the most memorable speech at that exposition was by Booker T. Washington of Tuskegee Institute reminds us that this was also the heartland of racial segregation.

For nearly a century after Reconstruction this was the political "Solid South," where whites didn't vote Republican and blacks didn't vote at all. In the 1930s its continuing poverty led President Franklin Roosevelt to call it "the nation's number-one economic problem."

During and after World War I millions fled Dixie, in one of the great mass migrations of human history, seeking opportunity in the North and West. In the 1960s the South was the setting for the stirring events of the civil rights movement, events that captured the attention of the world.

The fossil remains of this South can still be found. If you want to define the South as a poor rural region with oppressive race relations and undemocratic politics you can still do it. But the South's problems are increasingly the same as everyone else's. Dixie is a mere shadow of what it used to be; it has become a thing of shreds and patches—and most Southerners don't live there anymore.

*　　*　　*

Urbanization, industrialization, and the civil rights movement's successful assault on racial segregation have changed the South's economy and politics beyond recognition. The last fifty years have seen the emergence of a very different South. It occupies much of the same territory as Dixie, but that shouldn't blind us to the fact that it is an entirely new development—indeed, in many respects an entirely different region. Almost every unfavorable statistic that used to define the South has shown dramatic change.

Perhaps most striking have been the changes in Southern race relations. Only a generation ago the South's system of racial segregation was fixed in law, seemingly for all time; yet almost overnight it was dismantled by federal legislation and court decisions. With half of America's black population, the South elects two-thirds of the nation's black office-holders, and although black incomes in the South are still lower than white, they are approaching parity with black incomes elsewhere in the United States.

Economic and demographic statistics have also shown startling improvement. As late as the 1930s, per capita income in the South was half of that elsewhere in the United States. Personal income is still lower in the South (only Virginia and Florida are above the national average), but the remaining difference is small enough that it is largely offset by a lower cost of living.

Two out of three Southerners are now urban or suburban folk, and even most rural Southerners work in industry. The agricultural labor force has dropped from half of the total to under 5 percent, and Southern agriculture has increasingly become "agribusiness." (One telling statistic: 10 percent of the 1950 cotton crop was picked by machine; in 1970 the figure was 90 percent.) As the South has moved from agriculture to industry, its birth rate has declined; indeed, since the mid-1950s, it has been slightly *lower* than the US average.

The industrial development of the South is continuing. In the 1990s eight of the top ten states in the growth of manufacturing plants were in the South. In 1992–94 over half the nation's new jobs and ten of the top thirteen states in jobs added per hundred thousand population were Southern (the top three were North Carolina, Mississippi, and Kentucky).

Even in automobile manufacturing, the classic heavy industry, the South has been coming on strong since the 1980s. Tennessee now has Nissan and Saturn plants, Kentucky has Toyota, South Carolina BMW, and Alabama Mercedes-Benz. All told, these factories represent a $7 billion investment to create some twenty thousand well-paid jobs.

Foreign investment is increasingly important. There are forty-six German-owned companies in Spartanburg County, South Carolina, alone: the nearby section of Interstate 95 is known locally as "the Autobahn." One out of every eleven South Carolinians now works for a foreign-owned company, nearly twice the US average.

Interregional migration now flows *into* the South, not out of it, as the South's booming economy slows out-migration and attracts migrants from other regions. Shortly after 1960 more whites began moving to the South than were leaving it; a decade later, the same was true for blacks. Now more than one of every eight residents of the South was born outside it. In consequence, the South's population has increased rapidly. New York has now been replaced by Texas as the second most populous state, and Florida should knock it out of third place early in the twenty-first century.

When the South seceded in 1861, Karl Marx said scornfully of the Confederacy that it was not a nation at all, just a battle cry. He meant that the new country had no industrial base, no transportation network, no national press, no obvious capital city to tie it all together—none of what a *real* nation has to make it go. And Marx was right: one of the Confederacy's many problems was that it was trying to build these institutions while fighting for its very existence, and it never entirely succeeded.

But now there are dozens of regional publications, scores of regional trade and professional associations, hundreds of regional corporations. There is a sense—Marx's sense—in which the South is more of a nation now than when it was politically independent.

And Atlanta is its capital. Here is where regional trade associations have their annual conventions, where regional corporations are likely to be headquartered, where national corporations have their regional offices. Here is where the Southern correspondents of television networks and national publications are clustered. The *Wall Street Journal's* Atlanta office now publishes a regional supplement, and the *Journal Constitution* is the nearest thing the South has to a national newspaper. Atlanta is at the center of the South's transportation grid as well: its airport is the second-busiest in the United States, giving rise to the Southern joke that even if you're going to hell, you'll have to change planes in Atlanta.

This is the South of the future. Call it the "Southeast." This region barely existed before World War II, but it is all around us now. And it seems to be unstoppable, as its booming economy and surging population are translated into political power (primarily through the medium of the Republican Party, Dixie's old adversary).

But there is a reason to call it the South*east*. This is a smaller region than Dixie.

We can now see plainly a development that regional sociologists were predicting fifty years ago: Atlanta is not the capital of the *entire* historic South. The post-agricultural South has split down the middle into a southeastern region centered on Atlanta and a southwestern one that is essentially greater Texas. Dallas and Houston don't report to Atlanta the way Charlotte and Nashville and Jacksonville do. The western South has its own regional institutions, its own magazines and corporate headquarters, even its own edition of the *Wall Street Journal*.

To complicate matters still further, most of Virginia is now tied into the economy of the mid-Atlantic states to its north, much of Kentucky now looks to the Midwest, and Miami is becoming the de facto capital of a Caribbean region all its own.

*   *   *

So there is an old, agricultural South that is fading and a new, industrial South that is coming apart at the seams. Put that way, is there any reason, anymore, to talk about the South as *the South*?

Well, of course there is. Dixie was rooted in the cotton economy and the institutions that grew out of that. The Southeast, too, is defined by its institutions, most of them economic. But the South has always been as much a cultural region as an economic one. We speak of commercial activity in the Southeast, but not of Southeastern religion, Southeastern music, the Southeastern gentleman, or Southeastern fried chicken. The Southeast's future is as bright as Dixie's is bleak, but (as one historian has put it) the South is a region with more than a future, and its past lives on in its culture.

From the start the South has been the home of peoples whose intertwined cultures have set them off from other Americans. And where the economic and political story has been largely one of conflict, division, and separation; the tale of the cultural South is one of blending, sharing, mutual influence—and of continuing unity and distinctiveness.

Start with the fact that the South was settled primarily from Great Britain (especially from its "Celtic fringe" of Scotland, Ireland, and Wales) and from West Africa. To be sure, the native Indians made early and lasting contributions. It is impossible to ignore the French influence in Louisiana—and who would want to? Germans were an early and important presence in Texas and in Virginia's Shenandoah Valley. There are noticeable concentrations of Greeks in Florida, Chinese in Mississippi, and so forth. Acknowledge all that.

Still, Southern culture has been largely a matter of African Americans and Protestant whites of British descent borrowing from each other, imitating each other, shaping one another's attitudes, tastes, and values in ways both obvious and subtle. Black and white Southerners have created distinct but related cultures that are usually recognizable variations on a shared *Southern* culture. In the process, together, they have made the South a great seedbed—possibly *the* great seedbed—of distinctively American culture, inventing and exporting everything from Coca-Cola to rock and roll.

Here is where cultural differences persist in America. If you're looking for how the South is different these days, don't look at what people do from nine to five on weekdays. During those hours Southerners now do pretty much the same things everyone else does. Look instead at what people do in the evenings, on Sunday morning, Saturday night, and weekend afternoons. Look at tastes and cultural patterns that don't simply reflect how people make their livings, or how good a living they make. Look at things that are passed on from generation to generation within families, things that people take with them when they move on geographically, or move up economically. Look at things like manners, religion, cuisine, sports, and music.

When you do, you find a cultural South that is bigger than the Cotton Kingdom, one that encompasses both the Southeast and the Southwest (if not south Florida). Southern values and habits and practices are found in the Appalachian and Ozark mountains, in Texas and Oklahoma, in a great many areas marginal to the plantation South but settled by Southerners. Mapping cultural patterns makes it easy to figure out who settled most of Kentucky and Missouri, as well as the southern parts of Illinois, Indiana, and Ohio. Indeed, many of the same features can be found in scattered enclaves of Southern migrants throughout the United States—among Michigan auto workers, Southern blacks in Chicago and Harlem, or the children and grandchildren of Okies in California.

In nearly the entire South, for example, religious life is dominated by evangelical Protestant denominations (which makes the South unique not just in the United States but in the world). A religious solid South preceded the political one and seems to be outlasting it, because in this respect the South may be becoming even *more* different from the rest of the country. Almost nine out of ten Southerners are Protestant, more than half of those are Baptists, and the region is more Baptist now than it was in 1900.

And the South's fastest-growing denominations are even more unusual. Consider the Church of God in Christ (COGIC), for instance, a black Pentecostal group with its origins in the Mississippi Delta. At COGIC's centenary in 1997 it claimed some four million members, making it perhaps the least well-known of America's major religious groups.

The religious life of the Southern highlands and the Southwest is every bit as Southern as that of the Deep South. Early on, evangelical Protestants established their dominance in the Southern backcountry; as Southerners moved west and south, they took their religion with them. Not many people live in west Texas, but those who do are likely to be Baptist or Methodist or Church of Christ. The mountain South, too, is virtually indistinguishable from the rest of the region.

And when it comes to Southern music, the mountains and the Southwest are right at the heart of things. Although black musicians in the Deep South gave us jazz and the blues, the white songwriters and performers of country music mostly hail from a fertile crescent extending from the mountains of southwest Virginia through Kentucky and Tennessee to Arkansas, Oklahoma, and Texas. (Nashville's role in country music is well known, but the country-music center of Branson, Missouri—in the Ozarks just across the Arkansas line—has recently become second only to Las Vegas as a destination for American tourists.)

And when black music from the Deep South met white music from the southern uplands, in and around Memphis, rock and roll was born.

Both country music and traditional black music reveal in their lyrics another persisting cultural trait: a propensity for several sorts of violence. The FBI's crime statistics show that this is not just talk. The South has had a higher homicide rate than the rest of the United States for as long as reliable records have been kept, and the mountains and Southwest share fully in this pattern. But Southern violence is not random (it tends to be the kind of vengeance those songs are about), and it is usually directed outward (the South has the nation's lowest suicide rates).

Southerners have also displayed relatively conservative family and sex-role attitudes. These differences have surfaced in the legal system: Southern states were slow to enact women's suffrage; most never did ratify the Equal Rights Amendment; until recently few had state laws against sex discrimination. Although Southern women have actually been more likely than other American women to work outside the home (they have needed the money more), most often they have worked in "women's jobs"—as textile operatives or domestic servants, for example—and the percentage of women who work in predominantly male occupations remains lower in the South than elsewhere.

Some of these Southern characteristics go back to the early days of Dixie, if not to the British Isles and African savannahs from which so many of the South's people came. Many were mentioned by travelers in the antebellum South. But other regional folkways are of quite recent origin.

Occasionally Southerners have just appropriated pastimes invented somewhere else. American football, for instance, had its origins in New England, and it was not until Alabama beat Washington in the 1926 Rose Bowl that Americans were persuaded that Southerners could play the game competitively. Now, of course, the South provides far more than its share of players in the National Football League, and the tailgate party has become a Southern institution.

More often, however, new differences have emerged as Southerners have used their new resources and opportunities to express traditional values and tastes in new ways. Country music draws on old musical forms, but it took its modern form only after radio and the phonograph turned isolated rural folk into a mass audience. Similarly, stockcar racing reflects a historic admiration for daring and grace under pressure, but it appeared only after the whiskey-distillers of the upland South met the automobile.

Notice that the persistence of the cultural South does not require that Southerners stay poor and rural. Indeed, poor folks can't afford some of its trappings: new Southern phenomena from high-tech competitive bass-fishing to *Southern Living* magazine require technology, affluence, and mobility that simply did not exist in the South even a half-century ago.

No, mass society has made some inroads, but Southerners still do many things differently—and they keep inventing new ways to do things differently. In the past quarter-century the culture of the South has begun to adapt to migration into the region by unprecedented numbers of Northerners, Hispanics, and Asians. How these newcomers will be assimilated and how they will enrich the culture of the South are interesting questions, but *that* they will seems hardly in doubt. The cultural South has always shown remarkable resilience, and it will probably continue to do so.

*   *   *

The South is no longer defined by an economic system that exports raw materials and surplus population, while generating a variety of social and economic problems for itself. Some aspects of Dixie still linger, and a few of its legacies (notably a substantial black population) will be with us for the foreseeable future. But that South is largely—well, gone with the wind. And, for the most part, good riddance.

The South is now, more than ever, defined by its commercial and industrial economy, by the network of institutions that have emerged to serve it, and by the ever-increasing number of people who have an interest in making sure that it continues to exist. Here, however, the brute facts of distance and diversity conspire to reduce the South to a southeastern core, with the Southwest and south Florida and various borderlands taking their natural place with other regions or as regions in their own right.

But the South has always been and still is set apart by its people. Whatever else it has been or is becoming, the South is the homeland of people who think of themselves as Southerners. Some have even suggested that Southerners ought to be viewed as an American ethnic group, like Italian or Polish Americans, a people with a sense of group identity based on a shared history and a common culture. This is what W. J. Cash had in mind when he wrote in *The Mind of the South* that the South is "not quite a nation within a nation, but the next thing to it."

Geographers have come up with scores of criteria for locating the South, mapping everything from the kudzu vine to where people name their businesses "Southern" this and "Southern" that. But maybe the best way to define the South is with what Hamilton Horton calls the "Hell, yes!" line: you know you are in the South if that's what people say when you ask if they are Southerners.

I

The Journalistic Eye

The Mind of the South and Southern Distinctiveness

On the fiftieth anniversary of the publication of W. J. Cash's The Mind of the South, *the annual Chancellor's Symposium at the University of Mississippi was devoted to that influential book and its author. Cash was taking a lot of heat, but I wanted to compliment him on being right about some things.*

"I am not at all trying to lay out a thesis, far less to substantiate or to solve." This quotation is not from *The Mind of the South*. It comes instead from *Let Us Now Praise Famous Men*, another powerful book written a half-century ago by a Southern observer of the South, James Agee. W. J. Cash put a thesis on the table in a way that Agee did not—and in a way that I don't plan to, either. All I intend is to offer a few observations based on a dozen readings of the book since 1960 or so, a good deal of thought about it, and a few attempts to teach from it over the years.

Let me summarize that thesis of Cash's. He argued that "the South" (leave aside for now the question of whom *that* included) had exhibited a "fairly definite mental pattern," continuous throughout its history. This collective "mind" was characterized by romanticism and hedonism, on the one hand, and by individualism, on the other. It had been produced by the frontier and sustained after that by frontier-like conditions that Cash claimed to find in the plantation, in Reconstruction, and in the world of the textile industry. Cash discussed such "complicating influences" as regional conflict and the presence of an aristocratic tradition embodied in what he called "the Virginians." Nevertheless, he insisted that the South was *different*, and (despite its diversity) *solid*, set apart from the rest of the nation by its attitudes, values, and assumptions.

The Mind of the South does not explicitly state hypotheses and test them. That is, it is not a scientific treatise. In fact, it does not much resemble scholarship of any sort. As Bertram Wyatt-Brown has pointed out, Cash employed a lawyerly sort of exposition: giving examples, telling stories, appealing to his readers' experience and common sense; constantly making concessions, but never a fatal one; acknowledging exceptions and limitations, but always reverting to the main line of the argument. In other words, he wrote as an advocate, and his rhetoric is subtle, not to say slippery. Nevertheless, *The Mind of the South* is packed with propositions that could be subjected to empirical test, generalizations that are by their nature at least mostly true or mostly false. Whatever James Agee was doing—ethnography, premature New Journalism, or (as he said) a special sort of burglary or espionage—whatever it was, his book has not been held to the same empirical standards as Cash's treatise. In some ways Cash was bolder than Agee, and he has paid a price for his forthrightness, in the form of closer critical attention to what he was up to.

Much of that attention has been biographical in nature, and rightly so: Cash's circumstances unquestionably shaped and limited his view of the South. As C. Vann Woodward pointed out a generation ago, for instance, Cash wrote as virtually a life-long resident of the Carolina Piedmont, and that distorted his view. We should recognize that he also wrote as someone who aspired to be both a great writer and a member of the New South's smart set, and those aspirations affected both his prose and his opinions, not always for the better. Finally, let us concede that Cash wrote as a Southern white man of the lower middle class—particularly unfortunate origins right now. Everyone has to come from somewhere, of course, but viewed through the currently fashionable prism of race, class, and gender, both Cash and his analysis come up short.

Incidentally, some historians have made this last point at length, and I must say that it is passing strange to find them, of all people, trading in anachronistic criticism. Even a sociologist like me can recognize that times change and that, as Michael O'Brien put it, "Cash himself was a liberal in racial matters by the standards of his time, that is, he had adjusted his views to deprecate the enemies of blacks, but not yet altered his opinions to sympathize with black culture and personality." Fair enough—and so?

As for Cash's other limitations, I could point out that, when he wrote, the Carolina Piedmont and similar parts of other states were coming into their own, contesting the old plantation belt's economic, demographic, and even symbolic dominance of the South. I could also observe that, when Cash wrote, Southern white men of his class had attained a cultural and political hegemony that they had never had before, and have lost since. What Cash had to say may or may not have been true for Southern women, or for black Southerners—I will come back to this—but even if it was not, it is worth knowing about the mind of the white male Piedmont South. One could say that if we have to choose a race, class, and gender, Cash's combination is the most important one to hear from. One could say that, although I will not.

No, take all of those criticisms at full strength, and subtract from Cash's achievement the maximum allowance for all of his biographical limitations. The residue is still impressive. This is a good book. For a lower-middle class Southern white man from the Carolina Piedmont writing in the 1930s (if you insist), it is a *great* book. Besides, so far as I know, nobody from any other race, class, gender, or subregion has even tried what Cash tried. Give him credit for that.

*   *   *

What, exactly, did he do? We can evaluate his book in at least three ways: as a literary work, as an intellectual event, and, finally, as an empirical account and analysis of Southern history and culture.

C. Vann Woodward once observed that "social scientists, especially sociologists, seem to have a special affinity" for *The Mind of the South*. Maybe so. I do, anyway. Once I even went so far as to suggest in Cash's defense that it almost does not matter whether he was "right" or "wrong." "His South may not correspond perfectly or even very well to the real one," I wrote, "but it's certainly a fascinating place. . . . As a work of the imagination, *The Mind of the South* is a remarkable achievement—far better, as [Bruce] Clayton suggests, than any novel Cash was ever likely to write."

It is not so much his distinctive prose, although I admire that, too. Michael O'Brien has written that Cash's style, "like that of Thomas Wolfe, [is] best relished in youth," but I have learned by requiring students to read it that it is not to the taste of many readers of the MTV generation. Maybe those great rolling periods should be read aloud, so the snappy colloquialisms can punctuate them appropriately, but who has *time* for that, these days?

Anyway, Cash's real artistry lies in his daring conceptualization. Woodward observed that Cash himself "was merely illustrating once more that ancient Southern trait that he summed up in the word 'extravagant'"—and that is exactly what some of us like about the book:

27

not just the sound of its words, but the sweep and dash of its history, the boldness and the flamboyance and the very exaggeration of its characterizations. ("Softly; do you not hear behind that the gallop of Jeb Stuart's cavalrymen?")

Notice, though, that this tack tries to do for Cash what Louis Rubin did some time ago for the Vanderbilt Agrarians, Cash's contemporaries who wrote *I'll Take My Stand*. You say the description is inaccurate, the analysis all wet? Well, this is not history, or sociology. The "South" is an imaginative construction here, a trope. But, you know, both the Agrarians and Cash really were trying to engage in social analysis, and it is more than a little patronizing to tell them that they were not, never mind that you go on to say that they were doing something finer. Both books deserve to be taken seriously as what their authors intended them to be, even if that means savaging them. In any case, a good many readers have insisted on seeing them as something other than works of art.

Many, indeed, have taken *The Mind of the South* as gospel, which means that, right or wrong, it is undeniably important as an event in the South's intellectual and cultural history. For decades, it was the one book to read if you were only reading one. (In some circles, it still is. A while back I came across the Penguin edition in a Buckinghamshire bookshop, almost surely the only book about the American South in that little English village.) Some of Cash's great organizing concepts— "the man at the center," "the savage ideal," "the proto-Dorian bond," the "rape complex," and so forth—still shape our thought about the South, whether we like it or not.

Indeed, whether we *know* it or not. For better or for worse, many of Cash's broad-brush characterizations of Southern life and culture, stripped of their catchy labels, have become almost conventional wisdom among literate Southerners. The Trinidadian-Indian writer V. S. Naipaul, for instance, unwittingly paraphrased Cash again and again in his book *A Turn in the South*, as he quoted various Southerners' "observations." In fact, some of Naipaul's informants were probably repeating things that they had read or heard in college. Some of these ideas were not original with Cash, true, but he gave them popular currency. If we want to know where our ideas have come from, Cash's book is still required reading.

But it really does matter whether those ideas are right or wrong. Cash did ask to be judged, not as an artist or a walking intellectual event, but as a social analyst. As I have said, I think he was a pretty good one—although, Cash-like, we must allow the necessary qualifications and limitations. Some time ago, when *Southern Living* held an editorial conference at Ole Miss with the theme, "Where have we come from? Where are we going?", a curmudgeonly friend grumbled that he was more interested in the question, "Now that we're here, where the hell are we?" Well, all three questions are worth asking, and Cash addressed them all, with varying degrees of success.

Historians differ, obviously, about how good an answer Cash gave to the question of where we have come from. Maybe they always will differ. It is what they do. But at least Cash did some useful myth-busting. In particular, unlike his patron and fellow iconoclast H. L. Mencken, he was not captivated by the prevailing Southern view of life Before the War. His insistence that the Southern colonies housed a "rough young society" where "the test of a gentleman" was "the possession of sufficient property" was a useful corrective to the sort of misconception that led a student to tell me once in a paper about the aristocratic descent of white Southerners that "the gynecology of the Southern stock was very truly royal-like." Cash's account of "the Irishman" can be read alongside the sagas of Faulkner's Sutpens and Margaret Mitchell's O'Haras, and it may hold up pretty well as a social history of the settling of the Southern interior. In other respects, of course, his history is less satisfactory. The problem, however, usually seems to be that his account is partial, and how much that matters (except perhaps on Reconstruction), how misleading it is, often seems to be an open question.

The question of where the South was going Cash tried to duck. On his last page, he stated explicitly, "Of the future I shall venture no definite prophecies." But if we refuse to let him off the hook that easily, if we insist that his thesis implies continuity whether he likes it or not—well, whatever kind of historian he was, he made a lousy prophet. The changes since he wrote surely put the lie to his implicit predictions. In particular, he certainly saw little likelihood of dramatic racial change, much less of its coming about by black initiative. It is pointless to speculate about whether he would have adjusted happily to the postwar South, like some white Southern liberals, or been bewildered by it, like others, but there is no question that he would have found it surprising. Today's South is not one he could have imagined in 1940, much less predicted.

On the question of what the South looked like in his own time, though, I think he was a far better guide. The "mental pattern" he identified did characterize a great many Southerners, and some aspects of it—by no means all, not even most, but some—still do. Let us take a look what he had to say about those two allegedly major aspects of the Southern mind: romanticism and individualism.

* * *

His treatment of romanticism is the less persuasive. Frankly, I would like more evidence than Cash provides that the South's farmers and businessmen were any more romantic than farmers and businessmen anywhere else. Of course, many Southern *writers* have been romantic, and certainly Cash himself was. The assertion that the tough customers who built and ran the South were romantic came, after all, from a young man who burst into tears at Chartres cathedral.

There is a larger point here than simply the speculation that Jack Cash may have been projecting his own characteristics onto his fellow Southerners. As I said earlier, in sociological terms—race, class, gender, time, place—Cash represented an important population. In those respects, he was enough like other Southern white men to understand a great deal about them. But psychologically he was anything but representative. Consider the portrait of the artist that emerges from Bruce Clayton's biography. Here is "Sleepy" Cash, thirty-six years old, unable to hold a job for long, living with his parents. His recurrent attacks of neurasthenia and melancholia are notorious; he also suffers from goiter and (secretly) from fears of impotence. He seems to spend his days riding his bicycle, chopping wood, and dozing in the sun in front of the courthouse. He stays up nights talking with an unemployed Baptist preacher. He drinks too much, smokes too much, and probably doesn't eat his vegetables. In short, he is a mess. And hardly typical.

It is almost a sociological commonplace that marginality can produce the heightened consciousness required for social analysis. Cash's atypicality may sometimes have led him astray, but it may have led him to write his book in the first place—and when he got it right it may have been because he was far enough removed from the mainstream of white Southern life to see it whole.

When it came to *black* culture and personality, of course, Cash's understanding was obviously unsatisfactory. We should, however, acknowledge his remarks on the black influence on white Southerners. "Negro entered into white man as profoundly as white man entered into Negro," he wrote, "subtly influencing every gesture, every word, every emotion and idea, every attitude." Today, that is almost a cliché, and certainly that understanding is simply taken for granted in much recent scholarship on the South. We need to recognize, though, that in 1940 it was neither an obvious observation nor a popular one.

Since Cash's few references to religion also come under the head of romanticism and hedonism, this may be the place to remark on another empathetic failure. It seems to me that his treatment of Southern religion is almost willfully blinkered. Much of what he says about Southern religion is true, but so is much that he does not say. Another North Carolina journalist, Gerald Johnson, wrote once that "the man who will deny that religious admonition is the most powerful influence for public decency in the South simply does not know the South." But you will learn no more about that from *The Mind of the South* than from—well, than from the writings of H. L. Mencken.

If Cash was perversely obtuse when it came to Southern religion, though, I think he was right on the money in his discussion of civic pride, a Southern trait that shows few signs of abating. A recent study by Judith Blau has shown that, controlling for city size, wealth, and other factors, the South now has *more* than its share of museums, symphony orchestras, and other cultural institutions. Surely this burgeoning jungle of the *beaux arts* reflects less devotion to high culture for its own sake than the touching eagerness of our new urban elites to make their cities "world-class." What Cash wrote of skyscrapers in Charlotte could as well be said of World's Fairs in Knoxville and New Orleans, or the Olympics in Atlanta—that these towns have little more use for them than a hog has for a morning coat. How else to account for these undertakings, then, than as quests for civic glory, shaped by a taste for the grand gesture and the defensive desire to *"force [some] recognition* of our worth and dignity of character"? (That is Cash, quoting the Raleigh *News and Observer* from 1880.)

You know, maybe our business leaders really *are* more romantic.

*   *   *

Anyway, the other aspect of the Southern mind—what Cash called individualism and we might as well, too—is both better documented than romanticism, in the first place, and more clearly characteristic of Southern culture a half-century after Cash. Listen to Cash on the mind of the Old South: Its "dominant trait," he said, "was an intense individualism—in its way, perhaps the most intense individualism the world has seen since the Italian Renaissance." This trait was found, "mutatis mutandis," he said, at all levels of white society, from the planter, "wholly content with his autonomy and jealously guardful that nothing should encroach upon it," to "the farmers and the crackers [who] were in their own way self-sufficient, too—as fiercely careful of their prerogatives of ownership, as jealous of their sway over their puny domains, as the grandest lord."

Like other aspects of the Southern mind, Cash argued, this was originally a frontier trait, but it was preserved by the South's subsequent pseudo-frontiers, or frontier-equivalents. "Southerners in 1900," Cash wrote, "would see the world in much the same terms in which their fathers had seen it in 1830; as, in its last aspect, a simple solution, an aggregation of self-contained and self-sufficient monads, each of whom was ultimately and completely responsible for himself." (As Hank Williams Jr. puts it, a country boy can survive.) According to Cash, the "ruling element" in this tradition was "an intense distrust of, and, indeed, downright aversion to, any actual exercise of authority beyond the barest minimum essential to the existence of the social organism." In short, Cash believed that Southerners love politics but hate government.

There might seem to be a paradox here. How do you square individualism with the "savage ideal" of communitarian conformity? What is this—regimented anarchy? Cash offered no answer; indeed, he did not seem to recognize that there is a problem. Could this be because, in the South, there is none? Richard Weaver—University of Chicago philosopher, Cash's fellow Tar Heel, and the Agrarians' fellow traveler— suggested as much in an essay in which he distinguished between two *types* of individualism.

One type, which Weaver found exemplified by a New Englander, Thoreau, reflects the absence or rejection of cultural prescriptions. This is the modern individualism against which Alasdair MacIntyre contends in his book *After Virtue*, a form of social organization (if we can call it that) in which "I am what I myself choose to be." The other sort of individualism Weaver described is different: it is itself culturally prescribed. One is individualistic because one is supposed to be. Weaver took as an exemplar of this sort of individualism a Virginian, John Randolph of Roanoke, and I think this Southern, communitarian ethic is what Cash was observing. When he said individualism, he did not mean free-thinking nonconformity. He was talking about a norm of self-reliance, an anti-institutional orientation that says: you should be responsible for the welfare of you and yours. You should not be dependent on the government, the church, the labor union, the law-court—on "society."

A sociologist is inevitably reminded of Emile Durkheim's observation that some people kill themselves because they are adrift, without personal ties, but others, like Japanese kamikaze pilots, give their lives because they are too well integrated for their own good. Like suicide, individualism may be what is expected from well-socialized, well-integrated members of a community. Anti-institutional, that is, does not necessarily mean antisocial.

*   *   *

Notice Cash's male pronouns, by the way: each monad "responsible for himself." This is not just grammatical convention. When Cash spoke of "Southerners" he did mean white men, people very much like (but for the grace of God) himself. Consider this sentence: "No man felt or acknowledged any primary dependence on his fellows, save perhaps in the matter of human sympathy and entertainment." Cash surely did not mean that no black person or white woman felt or acknowledged dependence. Indeed, that was the role that the dominant social ideologies envisioned for them and, with considerable success, imposed upon them. Or take this passage, about the individualism of the plantation world: "[It] was full of the chip-on-the-shoulder swagger and brag of a boy—one, in brief, of which the essence was the boast, voiced or not, on the part of every Southerner, that he would knock hell out of whoever dared to cross him." Plainly, Cash did not mean "every Southerner" to include Southern blacks and Southern women. For a woman to reveal that attitude would have been unladylike; for a black to display it could have been fatal.

But to say that Cash was not writing about white women and blacks does not mean that what he said did not apply to them—"mutatis mutandis," of course. To say that they were supposed to be dependent does not mean that they always internalized that role, always saw themselves that way—and one readily available alternative has been to appropriate the self-reliant, chip-on-the-shoulder ideal of white men for themselves. It is significant that, among themselves, many black Southerners have admired a long line of heroic "bad niggers," from Stagolee and That Bully of the Town down to Superfly and Shaft in our own time. These are men who could teach W. J. Cash a thing or two about prickly individualism and autonomy. Black women, too, have had their pride and independence: think only of the story of Frankie and Johnny. As for white women—well, Scarlett O'Hara has shaped the self-image of a good many Southern women, if we can believe their testimonials. This is the same Scarlett who was once described as "J. E. B. Stuart in drag." Once upon a time, about the only woman celebrated in country music was the long-suffering dependent "angel," but these days Nashville offers a number of alternatives, from the good-timing, hell-raising good old girl to the super-competent, autonomous "good woman," who treats her man as no better than an equal. Even when it comes to violence—Thelma and Louise may be something new in the movies, but they have been hanging around country music for some time now.

If we take as our index of Southern-mindedness knocking hell out of people who cross us, both survey and crime data show that Southern women, although less touchy than Southern men, are more dangerous than Northern women—and blacks are the most Southern of us all.

*   *   *

Southern individualism is still with us, stated frankly in the lyrics of scores of country songs. It can also be found in Southerners' inclination to redress grievances privately, without recourse to third-party mediation. This means (as Cash recognized) that disputes are often settled violently—and that is what a lot of those country songs are about. Anti-institutionalism may also be reflected in Southern localism and familism, a preference for the known, tried, and true, as opposed to the distant and formal. It also marks and is probably reinforced by the Evangelical Protestantism to which most Southerners subscribe, a strikingly individualistic form of religion in which, as singer Tom T. Hall sums it up, "Me and Jesus got our own thing goin'. / Don't need anybody to tell us what it's all about." And, finally, individualism underlies the economic libertarianism of many Southerners, a self-help orientation that seems, if anything, increasingly common among Southern whites, and perhaps among black Southerners, too.

All of these attributes are more widespread in the South than elsewhere in the United States. You can deplore them—Cash did—but it is hard to deny that they exist. They show up as regional differences in everything from political attitudes to homicide rates, gun ownership to union membership. Some of these traits are more common among educated Southerners than uneducated ones, or among urban Southerners than rural ones. Laissez-faire economic views are even more common among migrants to the South than among natives, so Yankee immigration will not reduce *that* difference. In most of these respects, the South is not becoming more like the rest of the country: some of these differences are even larger now than when Cash wrote, and in other ways the rest of the country is becoming "Southernized."

True, a belief that says you are ultimately responsible for your own welfare fits poorly with the realities of a class-ridden society, but Cash maintained that the "yoke" of class "weighed but lightly" in the South. He did not deny that there were class distinctions in the South—indeed, as an aspiring 1930s intellectual he emphasized them. But he argued that there had been an "almost complete disappearance of economic and social focus on the part of the masses." More overstatement, perhaps, but can we agree that there was nowhere near as much class consciousness as there *should* have been? In explanation, he mentioned kinship ties, geographical and social mobility, the presence of a black underclass, and what becomes a recurring theme: the importance of Southern manners, which Cash claimed have served as "a balance wheel in the Southern social world and . . . a barrier against the development of bitterness"—or, you could as easily say, against the development of class consciousness. Again and again, Cash insisted that the Southern etiquette of class has deemphasized distinctions between rich and poor, just as the etiquette of race continually emphasized the gulf of caste. For all these reasons, Cash observed, "one simply did not have to get on in this world in order to achieve security, independence, or value in one's own estimation and in that of one's fellows." If not for that blind spot when it came to religion, he could have mentioned that, too, as a factor contributing to security and self-esteem.

*   *   *

Can anti-institutionalism of the sort Cash described survive in a complex, hierarchical, urban, industrial society like today's South? It is still with us, yes, but is that just because it has not been long enough since the passing of the frontier and its various surrogates? Will individualism soon be found only among fans of Hank Williams Jr., up the hollers? Perhaps, but let me suggest another line of thought. What was it about the frontier, after all, that encouraged individualism?

In part, it was the openness of the white Southern class structure, the fact that many Southerners had risen in it, apparently by their own efforts, and that even those who had not risen knew and were kin to some who had. Well, consider the fact that the South's class structure has never been more fluid than in the decades since Cash wrote. In 1940 roughly one Southern worker in six was in a white-collar, professional, or managerial job; half were farmers, the rest industrial workers. Now more than half of Southern workers do their work in offices. The South's per capita income has risen from half of that elsewhere in the country almost to parity. Those statistics mean that it is difficult—not impossible, but very difficult—to find adult Southerners who are worse off economically than their grandparents were. Can this explain the increase in economic libertarianism among Southerners? The message of self-help is better received in societies where many people actually *have* improved their circumstances.

Consider a related change: Almost overnight, in historical terms, the South has gone from a rural society, where only a third of the population lived in towns (and most of those towns did not amount to much), to a one where more than two-thirds now live in cities, suburbs, and towns; several Southern cities are among the nation's largest and fastest growing; and much of the countryside has been effectively urbanized. This *must* mean that many Southerners are rural-to-urban migrants or the children of such migrants. Is it fanciful to suggest that the Southern city is the latest frontier, with these uprooted rural Southerners as the new pioneers? Mightn't a frontier ethic of self-reliance serve such migrants well, in a new environment that is strange and in some ways threatening? Might this latest phase of Southern history be teaching some of the same lessons that Cash thought Southern history had always taught?

Finally, consider what many saw as the failure of major American institutions in the 1960s and 1970s. Could Vietnam, Watergate, Iran, assassinations, urban riots, economic stagnation, double-digit inflation, rising crime rates, urban decay—could these and a host of other distressing, frustrating, alienating developments have reinforced Southerners' distrust of large, distant, formal organizations? Some survey evidence suggests that they may have done so, and may even have led some other Americans to share that distrust.

But that is another book. Too bad Jack Cash is not here to write it, but the book he wrote is enough for one short life.

The *Times* Looks at Dixie

For as long as there has been a South, it has been compassed about by a host of observers and interpreters, both native and foreign. But most of the natives were out to defend their homeland or were working through their tortured relationship to it—in either case with a passion that often clouded their vision. Outsiders have been more likely to bring some objectivity to the task, and there have been a great many of them (2,703 books before 1955, by one count), but only a handful have captured not just the words but the music of Southern life. The most perceptive chroniclers of the South have often been hybrids, expatriates like Albert Murray or Fred Powledge, for instance, returning after many years away. They know the South well enough to recognize what's typical and what's bizarre (and what's both), but they also know enough about the rest of the world to know what's Southern and what's just human.

Peter Applebome has attained a similar state of productive marginality by a different, if increasingly common, route. In *Dixie Rising: How the South Is Shaping American Values, Politics, and Culture* he tells us that his relationship with the South began in the late 1960s when he came to Duke University as one of the many "snotty, privileged suburban college kids" at that fine institution. Now, with a wife related by marriage to the late Theodore Bilbo and two children who are "little Southerners even if their daddy is not," he confesses that he has become "someone who thinks he's a Yankee but hasn't lived in the North for twenty-one years, doesn't want to go back, and has come to the point where Southerners look normal and Yankees seem weirdly out of touch." (I commend to him a song by the Indigo Girls, "Southland in the Springtime," with its line "When God made me born a Yankee he was teasin.")

Not only has Applebome spent most of his adult life in the South, he has made his living by writing about it, most recently as a *New York Times* correspondent. I knew and respected his reporting for the

Times, but when I found him beginning his book with an account of a gathering of Southern Baptists at the Georgia Dome in Atlanta, I had some misgivings. Even the saintliest Yankee journalist would be tempted to portray this characteristic scene of the newest New South as a geek show, and Applebome does not entirely resist the temptation. As I read his mildly disdainful description of the Baptists' bumper stickers and big hair ("like it had been styled with a power blender and laced with Elmer's Glue"—and these are the *men*), the phrase "smart-ass New York media" came irresistibly to mind.

But this was a momentary lapse of sympathetic understanding on his part, a gesture to the thesis implied by his subtitle, that "the South is shaping American values, politics, and culture." Applebome's point is that these folks are on the cutting edge of political and cultural change in America. He goes on to list a variety of unfortunate and retrograde traits, observes that "such characteristics have always described the South," and asserts that "somehow, this now describes the nation." When it comes to politics, his argument can be summed up roughly as: Kirkpatrick Sale was right.

All this may have been more persuasive before the 1996 elections, but that doesn't really matter: Applebome barely mentions the subject again. Most of the rest of his book is devoted to what he does best, which is good old-fashioned reporting. His observations, his reflections on what he has seen, and his wry and sprightly prose put *Dixie Rising* in the front rank of travelers' accounts of the South, right up there with the work of an earlier New York journalist, Frederick Law Olmsted.

Applebome's travels have taken him from the "instant Dixie Cape Cod" of Seaside, Alabama, where "platoons of Atlanta lawyers and squadrons of Birmingham doctors' wives alight each summer to eat designer corn chips with peach melba salsa, drink piña coladas, and take seaside yoga classes," to what his host, a veteran of the civil rights movement, described as a "real SNCC wang dang doodle" outside Selma, to "drink some of that Black Panther piss." He has interviewed Southern politicians from a burnt-out George Wallace to Newt Gingrich ("a compulsively voluble quote machine and provocateur, sometimes brilliant, sometimes utterly out of control, speaking in a seamless barrage of sound bites like a computer programmed to provide good copy for reporters"). He has listened to the owner of a Mississippi country store explaining her permanent sign: HAPPY HOLIDAYS. ("We have a holiday every two months or so, so we just keep the sign up. It's almost Labor Day, ain't it?") He has drunk Budweiser with old boys in South Carolina as they extracted each other's teeth with pliers and debated the merits of labor unions (some "seemed to think that employers were such sorry assholes that unions were good," but another said "The way I look at it is that if a man hires me, and pays me his money, he didn't hire you to referee"). He has sat through enough church services to insure him a place in heaven, and has heard a "Christian music" executive describe the hundred-million churchgoing US adults as "the biggest niche market in America today."

Applebome is a great *noticer*, with an especially good eye for the weirdness treasured by those of us who love the South. (As Willie Morris told him at one point, it is the juxtapositions that drive you crazy.) Just for instance:

- In suburban Cobb County, Georgia, reminders of the battle of Atlanta and the lynching of Leo Frank cheek by jowl with the fifty-six-foot-high chicken decorating the former Johnny Reb's Chick-Chuck-'N'-Shake (now a KFC franchise) and Temple Kol Emeth, vandalized until an armed patrol of what the rabbi calls "the Jewish good ol' boys" of his congregation ran off the teenagers responsible.
- In Selma, a powerful black law firm known without irony as "the Jeff Davis crowd" (because its offices are on Jeff Davis Avenue), and a new civil rights museum in a building that used to be the headquarters of the White Citizens Council.
- Wilmington's black fourth-term sheriff (a New Age music fan) and a black brick mason who is the board chairman of the Historic Natchez foundation (a development "roughly comparable to an Arab running the Jerusalem Chamber of Commerce").
- Eudora Welty's favorite restaurant in Jackson, whose Greek owner celebrated Miss Welty's birthday by hiring a belly dancer with EUDORA WELTY, I LOVE YOU written on her stomach.
- A gathering of Christian nudists in Ocean City, North Carolina, and, near Dallas, Georgia, a proposed topless club featuring Klan memorabilia, which became instead the Georgia Peach Museum.
- In Nashville, sushi bars and microbreweries and a country-and-western transvestite cabaret called "Cowboys La Cage," but also "ragged, raunchy flowers" like Robert's Western World, offering "the most American music on earth played with berserk, merry abandon" by groups like BR5-49 (named from a Junior Samples routine on "Hee Haw"—and how's *that* for a postmodern lick?).
- New casinos south of Memphis with "the feel of spaceships full of money that had landed in the midst of the Delta poverty"; in Biloxi, more casinos—and the flourishing Jefferson Davis industry at Beauvoir, where $4.5 million in state bond funding is going to build a presidential library to put Davis "on a more equal footing with his peers who had operated out of Washington."

- At the University of Mississippi, an international conference on the life and work of Elvis Presley, organized by Ross Barnett's deconstructionist second cousin who teaches a course on Melville's Polynesian novels and Elvis's Hawaiian movies, a course called by undergraduates, inevitably, "Melvis."
- Old cultural wine in new virtual bottles on the internet: neo-Confederate web pages, innumerable Elvis sites, and the "front-porch cyber chatter" of the BUBBA list.
- In Moreland, Georgia, dueling museums that memorialize the birthplaces of Erskine Caldwell and Lewis Grizzard (too good a juxtaposition to ignore, and Applebome doesn't, devoting his last chapter to that fruitful contrast).

I make a cameo appearance in Applebome's book as a critic of the South-is-dead theory, but Applebome goes me one better, dismissing that view as simply a "crock" and observing that its advocates are mostly "liberals and writers who don't live there anymore." But if the South's not dying, what is it becoming?

Oddly enough, those misguided liberals and writers pretty much share the view of a crowd that Applebome calls the "neo-Cons" (that is, neo-Confederates), to be found at *Southern Partisan* magazine, in the secessionist League of the South, and hither and yon across the internet. Like the Hodding Carters and Marshall Fradys, these folks see the South as somehow *essentially* what it has been in the past, and thus as endangered, if not actually disappearing, and they simply assume that their version of the South is the only legitimate one—indeed, the only conceivable one.

Applebome plainly has little sympathy for the neo-Cons, but he does them the courtesy of taking them seriously, and he doesn't take the cheap shot of dismissing them as racists (although he observes—correctly, I think—that they can be "amazingly tolerant" of those who are). He recognizes that the killing of Michael Westerman would have been treated in the national media as the "shocking racial atrocity" that it was had the races of victim and killers been reversed, argues that "it's insane for either side not to make a distinction between those whose version of Southern heritage is just white supremacy in disguise and those immersed in the defining episode in the nation's history," and concludes that, "in a nation of historical amnesiacs, there are worse sins than passionate remembrance." (But a merciful forgetting, or ignoring, is what the South has often been about, as illustrated by Applebome's chapter on Honea Path, South Carolina, where the children and grandchildren of striking textile workers gunned down sixty years ago have to live with the children and grandchildren of those who killed them.)

Applebome acknowledges and explores the lasting power of the Old South myth, but he questions its present relevance. He feels much the same about a competing myth, rooted in the 1960s, in images of black struggle and white resistance. In Selma to attend the thirtieth-anniversary reunion of veterans of the Pettus Bridge encounter, he notes the yawning gap between the movement's ageing heroes and the younger generation, a cultural disjunction that troubles the old-timers, troubles Applebome, and should trouble us. He recognizes and ponders the real achievements and the real limitations of the civil rights move-ment, and observes that whatever problems face black communities these days, they are not just Southern, and it is not clear how helpful the imagery of the civil rights era can be in addressing them.

This is, by the way, only one of several unfashionable observations he has to offer on the subject of race relations. He also points out that the response to the mid-'90s church burnings was more newsworthy than the incidents themselves, observes that in most of the South most of the time ugly race hatred has been replaced by what he calls "the compulsive sort of Southern amity that doesn't so much transcend race as ignore it," argues that the creation of "majority-minority" congres-sional districts has had polarizing and generally unfortunate effects on Southern politics, and reports a growing nostalgia among many Southern blacks for the sense of community and self-determination lost with desegregation. (Here, too, he sympathizes with those who "would like to find the future in the past," but insists that "you can't get there from here, and in their heart of hearts most of them know it.")

So, if Applebome sees both the neo-Cons' version of the Old South and the civil rights era's racial morality play as shop-worn (not to say fly-blown) myths, long past their sell-by date, what is to replace them? It is hard to say, but whatever does will have to take account of the emergence of a *really* New South, an industrial-commercial, metro-politan region attracting migrants by the millions from other parts of the country and, increasingly, from abroad. Applebome observes that "one of the unmistakable truths of the South's current golden age is that it's not the grand old Southern cities like New Orleans, or Mobile, or Savannah, or Charleston, the most Southern cities in the South, that are leading the charge. Instead it's places like Atlanta, and Dallas, and Orlando, and Nashville, and Raleigh-Durham, and Charlotte [that] in the 1980s and '90s have been the most successful cities in America."

This is the South of Lewis Grizzard, not Erskine Caldwell, and Applebome appreciates Grizzard's status as a Southern mythmaker (although he notes his whiny tendencies—"as if nothing in life was so hard as to be a smart-assed white boy from Georgia"). Grizzard's South was a winner, a "world of beachfront condos on Hilton Head or Panama City, of wooded subdivisions full of glistening new Georgian homes, of Peachtree Road singles bars, of pregame tailgate parties at the Florida-Georgia football game." After his funeral, three of his buddies played a round of golf, in black golf shirts and one short of a foursome, "the missing man formation," and a handful of his ashes were scattered on the fifty-yard line of Sanford Stadium, home of the Georgia Bulldogs.

For better or for worse, this is the South where most Southerners live now, yet ironically it is the South that is least well-known and understood, even by those who live in it. It is also apparently where Applebome feels most at home. He even confesses that "I happen to love Charlotte, which may edge out Dallas and Atlanta as home to the purest strain ever discovered of the Southern booster gene." Still, he has some fun with Charlotte's insecurity, its nagging fear that it will not be thought "world-class," which sometimes leads to civic behavior that is sure-enough bush-league, like the *Observer* headline CHARLOTTE HITS BIG TIME: WE NEED 2 PHONE BOOKS and the 1970s Chamber of Commerce slogan "Charlotte—A Good Place to Make Money." Although "pessimism is about as much a part of the civic culture of Charlotte as communism," Applebome tracks down the village cynic, a man who carps that "the performing arts here are stock-car races" and "if somebody farts louder than somebody else, it'll be a world-class fart."

Well, the taste for a place that serves both God and Mammon with such enthusiasm is an acquired one, like that for Limburger—you have to get past the smell—but Charlotte does have some real achievements to point to, especially in the area of relations between black and white. Applebome explores these achievements, and even speculates that the new Southern cities' "blend of Yankee hustle and Southern charm" might make them "not just the nation's economic heart, but its best hope for racial peace as well."

A recurrent theme in *Dixie Rising* is provided by migrants to the South, who, like Applebome himself, find themselves becoming Southerners of a sort. Among those we meet are a successful real-estate developer from Illinois, raised by lapsed Presbyterian and Catholic parents, who now mans a Promise Keepers table after services at a biracial, nondenominational, twelve-thousand-member megachurch in suburban Atlanta, and the Ohio native who is now president of the Nashville company that owns Opryland ("the biggest hotel and convention center complex under one roof in the world," with two million visitors a year), The Nashville Network, Country Music Television, NASCAR broadcasting, Bass Pro shops, and who-knows-what-else this month. Applebome also chats with a natural-born troublemaker from Long Island now living in Georgia, a liberal Jewish woman who admits that "I like that people are more down to earth, more polite, that you don't have to walk around screaming and yelling and being rude, you know, the whole New York thing," but who nurtures a troubling suspicion: "It seems crazy listening to myself say this, but sometimes I think that a lot of the characteristics that come from some of this fundamentalist religious stuff that I hate also cause it to be so pleasant here."

To my mind, the most remarkable migrants in this book are the lesbian songwriter Janis Ian ("Society's Child"), interviewed in a Nashville latte bar called Bongo Java, who tells Applebome, "I walked off the plane in 1986 and thought, I'm home," and a black student from Grand Rapids who came to Jackson State "to see what it feels like to be in the majority" (he likes it) and who says, "I'll tell you, blacks in the South don't know how good they have it. I like Mississippi. I love Mississippi." (His father back in Michigan finds this baffling.)

It is gratifying to see that the South retains its remarkable capacity to assimilate newcomers, but of course migration does have a cultural down-side. Country-music singer Marty Stuart complains, for instance, that "country is such a huge industry now, that there are people coming to work in it every day who don't have a clue who Porter Waggoner is." And, ironically, several black Southerners express concern about the possible effects of migration on Southern race relations. Wilmington, North Carolina's leading Africanist, for instance, a native now retired after a career in New York City, believes that "with the influx of people from the North, the lines have hardened. [They] have brought some of the Northern attitudes toward race, which is many times a more brittle, much more exclusionary kind of thing." Similarly, Dorothy Counts, a black woman who attempted to desegregate a Charlotte high school in 1957, who has also come home after some years in New York, says that "I don't want other people to come in from other places and make things change. I don't want people who don't know what we've gone through to try to make Charlotte a different kind of place." Observations like these lead Applebome to wonder "whether the economic boom of the nineties is finally producing that idealized New South of prosperity and racial amity, or whether, in a cruel twist of history, interracial progress will hit a brick wall not because of the dissonant chords out of the South's past but because of the flood of Yankee transplants who have brought the casual, implicit, unreflective segregation of the North down South with them." The question is, will Charlotte and other Southern cities "stay Southern enough to keep the faith"?

Applebome closes his fine book with a visit to John Hope Franklin, the distinguished historian and possibly the last Southern gentleman, who clings to a vision of a redeemed, interracial South. Applebome recognizes that it is "more of a hypothesis than a caricature"—and that its time may have passed before it arrived—but he believes that you can still spy its outlines here and there, most importantly, perhaps, "in the routine courtesies and kindness and daily common ground of Southern life." Let's hope that he is right about that.

Among the Believers

In Dallas for the 1984 Republican convention, V. S. Naipaul noticed something odd. He knew little about the South, but he "had a sufficiently strong sense there of a region quite distinct from New York and New England" that he determined to return for a closer examination. His book *A Turn in the South*, the result, was published with such fanfare that no doubt most readers have at least heard rumors about what he found.

Naipaul originally thought his book would be about race, but that subject "quickly work[ed] itself out during the journey" and his topic became "that other South—of order and faith, and music and melancholy—which I didn't know about." At the end, he claims to have arrived at "an understanding of a whole distinctive culture, something I had never imagined existing in the United States." On the way, he heard and thought a great deal about race, which didn't work itself out all *that* quickly, and being a complete outsider licensed him to ask some heretical questions. He also reflects on historical memory and how it weighs differently on Southern blacks and whites, and he offers some unwittingly Cashian speculation about the effects of persisting frontier conditions, including an engaging hypothesis about why so many Southerners are fat.

But the core of Naipaul's disorderly book (I think) has to do with community, lost and regained. Time and again, among both blacks and whites, Naipaul met nostalgia. "The idea of a small community, where everyone knew everyone else and people were related—I had found that for many people it was part of the beauty of the ways of the past." He uses this to help explain what was for him the biggest surprise of all: the importance of religion in the South. The author of *Among the Believers*, an account of the non-Arab Islamic world, offers a striking observation: "In no other part of the world had I found people so driven by the idea of good behavior and the good religious life. And that was true for black and white." Naipaul concludes that many Southerners now rely on their churches for the identity and sense of belonging that are increasingly hard to get from families and communities.

He acknowledges exceptions. A couple of his informants were not hog-wild about that old-time community, or churches either for that matter. At the Nissan plant in Tennessee he reflects that maybe history can be "by-passed, just as in some quarters the old, too- demanding faith had been by-passed." But even in the Research Triangle of North Carolina, where the South is "seemingly abolished," a fern-bar waitress named Paula told him: "Well, you see. My husband and I had like a fight about a month ago. And he took half the stuff, and I had, like, well, the other half. But God gave me the strength to see that through." That, Naipaul suggests, is the New South talking.

This is good reading and, if nothing else, *A Turn in the South* is important as a cultural event. But one expected more from Naipaul. In its method his book is no different from a half-dozen other recent travelers' accounts. He wandered about, talked to some Southern- ers—famous and obscure, reliable and otherwise—and recorded and reflected on what they said. Most said interesting things, and many said them well. But some of what they said is well-known to the point of banality, and some of the rest probably isn't true. Naipaul acknowl- edges that his method depends on "accidents": "If I had met someone else my thoughts might have worked differently; though I might at the end have arrived at the same general feeling about the place I was in." Or then again, he might not have, and there's the rub.

Another problem: Naipaul is self-effacing to the point of invisibility. That's a relief, in some ways—this is not one of those travel books that is really about the traveler. But it means we can't begin to know how he affected what he heard. He tells us, for instance, that "Not a day had passed since I had come to the South without my reading in the newspapers about General Sherman, or hearing about him on televi- sion." Now, I go whole weeks without hearing about Sherman, and I have students who have apparently gone their whole lives (and some of the others think he had something to do with tank warfare). Could there be something about visiting foreigners that elicits such talk? Could Naipaul's questions have had something to do with it?

For a foreigner, Naipaul makes very few false steps, and most of them are minor, some charming. For instance, when he heard a TV evangelist plugging a book that answers the question "Will we be merry in heaven?" it set him off—"merry with wine, Merry Christmas, Old King Cole was a merry old soul"—when a Southerner would know that the question was "Will we be *married* in heaven?" Similarly, Naipaul understands Auburn's principal rival to be "Alabama State University," and he apparently believes that Virginia is a Northern state. (Of course, some Southerners do, too.)

A more serious problem is that an admittedly uninformed outsider, while his vision is not distorted by conventional wisdom, doesn't know when his informants are merely purveying it, as Naipaul's do on several occasions. To be sure, it is interesting when Naipaul sounds like Cash or Woodward, and it may even suggest that he is on to something. But he doesn't seem to be aware that some of his conclusions are recycled.

Moreover, as an outsider he is sometimes misled by Southern blarney or indirection. For just one example, his most notorious reassessment is an appreciation of the Southern redneck, excerpted in the *New York Review of Books.* Naipaul expected the worst (he had been told in New York that automobile associations give their members maps of the South that allow them to avoid areas of redneck infestation), but in Mississippi he was enlightened by an informant who "made me see pride and style and a fashion code where I had seen nothing, made me notice what so far I hadn't sufficiently noticed: the pickup trucks dashingly driven, the baseball caps marked with the name of some company." He came away thinking of rednecks as "a tribe, almost an Indian tribe, free spirits wandering freely over empty spaces," "people with a certain past, living out a certain code, a threatened species." Maybe so, and the Mississippian's panegyric is entertaining. But let's just say that it is not clear how seriously it was intended, although Naipaul took it to be in dead earnest.

What ought to have made this book truly exciting is its author's cosmopolitanism. A Hindu raised in Trinidad, resident for many years in England, widely traveled in the Third World—a man like that should see what other travelers have missed. Too often, though, what we get is mere place-dropping. Looking at cattle standing in a Georgia pond, for instance, "one might have been in India." At a Delta plantation house, "one might have been in Argentina, on an *estancia.*" Looking at the nearby workers' houses, "one might have been in some country in Africa—Kenya perhaps, if there had been hills in the background." The news that many Southern farmhouses once had swept-dirt yards inspires a bravura performance involving Japanese raked gardens, Congolese huts, and "the marks in dark sand of a *cocoye* broom . . . in the corner of a Trinidad Indian yard." Unelaborated and unexplored, these comparisons are just showing off, and sometimes they are even worse than useless. When Naipaul hears from an elderly white woman that blacks are devoted to their families despite their promiscuity, for instance, he free-associates: "That idea, about the importance of family, I had heard about in West Africa, in the Ivory Coast. It overrode the other idea—if it existed at all among Africans—of marital fidelity."

Occasionally, the book's comparative promise is almost fulfilled: when the Elvis cult provokes reflections on West Indians' identification with their political leaders, for instance; or when Naipaul observes that a Bible college teacher and New Right activist has the same training in theology and debate as many Islamic fundamentalist leaders; or when he speculates that brutal summer heat might contribute to "the almost Indian obsession of the South with religion, the idea of a life beyond the senses." And when a Confederate memorial inspires a reverie about the death of Ali and his sons—"Grief and the conviction of a just cause; defeat going against every idea of morality, every idea of the good story, the right story, the way it should have been: the tears of the Confederate Memorial are close to religion, the helpless grief and rage (such as the Shias know) about an injustice that cannot be rehearsed too often"—well, it's a thought, and one that suggests the book that might have been.

The "turn" of the title refers, in part, to Naipaul's changing impressions. One of the many surprises for him was when, well along, "I began to be aware of the great pleasure I had taken in traveling in the South." Since Naipaul coasting is sharper than most of us at full throttle, it is a pleasure to travel with him. But we learn less than he did, and less than we should have.

The Secret History of Civil Rights

The struggle for civil rights was one of the great morality plays of our time—indeed, one of the greatest of all time—and stage-managing that play was a major accomplishment of the movement and its allies in government and the media. But of course this struggle between black and white (literal and metaphorical) had its gray areas, its ironies and contradictions. As Rheta Grimsley Johnson writes in her foreword to Hunter James's *They Didn't Put That on the Huntley-Brinkley*, "Save us from more white sheriffs with potbellies battling it out with civil rights saints amongst the magnolias. It was more complicated than that. It is more complicated than that." The reporters who covered the movement knew that, even if they didn't always report it.

James, a retired newspaperman whose career spanned the era of the civil rights movement in Georgia, North Carolina, and Alabama, has set out to tell the "hidden story of the civil rights movement," to show how the movement worked itself out as "blacks and whites who had lived together as neighbors and sometimes as friends suddenly had to learn how to become friends and neighbors all over again in a different way." His book flags in places (his accounts of the Nixon and Goldwater campaigns don't add much, for instance), his command of the language sometimes falters (someone is "fomenting at the mouth," old Atlanta was "a polyglot of festering shantytowns"), and too many punctuation and spelling errors survived copyediting. His attempts to reproduce dialect are probably unfortunate: I don't question the accuracy of his rendition, but it sometimes gives an Amos 'n' Andy flavor to the proceedings. ("Dunno, boss. Can't rightly say. I reckon hit's jes goan depend on how all dis schoolin' turn out en whether dis city ever goan recognize dat we is men too en dat we got our rights jes like de white man has his'n.")

These flaws don't matter much, though. Basically James is just telling stories, and most of them are good ones. In my experience, old-fashioned working reporters are like small-town doctors and lawyers—worldly raconteurs, pleasantly cynical if they're not too sour—and James is one of the breed. His book sort of ambles from one good yarn or memorable character to another, and if it has a point it is just that, well, it's a funny old world.

Typical (speaking of sheriffs) is the quotation from Sheriff Bill Lee of Greene County, Alabama, that gave James his title. Lee, a former All-America tackle for the Crimson Tide, described how he saw his job:

> Keeping the whites off them, that's the main thing you gotta watch. I just let 'em talk, 'cause I'm used to it, and it ain't gonna hurt me none. But some of these whites, they ain't used to hearing that kind of talk out of niggers. They can say some real vicious things sometimes. But you gotta let 'em march. The courts have done said you gotta let 'em march, and I sure ain't gonna put up no barricade to try and stop 'em . . . sometimes I join right in and march with 'em. Sometimes I'll kneel with 'em and pray with 'em—whatever they want to do I'll join right in with it and go along. But nobody ever puts *that* on the Huntley-Brinkley.

James recognizes that Sheriff Lee was a decent man in his narrow way, and in James's account of the night Lee lost his job to a black insurgent named Tom Gilmore he laments the fact that his fellow reporters were shamelessly partisan. "I hated it when they took sides like that." But it must have been hard for outsiders not to. James quotes Gilmore in his earlier, activist days: "Sometimes when I'm in my bed at night and all the world is dark and all hope seems lost I ask myself, 'When is America gonna change? When is Greene County gonna change? When is Alabama gonna change? O Lord, when're we finally gonna be able to walk in this old world as free men and brothers?'" To which Sheriff Lee responded, "You see? Just plain vicious, that's all. . . . Just another cotton-patch nigger. That's all."

Not all of James's stories are movement stories, strictly speaking, although most have to do with race, one way or another, as most things in the South in those decades seemed to. He tells us, for instance, about Foley Watkins, a Winston-Salem shoeshine boy and numbers operator who angered a white barber by parking his Cadillac in the white man's customary parking place and refusing to move it. Soon after, Watkins mysteriously attracted the interest of the IRS and subsequently went to jail for nonpayment of sixteen years' worth of taxes. Not long after that, the barber was mysteriously murdered. The other barbers seemed to think he had it coming.

Some of James's best anecdotes come from his time in Atlanta, the pretentious capital of the New South, "the City Too Busy to Hate." We are introduced to "Mr. Million," a paper-products salesman alleged to be the city's one-millionth resident. Atlanta boosters sent Mr. Million on good-will missions to tell the North of their city's magnificence—until he moved to Pennsylvania.

Also in Atlanta, we meet "Big Gentry," a hard-drinking and not very bright laborer caught up briefly in the movement (to the dismay of his mama who wanted only peace and quiet and her own piece of land), and Lester Maddox, who chased demonstrators from his chicken restaurant with an axe handle, then sold over a hundred thousand souvenir axe handles (and hammer handles "for the toddlers"), before running successfully for governor.

But my favorite Atlanta stories involve the liberal *Constitution* columnist Ralph McGill and his many enemies. James once found McGill sharing a drink with Roy V. Harris, former speaker of the Georgia legislature and an old New Dealer turned race baiter, whose rabid stump rhetoric disguised a taste for classical music, poetry, and the study of history. Asked why he was being so chummy with "Rastus" McGill, his favorite bogeyman, Harris said, "Well, we talk, Ralph and I. . . . It's just that we have to be a little careful how we act in public. Wouldn't look right, you know, if we started acting too lovey-dovey. You know how it is. Me and Ralph—I mean, well, we *have* to keep up appearances."

Then there is James's account of the legendary last meeting between McGill and Gene Talmadge. One election night, the victorious Talmadge dropped in unexpectedly at the *Constitution* to find his old adversary in consultation with the sitting governor, Ellis Arnall, a wealthy Atlanta liberal who had beaten Talmadge four years before.

> "Give you a good whuppin' this time, didn't I, Ralph?" said [Talmadge] as he reached across the desk to shake hands. "Yessir. A real good whuppin' this time."
>
> McGill's voice failed him. Arnall was looking for a quick exit. He didn't find it. Talmadge stood pointing at him with his cigar. "Another thing, Ralph, this little fellow here wouldna beat me the last time if that black widow spider hadna bit me on the balls!"

But the Wild Man of Sugar Creek hadn't come simply to gloat: he had come to propose that McGill write his biography. He even had a title: *The Life of Gene Talmadge by His Old Enemy Ralph McGill.* (The book was never written.)

James moved on to Greensboro, North Carolina, where he encountered Ralph Johns, a former Hollywood bit player and double for George Raft, who ran a Greensboro clothing store to support his true vocation of crusading for left-wing causes. Johns apparently shamed four North Carolina A&T students into undertaking the historic sit-in at the Woolworth's across the street from his store, but never got the recognition he feels (and they agree) that he deserves. He has now returned to California and writes for an environmental weekly in Beverly Hills.

We also meet the young Jesse Jackson. As a football hero and student body president at North Carolina A&T, he was already a skilled manipulator of the media; already, too, a little careless about the facts. (That Jackson was not yet in Greensboro at the time of the original sit-ins is "just one of the things that's got all mixed up over the years," says one of the four participants.)

But the best of James's characters come from Eutaw, Greene County, Alabama, "a town so lost to the world that it was almost in Mississippi." It is there that we meet Lula, the live-in maid in an Alabama plantation house owned by the family of James's wife. Hired for fifty dollars a month to clean, garden, cook, and tend to an invalid old lady, Lula dismayed her employers by using the indoor toilet, eating at a "white" table, entertaining her guests in the house, and watching her soap operas on the family's television set. Despairing of teaching her correct behavior, "Uncle Dud" rehabilitated the old privy for his own use.

Uncle Dud is almost too good to be true. He also believed that the federal government should compensate the descendants of slaveholders for their losses at emancipation: "I still say it's a good fair debt that the government of the country owes the South. And they'd be well rid of it. Why, it's the right thing—the only honorable thing. And I'm bound to think they'd feel a whole lot better about themselves if they'd just go ahead and clear it off the books."

Eutaw was also home to O. B. Harris, a black merchant and chairman of the local NAACP chapter. Harris believed in the power of voter registration, and he opposed the demonstrations and boycotts brought to town by the young organizers of SCLC, the Southern Christian Leadership Conference. (They also brought signs left over from other demonstrations in other towns. "Integrate the Bowling Alley!" said one.

There was no bowling alley in Eutaw.) James tried to interview Harris after he was kicked out of office for being too moderate, but Harris said that he was saving most of his material for his own book, to be called *Uncle Tom Speaks Out*.

Harris was succeeded as NAACP chairman by a forty-seven-year-old preacher named William McKinley Branch. Like so many black preachers, Branch was a powerful speaker, and James gives us some samples. In support of a boycott: "Stay outa them white men's stores. Let them balonies rot. Let the cheeses rot. The vegetubbles and the fruits and the fresh meats, let all them things rot." But also: "I believe we are made of the same order other men are made by . . . I believe that we can be stronger and better, and the world made stronger and better because we have lived."

The boycott was supported by a good many of what Southern white folks used to call "outside agitators," including SCLC's Hosea Williams. Williams came to rally the local troops and, while he was at it, to needle a prominent white lawyer: "Why, I'm surprised at you, Mr. Banks. Here you are a graduate of the University of Alabama and you don't even know the proper pronunciation of *Negro*? KNEEgrow, Mr. Banks. KNEE . . . KNEE, Mr. Banks. Think of your knee. It's what you Episcopals get down on when you pray for us nigras." (A bum rap, by the way: People who pronounced "piano" *pyana* pronounced "Negro" *nigra* quite naturally and without malice—one reason I was glad to see the preferred usage change to "black.")

The boycott worked, but what made it work was outside help of another sort: an outsider named Andrew Marisette organized teenage boys into "goon squads" to tear up grocery bags and to intimidate, sometimes to beat, black folks who didn't cooperate. Looking back, a local preacher observes, "Yeah, I guess you might say there's lots of things we did that was against King's guidelines, all right enough. But we saw it took that technique to get the thing over, and so we contraried a lot."

Greene County was no stranger to violence. Civil rights demonstrators had been threatened with chain saws and sprayed with poison from a crop-dusting airplane. But over time the violence directed against Greene County black folks increasingly came from other blacks. One of the most painful conversations in this book is with Wes Taylor, an aged black man whose young daughter was blinded by shotgun blasts from enforcers, out to get those who did not vote the insurgent line. "Why'd dey pick me out, cap'n?," Taylor asks. "Why'd dey want to go en shoot my little girl?"

In Greene County neither the worst fears of whites nor the highest hopes of blacks have been realized. Some whites have left the county, but the feared mass exodus never happened. Economic power is still solidly in white hands, political power now in black. Although there has been a measure of rapprochement (over the objections of some diehards, both black and white), there has been nothing like redemption, and James makes bitter fun of some writers who wrote that story prematurely.

His book ends, oddly, in a different Alabama town, with the old story of the rape of a white woman, racial tension, rumors flying, muttered threats—and a lynching that doesn't happen. That, he suggests, is progress, of a sort. Even those of us who are more optimistic than he can agree with that.

The Smoke Never Clears

All freshmen entering the University of North Carolina in the fall of 2000 were assigned Tony Horwitz's book, Confederates in the Attic: Dispatches from the Unfinished Civil War. *I got to talk to them about it.*

I first met Tony Horwitz some years ago at a Southern Historical Association convention in Louisville. I was moderating a panel on the meaning of the Confederate flag. It was basically a debate between Professor Clyde Wilson, editor of the Calhoun papers at the University of South Carolina and a founder of the League of the South, and Julian Bond, the well-known civil rights activist who was then a professor at the University of Virginia, not yet chairman of the NAACP. The discussion was polite, but—not surprisingly—there was no meeting of the minds.

After the panel was over, an innocent-looking young guy from the audience approached me and introduced himself as Tony Horwitz—a name that didn't mean anything to me. As I recall, he asked some rather naive questions, and I pontificated a bit for him. Only later did I realize that I had been reading his dispatches from the South in the *Wall Street Journal* for some time. I also realized that he was neither as young nor as naive as he appeared to be.

That innocent and engaging curiosity is a mask that conceals a deft reporter, even a sly one, a man who encourages people to say more than they mean to, maybe more than they should. This is after all a journalist whose beat for many years was the Middle East, a place not known for innocence. (He wrote a book about it called *Baghdad without a Map*, undoubtedly the funniest book ever written about Iraq.) After that Tony served as the *Wall Street Journal*'s European correspondent, working out of London, then came back to the States and settled in northern Virginia, reporting on national affairs for the *Journal*, work that won him a Pulitzer Prize.

After we met in Louisville, Tony and I became that odd modern phenomenon: email buddies, sort of electronic pen pals. We turned out to have a lot in common: interests in the South, of course, but also in England and the Middle East, where we had both lived. Most of our "conversation" was online, but my wife and I had lunch with him once in Washington, and he stopped by to visit when he was in North Carolina. Later we got to know his wife, Geraldine Brooks, an Australian who is an accomplished writer herself, author of *Nine Parts of Desire: The Hidden World of Islamic Women* and of a marvelous memoir called *Foreign Correspondence.*

I knew that Tony was working on a book about the Civil War and historical memory. Many of his newspaper articles fed into that interest. (They usually appeared in the front-page-center slot that the *Journal* reserves for "quirky" material.) When Tony asked me to read the manuscript of *Confederates in the Attic* I gladly agreed. I corrected a few typos and suggested some structural changes—none of which he made, as far as I can tell, but he is the best-selling author, not me. I also wrote a promotional blurb for the back cover of the first edition, replaced on later printings by a quotation from one of the book's many rave reviews.

Not all the reviews were raves, and I'll get to that in a minute, but for the most part, the book was well-received. After it was published Tony left the *Wall Street Journal* to write for *The New Yorker*, mostly on Southern topics ranging from the futile search for Eric Rudolph in western North Carolina to the wretched yuppie excess of the Inn at Little Washington in northern Virginia. I think he grew tired of writing about the South, though: his next move was to spend a year with Geraldine and their son in Australia—about as far from the South as possible—where he worked on a book about Captain Cook. But we in the South can be grateful that we had his attention as long as we did. Even if I didn't know and like its author, I believe I would find *Confederates in the Attic* valuable (more for the questions it raises than for the answers it gives), and of course the book's a lot of fun, too. It sometimes made me laugh out loud.

Not everyone agrees. Some defenders of the Confederate faith have assailed Tony for his treatment of the last Confederate widow, among other evidences of what they see as disrespect. On the other hand, a few academic historians have also criticized him, charging him with guilt by association, for being *too* respectful of some folks they find disgusting. That Tony could hang out with these yahoos, even "spoon" with them, yet not condemn them strikes these folks as politically irresponsible. At one point when Tony was being fired on from all sides

I reminded him of Nathan Bedford Forrest's response to the news that the Yankees were both behind his position and in front of it. General Forrest's command was: "Attack in both directions."

I think most of Tony's critics suffer from ideological tunnel vision and are seriously humor-impaired. But there are a few folks whose dislike for the book I take more seriously. These are men and women who feel that *Confederates in the Attic* presents the South as a sort of American freak show, and resent that. One of my good friends in Chapel Hill, a man I admire very much, declined on these grounds to conduct a discussion group about Tony's book. (I told him that if he thinks Tony was hard on us he should see what he wrote about Iraq.) Certainly this book introduces us to some odd people, many of them on the fringes of Southern life, a few of them on the fringes of sanity. But Tony doesn't present them as in any sense *representative* Southerners—in fact, he explicitly denies that they are. He recognizes that to many Southerners these days the Civil War is as remote as the War of the Roses.

A hundred years ago, things were different. In 1900 a Southerner *was* someone who stood up for "Dixie," saluted the Stars and Bars, and honored the Lost Cause and its heroes. Of course, this definition excluded a good many white residents of the South and nearly all black ones, but their views on the matter carried no weight. Tony's book amply demonstrates that this version of Southernness is still with us, but my guess is that most Southerners see the folks that Tony hung out with as something like living fossils. So do I. But in education fossils do have their uses. One purpose of a liberal education has always been to liberate students from their own cultural parochialism. You study the Greeks and Romans, or the Trobriand Islanders, or the Aztecs, to learn what is human and universal, but also to enter imaginatively into cultures in which practices like slavery, infanticide, or human sacrifice were normal, everyday practices, accepted by good and decent people. The point is not to bask in our superiority to ancient or primitive cultures. Far from it. Ideally this process raises the question of which of *our* taken-for-granted institutions will someday be seen as self-evident abominations.

I tell university students that whatever their individual backgrounds may be, whatever their "heritage"—Confederate American, African American, Yankee American, or something else altogether—they have the opportunity to explore it in college. But one of the best ways to deepen your understanding of your own culture is to understand as best you can some *other*, very different worldview—not to accept it, but to understand how someone could. One lesson of Tony's book is that you don't have to go back in time or to another continent to find striking contrasts to the dominant, modern, American view of things.

A more obvious, less rarified way to read the book, though, is for the questions that it raises about the South, questions that are central to our common life in this region in this new century. What does it mean to be "Southern"—if, indeed, it means anything these days? Is there one "Southern heritage" or many? Who gets to decide what that phrase means?

Beneath the book's account of its author's misadventures and encounters with colorful characters lie serious considerations of historical memory and myth—"myth" not in the sense of falsehood, necessarily, but meaning simply the story people tell about their past. Groups *will* have stories about themselves and their history. Indeed, many groups are created, defined, by such stories—more or less accurate, more or less flattering, more or less useful. People die for myths, and for the symbols that evoke them—for things like flags. Some versions of history should bear a warning label: "Danger: Harmful or fatal if swallowed."

How are we going to deal with a past that, like most peoples', is a mixture of triumph and tragedy, grandeur and squalor, oppression and accomplishment? Twenty-five years ago, Tanya Tucker sang a country song called "I Believe the South Is Going to Rise Again," in which she called on Southerners to "forget the bad and keep the good." Can we do that? Can we accept a sort of no-fault history and move on? Sounds nice, but one lesson of Tony's book is that we are going to have some trouble sorting out the good and the bad to everyone's satisfaction. If you don't find *Confederates in the Attic* thought provoking, you must be brain-dead.

One Tough Lady

There is nothing fashionable about Florence King. She lives in small-town Virginia, likes being called a spinster and defends cigarette smokers. The only thing even remotely trendy about her was the lesbianism she wrote about in *Confessions of a Failed Southern Lady*, and she gave that up when it took on political overtones. "I don't mind being regarded as perverted and unnatural," she writes in this new book, "but I would die if people thought I was a Democrat." (Wait. You haven't seen the photograph on the cover of this book. It makes the smiling author look like that adolescent nightmare, an omniscient junior-high teacher. The .22 pistol she's holding makes it even more obvious that this is a woman you don't want to mess with.)

Some in our parts remember Miss King as a women's page writer for the Raleigh *News and Observer* in the mid '60s, but I first encountered her delicious prose in *Southern Ladies and Gentlemen*, published in 1975 and still one of the funniest ethnographies of the modern South. That book and several more, written under various names including her own, were followed in 1985 by her semiautobiographical *Confessions*, then by a volume of social criticism called *Reflections in a Jaundiced Eye*, a splendid collation of anecdotes and judgments, literary and political. When a wimpy interviewer suggested that *Reflections* revealed "a new, more strident persona" than the author of *Confessions*, Miss King cheerfully acknowledged the change, and chalked it up to The Change. Menopause, she said, had clarified her thinking. Whatever the reason, I thought the Florence King of *Reflections* was the most engaging yet: an author who knew her mind, stated it with wit and precision, and really didn't care whether you agreed or not.

Lump It or Leave It, as its title suggests, is more of the same. Which suits me just fine, because Miss King often and admirably expresses views that I agree with, or will from now on. No doubt some other readers will find her a trenchant social critic and a wickedly funny lady even as they disagree with her. And I am sure some right-thinkers will be scandalized: some by her language, some by her opinions. You will know who you are before I finish quoting, and there is no reason you should like Florence King: She certainly doesn't like you.

Besides menopause, firearms, and cigarettes, Miss King champions a variety of such apparently lost causes as Robert Bork and school prayer. She is moved to greatest eloquence and ingenuity, however, by what she *doesn't* like. For example, she has decided that the noble experiment of coeducation has failed. When "males and females haunt each other twenty-four hours a day," she writes, "the sexes see far too much of each other and have gotten on each other's nerves. The rise in homosexuality in recent decades has less to do with sex than with rest cures." It's a thought.

Miss King offhandedly refers to her book as "this new volume of anti-Americana," but if this be anti-American, then so are Walker Percy's *Lancelot*, Tom Wolfe's *Bonfire of the Vanities*, George Garrett's wonderfully vicious *Poison Pen*, and the Agrarian manifesto *I'll Take My Stand*. Like the Southerners who wrote those books, Miss King is offended by the sheer trashiness of contemporary American civilization. "Anything is possible in a madhouse," she writes, "even a very small madhouse, and the one I'm talking about stretches from sea to shining sea." She has little use and less mercy for a culture where personal ads say stuff like "Handsome masochist, 28, seeks disciplinarian to tie me up, beat me with cat o' nine tails, dunk me in ice water, ram me with baseball bat, and stick arrows in me for St. Sebastian fantasy. Nonsmokers only." The new, aerobic Puritanism annoys her even more than the old-time variety.

She laments the decline of the "Do Right" ethic which used to form the character of well-raised Southerners. This was not the last word in morality ("Being kind to slaves, making *good* bootleg whiskey, and never shooting a man in the back all came under the heading of Do Right"), but it did give some guidance, more like a compass than a map, "permitting us to practice situation ethics from an unshakable moral base." Its passing means that some ethical eccentrics now get better hearings than they deserve, and Miss King seeks out and destroys a number of them. The writer Jan Morris, for instance, who is soft on incest: "Granted, Morris is an idiot, but idiots get a lot of respect in America."

This is a woman who does not suffer fools, and she is evenhandedly impatient with cant from her own end of the political spectrum.

She has great sport with America's newly discovered enthusiasm for "Trad Vals"—traditional values: "Lest anyone doubt that Trad Valhood is powerful, remember this: It made Jesse Helms go to an art gallery." And she puts her finger on a central dilemma of *fin de siècle* America: "Americans are presently longing for high moral standards and the security they bestow, but our love affair with freedom and individualism gets in the way. We are unwilling or unable to see that such standards require a mentality that accepts and derives comfort from ironclad rules that make no sense, and explanations like 'just because.'"

Florence King has such a mentality herself and she flaunts it on the subject of flag-burning: She opposes it not because she loves the flag ("The American flag means nothing to me except that 11 of its stars represent the Old Confederacy") but because flag-burning should be something that simply is not done. She says she dreams of someday "rescuing Old Glory from a pyromaniac and bellowing, 'Shoot if you must this old gray head, but spare this Yankee rag.'" I have quoted so many of Florence King's words that I should probably split my check with her, but there is much more where this came from. We are dealing here with a major-league curmudgeon. Florence King is an unapologetic elitist, but her elite is the same one Thomas Jefferson celebrated: a natural aristocracy based on talent and hard work. She scorns anyone who would substitute mere wealth or credentials or political correctness for genuine accomplishment, and on the subject of Americans' dirty secret, social class, she is deadly. She writes, for instance, about the "latest bromide," which has it that "whites are no longer prejudiced against blacks as blacks: discrimination is now a matter of class rather than race."

How many have heard that, even said that? But here comes the sucker punch: "Where else but America could you banish social guilt by identifying yourself as a snob?"

A South That Never Was

When it comes to reviewing books I try to go with the rule "If you can't say something nice, don't say anything at all." For most authors writing is such hard and unrewarding work that if I don't like a book I get for review I usually just send it back. When I tried to do that with this one, though, the editor persuaded me to say why I disliked it so much. My review won the Dictionary of Literary Biography Yearbook's *annual Tomahawk Chop Award for 1995.*

I wanted to like *The South*, by B. C. Hall and C. T. Wood. The authors are Arkansas boys who have some good stories and know how to tell them. They have talked with other good talkers, too, like singer-songwriter Tom T. Hall ("Picking up a snake down here is the same thing as lighting a candle") and an Atlanta hotel doorman (who, when asked if his city is still part of the South, observed, "Well, wherever you go, there you are"). They have turned up an unidentified early explorer who declared that "Arkansas is not one of the places that Jesus Christ died for," and this wonderful folktale fragment:

"Had a high old dream last night. Dreamt I was in hell."

"Rough country?"

There is good stuff in here about the South's outlaw tradition and the region's flourishing marijuana economy, and about Bill Clinton's corrupt and decadent home town of Hot Springs. I would enjoy an evening swapping stories with these guys. But that doesn't mean that they have written a good book.

It begins in Virginia, moves south and west, then back along the Gulf Coast to finish in Key West, an itinerary that roughly parallels the chronology of settlement. Each chapter offers a little geography, a little history, an interview or two, some amusing gossip, often a few memorable images to take along as souvenirs. At first glance, this looks something like a down-home version of John Gunther's *Inside U.S.A*, but the introduction suggests a higher standard, evoking W. J. Cash's *The Mind of the South*. Hall and Wood do use "the savage ideal" (Cash's catchy phrase for Southern intolerance) to lambaste a string of Southern bad guys from those old adversaries Andrew Jackson and John C. Calhoun to a newer crop that includes Jesse Helms, Jerry Falwell, and Rush Limbaugh (from Cape Girardeau, Missouri). Aside from that, however, their homage to Cash is mostly a matter of sharing his tendency to purple prose and his contempt for Southern folk religion. Both are evident in passages like this one: "Though Christianity was born with Paul of Tarsus, for God-fearing Southerners it was truly born in the Great Awakening and reborn in the Great Depression. Then it was that the Great Speckled Bird hatched a passel of orphans: the splinter-berserker-shaker-snakehandler-self-whipping-hairshirt-tortured-acid-drinking-orgiastic-lunatic fringe of evangelicals on the Southern religious stage."

You might ask yourself what the poor Shakers are doing in there, and if there are any hairshirt–wearing evangelicals in Dixie I'll drink some acid myself. But it *sounds* good.

And that's this book's real problem. Precision and even accuracy are well down the list of its concerns. Phrases like Black Belt, shotgun shack, gutbucket guitar, hard-shell Baptist, closed shop, and relative deprivation all have specific, even technical, meanings, for instance, but Hall and Wood refuse to be constrained by that. Just so, the Roman Catholic Church is not a sect, Pat Robertson is not a Calvinist, the Africans unloaded at Jamestown in 1619 were not legally slaves, L. Q. C. Lamar was not a redneck, and a waltz is not a two-step even when done by Cajuns.

This nonchalance begins on the fly-leaf (Georgia's demagogic Talmadge was Eugene, not Herman) and things go downhill from there. The stars of North America were not "strange" to European astronomers. The Shenandoah River does not flow "down from Harper's Ferry." Raleigh is not in North Carolina's "Triad," the "Grand Strand" does not reach from North Carolina to Florida, and Erskine Caldwell's birthplace of White Oak, Georgia, is not anywhere near Augusta. Tupelo is not a "delta town," Tougaloo is not a land-grant college, Pensacola has no eighteenth-century mansions, and Jacksonville is the largest city in Florida only if we are talking about acreage (and it is not clear that we are).

Continuing: The Van Burens were not among the First Families of Virginia, Jefferson's views on slavery did not "condemn him utterly in the eyes of his fellow Southerners," and the abolitionist movement was not responsible for outlawing the importation of slaves. Jefferson Davis was not captured in Lynchburg and did not die "scorned" by his fellow Confederates. "Countless thousands" of blacks did not die in the siege of Richmond, and Joe Johnston did not lead "the last army of the South." Kentucky was not Reconstructed, Andrew Johnson did not come from South Carolina, the Yellow Rose of Texas was not originally a flower, and is the name of Henry Clay really "all but forgotten today"?

Want more? The Acadians were not Huguenots. Charleston's "claim to gastronomic delight" is not key lime pie. Lynchings were not "on the rise" in 1934, and W. J. Cash's book did not make him a "pariah." Atlanta's population in 1900 was not a million, the Duke family did not own "the entire hydroelectric power systems of North and South Carolina," and Delta Air Lines was not formerly Southern Airways. H. L. Mencken was not any kind of Anglican, and Norman Thomas never "sign[ed] up with the vision of Marxism." Nobody was listening to rock and roll in the 1940s, the Grand Ole Opry was not all-white, WSM was not Nashville's rhythm and blues station (WLAC was), and Otis Redding did not sing "Southern rock."

It gets even stranger: The conservative Nashville Agrarians never turned to "W. E. B. DuBois's practical vision"—whatever that means— and they were not "followers" of Donald Davidson. The "prevailing view" even of the "redneck South" has never been that blacks do not have souls. Being bitten is not a sign of a snake handler's worthiness. And I don't know what it means to say that Vulcan was "a misshapen Norse Roman god."

And downright bizarre: Coon hunting did not evolve as a postbellum substitute for slave-catching. Robert E. Lee did not ride Traveler into the lobby of San Antonio's Menger Hotel "just for the hell of it" or for any other reason. And surely "the spiritual father of the counterculture" was not Kingman Brewster, president of Yale.

These are just things I happened to know, or was curious enough to look up, and Lord knows what I missed. Maybe errors like these are trivial taken one at a time, but their cumulative effect soon had me scrawling "NO!!!!!" in the margin. Of course, if you don't know anything at all, this book could be fun to read—and there is the problem. When you're finished you will know a lot. And much of it won't be true.

As Hall and Wood ask at one point, however, "What's truth in the South but a secondhand emotion?" What, indeed? The late comedian Dave Gardner is one of the Southerners this book celebrates, and here is what Brother Dave would have called a "weird thought": Could this be some deep postmodern good-old-boy put-on? Could it be perhaps a test of Faulkner's observation about Yankees' "gullibility," their "volitionless, almost helpless capacity and eagerness to believe anything about the South not even provided it be derogatory but merely bizarre enough and strange enough"? Be that as it may, the favorable reviews in *Publishers Weekly* and *Library Journal* suggest that old Bill knew what he was talking about.

II

History And Historians

American Weed

The hard-pressed lobbyists of the Tobacco Institute should be pleased. In *Tobacco Culture*, subtitled *The Mentality of the Great Tidewater Planters on the Eve of the Revolution*, T. H. Breen, one of our best historians of the colonial period, argues, in effect: no tobacco, no United States. If that doesn't wrap sotweed in the flag, nothing will.

Tobacco Culture looks at the Revolutionary generation of Virginians as they saw themselves—as men whose lives depended on successfully growing and selling tobacco. Then it asks how such men came to take up arms and to risk their lives in a struggle for political independence. On the way to his answer, Professor Breen gives a vivid portrait of life among the tobacco grandees of eighteenth-century Virginia.

Many of us, of course, at least think we know something about these men already. We have seen their homes: Berkeley and Shirley and Carter's Grove and others are still standing (some indeed are still growing tobacco), and they have become popular tourist spots on the way to Williamsburg and Jamestown. But the images of eighteenth-century life that these estates provide are misleading. "Ol' Virginny" was a place of lavish hospitality and gracious living, to be sure, but it was also, and primarily, a place of working farms, a place where not only a man's income but his social standing and even his self-esteem depended in large measure on the quantity and quality of the crops he made.

Breen argues that accumulating debt to London merchants and tobacco buyers was at the root of the revolutionary impulse in Virginia. "If the [Virginia tobacco] planters' perceptions of debt and their fears over the loss of personal autonomy were not sufficient causes for revolution," he writes, "they were certainly necessary." His case is a subtle one, though: Washington and Jefferson and Patrick Henry were not just deadbeats who wanted independence in order to welsh on their debts. As in most agricultural societies, in Virginia credit was a necessary aspect of the economy. Debt was a more or less taken-for-granted condition. What irked the Virginians was not the debt itself, but a difference between them and their distant creditors about what debt *meant*. The Londoners viewed it much as most of us probably would—as a business matter. But Breen shows that to the Virginians it was something else altogether. By their code, a loan was a personal favor, an expression of friendship and patronage, an informal arrangement between gentlemen. Loans were to be paid back, of course, but not to be pressed. If they were not repaid, presumably there were good reasons why not; to assume otherwise would be to question the honor of one's debtor. This has a quaint, premodern ring to it now, but of course the Virginians didn't see themselves as quaint or premodern: to them, this was simply how things were.

After 1750, Breen shows, the planters found themselves increasingly in debt. On the farm, when tobacco prices were low, they borrowed to buy slaves to expand production. In the home, they borrowed to buy new necessities that would formerly have been seen as luxuries. And when their British creditors got nervous and reluctant to lend them more, they saw this as betrayal. "Merchants have no gratitude," Landon Carter complained in 1768; it didn't matter that he had been dealing with them for years. Increasing debt came to be felt as increasing dependence—and dependence not on other gentlemen but on money-grubbers who did not play by Virginia's rules, who didn't understand the etiquette of debt. The tobacco growers were threatened where it hurt: not just in the pocketbook, but in their honor, in their treasured sense of autonomy and independence. They began to feel like—well, like slaves.

This was the situation into which the rhetoric of republicanism fell, like a spark into tinder. Many planters grasped at the language of independence—not just for the colonies but for the individual colonists—and many of their names adorn American history textbooks today.

Breen makes this argument eloquently, and with a wealth of detail, anecdote, and documentation. Unlike many historians these days, he doesn't seem to be writing mainly for other historians. His book can be read with profit by those who don't know or care about historians' intramural squabbles, and it *should* be read by anyone who cares about the antecedents of the revolution. It is pleasantly illustrated with maps, engravings, and commercial documents of the period.

Slaves View Slavery

Writing in the 1950s, Richard Hofstadter called for the realization that "any history of slavery must be written in large part from the standpoint of the slave." It is perhaps some measure of progress that this point should seem obvious to most present-day readers. When Hofstadter wrote, however, no really satisfactory attempt had been made to address the question of how slaves experienced slavery.

At that time, the field of slavery history was dominated by the work of Ulrich B. Phillips and his students. Phillips was a Georgian who, in two remarkable books and a number of articles, essayed a comprehensive study of the structure of slavery in the antebellum South. Even Phillips's critics are compelled to acknowledge his contributions, but they have claimed that he failed in several respects, particularly in his treatment of the slaves' response to slavery. Hofstadter argued that the impression one gets from Phillips's writings is very close to the slaveholders' view of the slave "as a singularly contented and docile 'seriocomic' creature." If a scholar who did not share Phillips's preconceptions were to do as intensive a study, Hofstadter asserted, he would arrive at a "materially different version of the slave system." It is perhaps the case that if such a scholar restricted himself to Phillips's sources he would have little basis for *any* reliable conclusion about what it was like to be a slave, for Phillips relied primarily on plantation records, and slaveholders' journals and letters. It should be obvious that such sources are poor guides to the attitudes of slaves and to the details of what private lives they could wrest from the system.

The principal reason for slaveholders' inability to testify accurately in these respects is the early mastery by slaves of what sociologists would later call "impression management," an art universally cultivated by subordinates. Many aspects of everyday life and thought in "the quarters," particularly those contrary to the white folks' desires and preconceptions, were carefully shielded from observation (sometimes with the aid of magic). The shock reported by many slaveholders when

71

"devoted" servants defected to the Union army and the remarkable trust that many runaways reported having exploited are evidence of the success with which some slaves, at least, concealed their real feelings about slavery and "old massa." The more perceptive slaveholders only realized more fully the extent of their ignorance; one South Carolina plantation mistress, for example, speculated in her journal on what was going on behind the "bronze masks" of her slaves.

A different objection to over-reliance on documents left by slaveholders is that the plantations for which they are available are unrepresentative, "the upper crust of the upper crust." Hofstadter showed that the plantations Phillips studied were among the largest—over a hundred slaves apiece—and that such slaveholders held only about 10 percent of all slaves and were fewer than 1 percent of all slaveholders in the South. Discussing ways to overcome this bias, Hofstadter suggested greater use of travelers' accounts of the Old South. It is ironic that Phillips had held such accounts suspect partly on the grounds of the atypicality of *their* observations and their inability to "distinguish what was common in the system from what was unique in some special case."

Phillips also distrusted such accounts because he was extremely sensitive to the antislavery bias of most such travelers. He felt particularly that those who wrote for publication were "propagandists of one cause and another, and as such set their spectacles upon their readers' noses." (His critics claim Phillips was too scrupulous: he did not begin to exploit the exceptional works, such as those of Frederick Law Olmsted, which achieve credibility despite the commitments of their authors.)

As testimony on the experience of slavery, travelers' accounts have still another shortcoming. Such information as travelers gathered must have come, ultimately, from slaves themselves, and here again the disconcerting propensity of slaves to tell the white man what he wanted to hear clouds the evidence. Proslavery travelers were inordinately likely to encounter evidence that slaves were generally well-treated and content, while abolitionists were likely to be told of terrible suffering and incipient revolt. The antislavery writer James Redpath, for instance, acknowledged that "the slaves often told me, at first, that they did not care about freedom," but reported that "never yet have I met with one who did not finally confess that he was longing for liberty."

In general, then, documents left to us by contemporary whites are at best of uncertain reliability as guides to the slaves' viewpoint. First, the slaves told whites what they thought the whites wanted to hear. Second, the mechanisms, which latter-day social scientists have called "selective exposure," "selective perception," "selective interpretation," and "selective retention," operated to ensure that the whites' stereotypes would not be upset. Finally, those partisans who wrote for publication must be suspected of what might be called "selective reporting," until their innocence is established.

The obvious solution would seem to be to turn to documents left us by blacks themselves. Needless to say, very few are available written by slaves while enslaved. Most slave states had laws against teaching slaves to read and write, and those who did manage to learn had neither the time nor the inclination to keep journals. The few slave-written letters that we have reveal little of interest to the historian. The bulk of the material written by blacks prior to emancipation is in the form of autobiographies (often "ghostwritten") and letters by fugitive slaves— not very reliable testimony on the general experience. As a number of works on the Underground Railroad have documented, escape to free states was an extremely unusual response to slavery. It is difficult to say whether runaways, in general, had had a worse time of it than other slaves (as many runaways claimed) or a better (as many slaveholders of the "give-'em-an-inch-and-they'll-take-a-mile" school claimed), but it is certain that they felt more strongly the injustice of the situation than did those who stayed put. If fugitives in general were an atypical lot, how much less typical must have been the characters and experiences of those who chose, and were able, to write about their lives. More-over, whoever recorded the fugitive's experience, whether himself or an interviewer, was likely to have done so in order to score points in the national debate, and to have selected from the available material accordingly. As Phillips noted in dismissing such sources, "ex-slave narratives in general . . . were issued with so much abolitionist editing that as a class their authenticity is doubtful."

Fortunately for the historian of slavery, however, a class of sources not available to Phillips furnishes a somewhat more accurate picture of the South's "peculiar institution" as seen from "the standpoint of the slave." In the 1920s American sociology, dominated by the "Chicago school" of ethnographers, was engaged primarily in detailed descrip-tion of various American subcultures—the small-town Midwest, the big city Negro ghetto, the underworld of petty thieves, and so forth. Influenced by this work, with its emphasis on representativeness, accuracy of recording, thoroughness of detail, and avoidance (in prin-ciple, at least) of moral judgment, a number of investigators returned (shortly after Phillips's last book was published) to the collection of ex-slaves' narratives. Their aim was not so much to forge these materials into weapons against ideological opponents as simply to record this invaluable source material while it was still available.

Although such collections were initiated by academic researchers at Fisk and Southern University, the best-known is probably that undertaken by the WPA Federal Writers Project. Ranging over most of the South, this group sought out more than two thousand surviving ex-slaves and recorded verbatim their recollections of everyday life under slavery, of the war, and of emancipation. The transcripts of these interviews have been used extensively by later historians, and excerpts have been published as *Lay My Burden Down*. In *Life Under the "Peculiar Institution,"* Norman Yetman has brought together over a hundred of these narratives, in their entirety, and from them the general reader can begin to piece together an answer to the question of what it was like to be a slave. Those with strong preconceptions will not be happy with this evidence, for the picture is one of great variety in both situation and response. The question of whether slaves were content—which many contemporary controversialists viewed as crucial—seems not to be answerable in general. There are slaves here who see their masters as sadistic tyrants and others who see them as benevolent Christian autocrats; there is seething resentment and genuine devotion; docile compliance alternates with foot-dragging and sabotage.

When slaves report satisfaction with their situation, the basis for this satisfaction is worth examining. Most often, it seems, slaves assessed their well-being by comparing their lot with that of slaves on nearby establishments. A slave who was apparently content reports, "When we would look and see how the slaves on the joining farm was farming 'twould almost make us shed tears," while one who was disgruntled tells us, "Now, Old Marster Goforth had four sisters what owned slaves, and they wasn't mean to them like our Old Marster and old Mistress." An indictment of the slavery system could be based on the extent to which it restricted many slaves' grounds for comparison. (In fact, Richard Wade has argued that slavery was incompatible with city life partly because the urban scene provided more varied reference points—in the form of free blacks and poor whites—than did the countryside.) As one of the ex-slaves in Yetman's book puts it: "If I had my life to live over again, I would die fighting rather than be a slave. I don't want no man's yoke on my shoulders no more. But in them days, us niggers didn't know no better."

Yetman supplements these reminiscences with a fine essay on the history of the Slave Narrative Collection, an evenhanded discussion of possible bias in the selection of ex-slaves to be interviewed, a description of how he chose the narratives for this volume, and photographs of great poignancy. An appendix lists the name and race of each interviewer on the project, a valuable aid to assessing the reliability of these reports. If, as students of public opinion polling have demonstrated, white interviewers still lead black respondents to distort their reported attitudes, one can imagine the effects on ex-slaves in the South in the 1930s. One should be skeptical of a report like the one (quoted in *Lay My Burden Down*) that concluded: "all in all, white folks, then was the really happy days for us niggers." The camouflage taken on in slavery times was apparently still functioning two-thirds of a century after emancipation.

Of course these narratives are not without their own drawbacks as evidence on the experience of slavery. As the editor of another collection of ex-slave testimony reminds us: "The passing of the years, the early age of witnesses at the time, and the bitterness against the institution of slavery might be arguments against the historical accuracy of everything which follows," and, moreover, the reader must beware the tendency to remember the unusual rather than the mundane. Even outright fantasy sometimes appears in these accounts. By and large, however, a discerning reader can weigh the whole of an individual narrative and arrive at some judgment of the narrator's credibility and reliability. A surprising proportion of these narratives are coherent, detailed descriptions of life in slavery, recorded as delivered by those who knew it best.

Slipshod Totalitarianism

Thirty years after the previous review was written, the question of how slavery was experienced was still vexing historians, and new ways to look at it were still being devised.

Susan Petigru King spoke for many other slaveholders in the American South when she remarked, "I know that [slaves] have as much contentment in a general way and in their way as we have." This belief coexisted strangely with slaveholders' concerns about slave revolts and runaways, but it was essential both to their peace of mind and to their argument with abolitionists, and it was not just self-serving fantasy: a great many slaves found it prudent to appear content, and apparently some even were. Of course, millions seized the chance of freedom as soon as invading Union armies made it possible (and scores of thousands promptly enlisted in those armies), which would seem to have answered once and for all the question of whether slaves in general were contented, but within decades the slaveholders' view made a startling comeback. Scores of sentimental plantation novels and innumerable popular songs both shaped and reflected white Americans' views of the Old South, and by the 1930s those views had received the academic imprimatur of historians like Ulrich B. Phillips, whose treatment of slaves' response to slavery, in works like his Pulitzer Prize-winning *Life and Labor in the Old South* (1929), was later characterized by Richard Hofstadter as virtually "a latter-day phase of the proslavery argument."

But even at the time there were dissenting voices, and of the dozen or so major works since the 1950s that have reexamined Southern slavery from every conceivable angle, only Stanley Elkins's bold, if wrong-headed, study of slave psychology, *Slavery: A Problem in American Institutional and Intellectual Life* (1959), has even suggested that slaves did not long to be free—and Elkins's argument is not that slavery was benign, but that it was so terrible that it "infantilized" its victims. Both this scholarship and broader changes in the political climate have now

77

made it almost impossible for any serious student—any undergraduate, for that matter—to believe that most slaves were content under the yoke.

In *Runaway Slaves: Rebels on the Plantation, 1790–1860,* John Hope Franklin and Loren Schweninger add another nail to the coffin of that argument. Drawing on petitions to legislatures and courts and on a data base of several thousand advertisements for fugitive slaves, they provide an amazing wealth of detail on the backgrounds and experiences of bondsmen and bondswomen who were so discontent with slavery, or at least with their particular experience of it, that they simply ran away.

There were apparently hundreds of thousands of such fugitives. Franklin and Schweninger argue convincingly that more than fifty thousand slaves (a conservative estimate) took flight each year. This works out to a shade more than 1 percent of the South's four million slaves, and over a period of decades it must have added up to a substantial fraction, even allowing for the fact that, as the authors show, many runaways were repeat offenders.

Numbers aside, what is impressive about these runaways is their sheer variety. Again and again Franklin and Schweninger offer a generalization—for instance, that young men were overrepresented—and then swamp us with counterexamples. And beyond demography it is hard even to generalize. Some slaves lit out after enduring unremitting cruelty, others when "good" treatment was (or was about to be) replaced with bad; still others were relatively privileged, and exploited their privileges to make a run for it. Some were consistently defiant, often in the face of repeated punishment; some were more devious, planning their escapes behind a smiling facade; some were simply opportunistic, seizing unexpected chances to flee.

After escaping, some sought families from whom they had been separated; some hid out in nearby swamps or forests; some headed for Mexico, or Florida, the free states of the North, or Canada. Many were on their own, but others joined up with other runaways, or were aided by the slave community, or by free blacks, Indians, or renegade poor whites, even occasionally by slaveholders who saw the chance to get some labor without having to purchase it. Most were soon captured, or returned voluntarily, but others stayed gone for months, or years, or never returned.

The picture of slavery that emerges from this volume is of a system that was oppressive, often brutal and bitterly resented, but not terribly efficient. As totalitarianism goes, slavery in the United States was a rather slipshod proposition. Slaves' freedom was severely restricted, to be sure, but many found ways to play whites off against each other, to negotiate with or to intimidate or to deceive their owners, to accumulate resources against the day that they could make a bid for greater freedom. And not least among those resources was the trust of masters who believed that their slaves were content: again and again, slaveholders complained about "disloyal," even "ungrateful" slaves who betrayed that trust by running away.

Still, whether for fear of whipping, branding, mutilation, or sale, because of ties to family and community, or from ignorance of the alternatives, only a minority of slaves became runaways, and only a minority of that minority headed for free soil. The slavery regime's system of patrols, passes, slave-catchers, and bloodhounds ensured that few of those reached it, and only a tiny minority of them—about seventy, William L. Andrews tells us in his introduction to *The Civitas Anthology of African American Slave Narratives*—wrote about their experiences for publication.

Even if we do not accept Ulrich Phillips's claim that abolitionist editing makes most of these accounts suspect, the authors of these narratives were so unusual that one inevitably suspects that their stories are, too. But several of those collected by Andrews and his coeditor, Henry Louis Gates Jr., achieve credibility despite these reservations, and nicely reinforce conclusions suggested by Franklin and Schweninger. And the fact that Andrews and Gates are professors of literature suggests another reason to make these narratives more widely available: most of them are gripping stories, well-told.

In a previous volume, *Pioneers of the Black Atlantic*, Andrews and Gates published five representative and popular narratives from the period 1772–1815. Their second collection reprints seven of the most compelling and influential specimens from between 1831 and 1861. As Andrews notes, those by Frederick Douglass and Harriet Jacobs are among the most widely studied and read American texts from the middle of the nineteenth century, but the others, though all in print, are less well known these days. The editors have modernized (and Americanized) spelling and italicization, and Andrews provides some background for each selection, but otherwise these are simply the texts as originally published. A few explanatory notes would have been useful (e.g., the name of the congressman who fathered Harriet Jacobs's children), but this volume does bring these stories together conveniently for the general reader, and makes easy the kind of comparison that Andrews sketches in his introduction.

The two earliest selections fit least well. *The History of Mary Prince* (1831) is important by virtue of being the first slave narrative written by a woman, but Prince was enslaved in the West Indies, not the American South, and she obtained her freedom when her master took her to England where, by law, she was free simply to leave his service. *The Confessions of Nat Turner* (also 1831), supposedly transcribed by a white lawyer as Turner awaited execution for leading a rebellion in Southampton County, Virginia, is also historically important, but it tells an even less typical story.

The last five accounts, however, are variations on a single theme, recognized as a genre as early as 1849 when the Boston clergyman and abolitionist Ephraim Peabody discussed it in an article in *The Christian Examiner*. The "fugitive narratives" of Frederick Douglass (1845), William Wells Brown (first published in 1847; this is the expanded, 1849 edition), Henry Bibb (1849), William Craft (1860), and Harriet Jacobs (1861) are similar in form: each tells of misery and oppression as a slave, the break for freedom, the dangerous journey north, and the happy ending on free soil. But, as Andrews observes, even among these writers there is a great deal of variety, from Douglass's self-portrait as "heroic resister," to Brown's "slave trickster," to Bibb's "picaresque road narrative," to Jacobs's indictment of "the patriarchal institution" from an exploited woman's point of view.

In this anthology, as in *Runaway Slaves*, many different kinds of men and women appear, but none who is docile or cowed or content. Of course, both books deal only with those who were discontented, and enough to act on it, but they certainly support the proposition that few slaves ever accepted the legitimacy of their own enslavement. That, given the opportunity, and a reasonable chance of success, nearly all would have chosen freedom has not been universally self-evident, but it was obvious to Mary Prince. "I know what slaves feel," she wrote. "I can tell by myself what other slaves feel, and by what they have told me. The man that says slaves be happy in slavery—that they don't want to be free—that man is either ignorant or a lying person."

Southern Intellect

Daniel Joseph Singal, whose book *The War Within* began its life as his dissertation at Columbia University, likes to tell of the time he told one of his professors that he was writing about Southern intellectual history. "Oh," the man replied. "is there any?"

Well, no fewer than three recent books testify to its existence, and demonstrate that writing it is becoming a minor industry. Of the three, the most interesting and troublesome (because the most ambitious) is Michael O'Brien's *All Clever Men, Who Make Their Way*. Fred Hobson, editor of *South-Watching: Selected Essays by Gerald W. Johnson*, and Thomas Daniel Young, in *Waking Their Neighbors Up: The Nashville Agrarians Rediscovered*, are dealing with twentieth-century figures, members of the remarkable interwar generation of Southerners, and most people—at least most beyond the Upper West Side of New York—would acknowledge that they have something to write about. O'Brien has written about that generation of Southern intellectuals himself, in *The Idea of the American South*, but in his new book he takes on the more demanding assignment of reclaiming the intellectual history of the antebellum South. And here it is not only Columbia professors who will ask whether there is any.

O'Brien's reclamation project proceeds on two fronts. He offers us, first, a twenty-five-page introduction, "On the Mind of the Old South and Its Accessibility," then fourteen essays by as many antebellum Southerners, his candidates for representative intellectuals of the time and place. The essays were chosen, he reports, to allow examination of the "reception and understanding of new ideas" in the Old South.

No doubt most reviewers will concentrate on the introduction, and I am no exception. O'Brien's essayists address an impressive range of topics, and drop a good many impressive names, but to say whether they were au courant or not would require familiarity not only with the ideas and intellectual figures the essayists discuss, but with the state of discussion about them at the time. Who has such familiarity with all, or even most, of these topics?

Maybe O'Brien does. The essays have been "closely annotated to help the reader appreciate the texture of each piece," and the erudition revealed in the notes is awesome. (And sometimes surely tongue-in-cheek. One of my favorites is a footnote to an unattributed quotation that says "This is not Burke.") Perhaps O'Brien can say with conviction that these essays were good intellectual work for their time, but I suspect that most readers will have to take his word for it. I do note, however, that these essayists were discussing the ideas of Sismondi and Bancroft, Emerson and Schlegel, Hawthorne and Hegel—not vice versa.

Of course, most intellectual work, in every time and place, has been comment on the work of others and of no great originality, but that is not ordinarily an impediment to reputation. If these essays are indeed good work, and representative of a larger body of good work, the explanation for the Old South's reputation as "superficial, unintellectual, obsessed with race and slavery, enfeebled by polemic" (as O'Brien summarizes it) must be sought elsewhere. In his introduction, O'Brien suggests a number of reasons, some of them having to do with the institutional nature of antebellum intellectual life, others with the agenda of twentieth-century scholarship.

O'Brien argues that the life of the mind in the antebellum South has been inadvertently misrepresented by the two groups, historians and literary critics, whose business it ought to be to tell us about it. The critics, by following the lead of Allen Tate rather than Vernon Parrington, have concerned themselves almost exclusively with "imaginative literature" and, finding little of any worth in the South before the Civil War, have written off that era as intellectually negligible (rightly so, of course, in their terms). Historians, O'Brien maintains, have suffered from a similar sort of tunnel vision, concerned with the rhetoric of Southern nationalism and the ideology of race and slavery—that is, with the antecedents of the Civil War. Unlike the critics, historians have found much to study, but at the price of implying that Southerners thought and wrote about nothing else. O'Brien even ventures a quantitative assessment: something less than 20 percent of the articles in the periodicals he examined (excluding *DeBow's Review*) deal with slavery or even with politics broadly defined.

O'Brien notes some recent attempts to put this situation right, but observes that the reconstruction is hampered by the nature of the Old South's intellectual life. The fossil remains of that life are to be found in periodicals, in articles written by self-effacing, sometimes anonymous, almost always "amateur" authors—lawyers, clergymen, politicians, physicians, teachers, and (one remarkable example here) a plantation mistress. Before we can assess them intelligently the texts have to be assembled, because, for instance,

> one can read about a George Frederick Holmes, but not Holmes himself without elaborate effort. One can, it is true, go to the bibliography in Neal Gillespie's biography; jot down the essays that Holmes published anonymously and prolifically; proceed to the appropriate volume of the *Southern Quarterly Review* or *Methodist Quarterly Review*, if your library has it; and read Holmes. The hardiest student might choose to risk the hazards and inconveniences of interlibrary loan. He may care to peer into the gloom of a microfilm machine. And he might not. It is easier to read Emerson, and that is what he does. Life is short and scholarship is long to waste upon an intellectual culture that all agree is scarcely worth a nod.

The result, O'Brien argues, is that nobody really knows whether that culture was negligible or not. We do not even have the raw material at hand to argue about it.

> I could airily pronounce Holmes's essays exceptionally interesting. The reader could not make an informed response. He has not read Holmes. He could, of course, make an uninformed response and well might. But Holmes would remain my critical prisoner. . . . If I say absurdities about Walden Pond, an informed skepticism can be expected. But I could pronounce a series of idiocies about Holmes— that he was a closet abolitionist, that he once raped his daughter and this explains his abomination of Herder, that he wrote with purple Bollandist ink lives of the saints—and need only await chastisement from Holmes's biographer, a small audience.

This book, O'Brien would be the first to acknowledge, is not even a significant contribution to the textual work that needs to be done. It is an extended argument, with illustrations, that the Old South had a significant intellectual culture, worth the effort of uncovering. Is the argument persuasive? That largely depends on what is meant by "significant."

On this evidence, these were well-read and thoughtful individuals, with a wide range of interests—not at all the narrow, slavery-obsessed bigots that O'Brien has implicitly set up as the straw men of his argument. They were not, so far as I can judge, greatly original thinkers, but they were intelligent critics and consumers of the ideas of others. Were some antebellum Southerners thinking and writing interesting things that had something to do with what was going on elsewhere in the world? Apparently (although the extent of that activity must await further research).

Did it matter? Not much, I would guess. The same factors that make access to these antebellum writers difficult for modern scholars must have reduced their impact on their own time. Although they had some of the characteristics of a modern intelligentsia (nearly all were urban, for instance), they lacked its apparatus: that network of publishers, commentators, acolytes needed to amplify and propagate ideas and reputations. Some recognized this—O'Brien quotes Holmes, for instance, on the advantages of collected essays over the sort of fugitive publication he was doing—but many apparently preferred it that way. Writing, perhaps anonymously, in periodicals of limited and regional circulation, attracting little attention, was the approved style. In one of the essays reprinted here, Richard Henry Nisbet wrote that "American authorship, like American politics, is fast becoming a trade," and the disdain implicit in that observation suggests why it was happening less rapidly in the South.

In any case, O'Brien claims that all he wants to do is raise some questions that we have been too ready to assume answers to, and his book certainly does that. It is, in addition, a pleasure to watch him at work. Another of his footnotes remarks that Hiram Powers's neoclassical statue of Calhoun "was shipped from Lisbon in 1849, but its carrier, the Elizabeth, sank . . . on 19 July. The statue went down with, among other things, Margaret Fuller. It, though not she, was salvaged at the behest of the Charleston authorities in late 1830 and arrived in Charleston on 12 November 1830."

This sort of casual bitchiness is fun when it is at Margaret Fuller's expense, but I find it less amusing when directed against my friends, as when O'Brien patronizes the "social circle" of contemporary Southern literary critics. Nevertheless, he does not spare himself. Surely John Holmes Bocock's essay on Emerson was included simply for the sake of Bocock's observation, "Things which are small things, or even nothings, when reduced to their adequate terms of expression, have often been made to appear great things, by being thrown loosely out, in florid, and mystic, and deep-sounding sentences, with a scrap of Greek in the frontispiece, after the manner of Coleridge and Bulwer, or a few lines of wild, enigmatical English verse, after the manner of Waldo Emerson."

This in a book with a Latin dedication and some lines from Byron at the front. Any reviewer who fails to mention Bocock's remark can be assumed not to have read that essay. (O'Brien's enigmatical title, by the way, is from Byron's "Epistle from Mr. Murray to Dr. Polidori," and it makes more sense than you probably suppose.)

*   *   *

Whatever may have been the case in the Old South, by the 1920s the intellectual had clearly emerged as a recognizable social type in the South—so much so that one of them could capitalize the label and complain that no one took them seriously: "The Intellectual in the South is merely an eccentric. His weight, in the estimation of the rulers, is scarcely that of a feather." That complaint, of course, is one of the marks of the type. The writer quoted is the journalist Gerald Johnson, whose essays on the South have been collected in *South-Watching*, with an intelligent and helpful introduction by Fred Hobson.

When discussing Johnson, a good many comparisons come to mind. H. L. Mencken, his mentor, obviously influenced his style, and helped him in his career. Although Johnson did not attain Mencken's reputation, he was as good a writer, which is saying a lot. As an observer of the South, he was superior. The down-home truths scattered through his essays suggest that Hobson is right to believe that Johnson could have written at least as good a book on the South as his contemporary W. J. Cash did. That he didn't write it is a pity, and may account for why Cash was better known decades years after his death than Johnson three years after his.

Johnson was a Southern liberal, of a sort now vanishing—like Cash, and like his friend and sometime colleague Howard Odum. He could have been writing a job description for himself when he wrote in Odum's *Social Forces* that

> the South must develop its own critics. They can criticize most effectively, in the first place because they have the Southern viewpoint, and can therefore be understood, and in the second place because they have the most reliable information, and therefore can most frequently spot the joints in Southern armour. [But] they must be critics, not press-agents. Too much has been said of the South's need for "sympathetic" criticism. This demand has resulted in some so-called criticism that is sympathetic, not with the South, but with the South's least admirable traits, with bigotry, intolerance, superstition

and prejudice. What the South needs is criticism that is ruthless toward those things—bitter towards them, furiously against them—and sympathetic only with its idealism, with its loyalty, with its courage and its inflexible determination. Such criticism will not be popular. . . . But it will be respected and in the end admired.

There is much here to respect and to admire, and not least the man's ability to write. His voice varies from one essay to another, from skin-'em-alive Menckenesque to the preachy, almost pious (suggesting by exemplification another influence of evangelical religion on the South), but all of these essays are good reading still, and several are jewels.

Indeed, the editor, a professor of English, argues that Johnson's essays deserve to be read in college literature courses. He observes that journalists like Addison and Steele, and social critics like Carlyle and Arnold, get that treatment, but laments that "social criticism, like journalism, it seems, should be a century in the past and preferably across the ocean before it qualifies as belles lettres." Johnson himself had no apologies to make for being a journalist, and he held his professional colleagues to high standards. In one essay, he observes that the "sudden fecundity" of the South in producing "literary artists" was paralleled by an equally remarkable efflorescence of capable Southern journalists. "They are part of the renaissance," he insisted. "Their contribution to the life of the South affects its economics, its science, its mechanics, but in itself it is no more economic, scientific or mechanical than is the 'Perseus' which Benvenuto Cellini contributed to Florence of Lorenzo de' Medici."

One need not have quite so grandiose a view of what Johnson and his colleagues were doing to recognize that newspapermen—and women—were an important part of the intellectual ferment of the interwar South. Johnson lists a number of examples, but modestly excludes himself. Anyone thinking about a study of the subject should silently slip his name into that list—near the top.

*   *   *

One of Johnson's longstanding conflicts was with the Vanderbilt Agrarians, the authors of *I'll Take My Stand*. In retrospect, it is perfectly clear that he and they had a great deal in common—all were urban, college-educated, "modern" young men; all shared a distaste for boosterism, Babbitry, and much of the emerging culture of the industrial and commercial South; all believed that there was such a thing as "the Southern viewpoint"; and all loved the South, in their several ways. But at the time it certainly seemed that they were ranged on opposite sides of a mighty conflict. In *Waking Their Neighbors Up*, Thomas Daniel Young quotes from a letter from Donald Davidson to Allen Tate, reporting that Johnson had been asked to contribute to the volume that was to become *I'll Take My Stand*, but that "his answer showed that he didn't understand what we were talking about."

Many people have had that problem, of course. One reason is that the Agrarians were doing several things simultaneously (and some of them probably unintentionally). At least since the paperback reissue of *I'll Take My Stand* in the 1960s, with Louis Rubin's appreciative foreword, sorting out and evaluating the various aspects of this protean work have engaged the attention of some of the best literary critics working in the South today, and in 1980 the fiftieth anniversary of the original publication saw a new spate of reassessments. In that year also, fittingly, the Lamar Memorial Lectures at Mercer University were delivered by a long-time student of the Agrarians, Thomas Daniel Young. *Waking Their Neighbors Up* is based on those lectures.

Probably wisely, Young assumes that his audience knows little about his subject, and fills them in. There is little in his account of the origins of *I'll Take My Stand* that is new to readers of, for example, his biographies of John Crowe Ransom and Donald Davidson, but it is pleasant to retrace this history with a literate and congenial guide. Young's second chapter, the core of the book, is a rhetorical analysis of the essays in *I'll Take My Stand*. (It necessarily summarizes their arguments, and might serve as something of a pony—although of course it is not meant to be a substitute for the original.) The Twelve Southerners, it appears, used almost that many modes of presentation in making their points—which makes it wonderful indeed that the book coheres as well as it does. Young's concluding chapters discuss the continuing relevance of the Agrarian critique and (given that, ironically) examine the dissolution of Agrarianism as a movement, or at least the beginning of one. Young has some instructive things to say about how the Agrarians' view of things was both like to and different from that of Emerson and Thoreau.

*   *   *

Young's little book is a worthwhile addition to the ever-growing library of works about the Agrarians. Fred Hobson and Michael O'Brien each suggest, perhaps inadvertently, another direction to take in the attempt to explain the cultural explosion of which the Agrarians were so conspicuous a part. Hobson's way is to give greater attention to figures like Gerald Johnson. As Johnson himself observed, Southern journalism in the 1920s was almost certainly fed by the same springs as the literature of the period. Call it a parallel renaissance or part of the same, understanding Johnson and Cash and the others ought to help us understand their contemporaries who turned to imaginative literature rather than social criticism and reporting. O'Brien's book suggests a different tack. Like those Young Turks who have been arguing that the economic elite of the New South had more continuity with that of the antebellum South than C. Vann Woodward allows, O'Brien implies that there is a sense in which the intellectuals of the South after World War I were not such a new thing as they and others since have supposed. I am oversimplifying, of course. In *The Idea of the American South*, O'Brien himself argued that they were a "new thing," in many ways. But he now contends that they had some antecedents worthy of our attention, and if he is even approximately right, an obvious question is how they are related to those antecedents. As I wrote at the outset, O'Brien's book is interesting, and troublesome. All three books should be read by students of Southern intellectual history—and by anyone who doubts its existence.

Southern Studies Abroad

Consider these events of a single, recent academic year in Europe. In September, a four-and-a-half day convention in Bonn heard forty-one papers on the history and literature of the American South. In February, University College, London, sponsored a symposium on "Race and Class in the South." In March, a gathering at the University of Burgundy attempted to assess the "Southernness" of Eudora Welty's fiction. In April, a conference in Seville examined such topics as "Images of the South" and "The Southern Lady." An August meeting in Reykjavik on contemporary Southern literature heard papers on Welty, Barry Hannah, and Lee Smith. Add the fact that a little volume called *The American South: Portrait of a Culture*, first published for overseas distribution by the Voice of America in 1979, went into a new edition, having set a record for demand. What is going on here?

The vigorous activity of a group called the Southern Studies Forum of the European American Studies Association is both a symptom and a cause of this flowering of interest. The Forum's first meeting was held in Genoa in January 1990, and *The United States South: Regionalism and Identity*, edited by two of the organization's founders, presents the proceedings of that meeting. A dozen Europeans—Italians, Germans, Englishmen, a Dutchman, a Dane, and an Austrian—presented papers on subjects ranging from the Percy family to Jewish Southerners, from Edgar Allen Poe to the New South Creed. They were joined by six visiting scholars from US universities who spoke on the Chapel Hill regionalists, antebellum Southern localism, Rose Cecil O'Neill's cartoons, Tennessee Williams, higher education for Southern women, and an overview of the last fifty years of Southern history.

The papers cohere no better than is usual in such symposia, but they are, for the most part, good work. (Among those I have not mentioned, I particularly enjoyed one that examined Mark Twain's ambivalent relation to the South.) Still, most American readers will probably be attracted to this symposium less for its content than because its novel venue and its multinational cast of characters would seem to offer a chance to see how European and American versions of Southern studies differ. Alas, however, any national differences are overlaid and obscured by disciplinary ones: most of the European contributors are literary scholars, most of the Americans historians (the British characteristically waffle, and split evenly).

Why does the study of the South in Europe seem to be so largely a literary affair? That the sources for literary study are relatively accessible means, of course, that it is possible to be a serious student of Southern literature without ever setting foot in the South. Obviously, it is far more difficult to study Southern history that way. Writing Southern history as Americans write it requires frequent access to archives in the United States, beginning ideally during one's graduate schooling, and how many foreign graduate students have the resources or even the inclination to undertake such study?

If we want foreigners to write Southern history, we may have to recruit and train them ourselves, at least until they have well-funded American history graduate programs of their own. But another possibility, more interesting and probably more likely, is that European Southernists and would-be Southernists could draw on sources (colonial and diplomatic records, for instance) to which they have easier access than US scholars, producing thereby not just more Southern history, but a different *kind* of Southern history. They could, in other words, heed Booker Washington's advice to Southern Negroes and cast down their buckets where they are.

That might not be bad advice for European students of Southern literature either. Those represented in this volume may write better English than many of their American colleagues, and they seem less disposed to theoretical cant (although there were no French participants), but otherwise most of their papers would be right at home at a meeting of the South Atlantic Modern Language Association. The best of this work is very good indeed, but there little that is *European* about it, and that seems . . . not a shame, exactly, but a missed opportunity. Two interesting papers in this volume are accounts of European travelers in the South: William Bartram, an eighteenth-century Englishmen, and Carlo Vidua, a nineteenth-century Italian. As these papers suggest, European Southernists can examine sources, trace connections, do comparisons, document influences that Americans are less well situated to carry off.

With this carping reservation, however, this volume is welcome evidence that the death of the South has been greatly exaggerated. At least as an object of study, it is apparently alive and well, and living in Europe.

III

Friends And Masters

C. Vann Woodward

In the fall of 1973, I was teaching at the Hebrew University of Jerusalem—or would have been, if the Egyptians and Syrians hadn't invaded four days after we arrived—when C. Vann Woodward came to town to deliver a series of lectures. I had to tell my department chairman what the "C" stood for, so he could get some posters made. (Cecil, Charles, and Comer—the right answer—would all be different initials in Hebrew.) Most students and faculty were still mobilized when the Woodwards arrived, so my wife and I were assigned to entertain them, the start of a casual friendship that lasted until Vann's death in 1999. To publicize the lectures, I reviewed Woodward's most recent book for the Jerusalem Post.

For many readers American history has a lot in common with science fiction, or moral philosophy. For most of the world, the first century and a half of the American experience—at least as it is represented in the American consciousness—has very little to do with the world as they know it. American society has escaped, or Americans have believed until recently that it had escaped, much of what must seem to others inescapable aspects of the human condition: extreme poverty, insoluble moral dilemmas, defeat in war and occupation by foreign armies, powerlessness and frustration and the knowledge that things will be worse before they get better, and they may not get better at all.

In this context, the American South has served as a Gulliver, considered a freak by those who are themselves a little unusual: a slaveholding folk within a free society; poor and agrarian in a wealthy, industrial nation; a God-fearing island within a largely secular culture; conquered, occupied, and exploited in a country that used to boast that it had never lost a war. But, like Gulliver, it is only in a bizarre context that the South looks odd at all, so that many readers of William Faulkner, for example, find that the history of the South speaks more of things they know—if not of things they desire—than most American "national" history.

This argument—that Southerners are after all *human* (as Califor-nians, for instance, may never be) and that the South has often been "un-American" simply by being like the rest of the world—has been both developed and applied by C. Vann Woodward, unquestionably the best historian of the American South writing today. He made the point most explicitly in his book *The Burden of Southern History* (1960), but again and again in his writings, one finds the Southern particularity speaking to the human generality. It looks like a happy accident: like his fellow Southerner Faulkner he seems to be setting out simply to write about men and events, but these just happen to implicate themes of universal significance. When "the facts speak for themselves" with such striking applicability, one knows there is an accomplished puppet-master somewhere pulling the strings, and Woodward is in fact an accomplished narrative artist.

Woodward obviously believes, with Lord Acton, that history is "weighty with inestimable lessons that we must learn by experience and at a great price, if we know not how to profit by the example and teaching of those who have gone before us." But drawing lessons from the past is almost as risky as failing to do so. Woodward has succeeded because, as David Potter, another distinguished American historian, has observed, he combines a "capacity for perceiving the meaningful item and for construing his material broadly" with "a solid command of freshly mined data." This combination makes for great academic history, and Woodward's string of prizes and offices testifies to his commanding position in his discipline. His painstaking research has established his interpretations of late nineteenth- and early twentieth-century Southern history as the new conventional wisdom on the subject. In the United States, Woodward probably finds his largest audience, however, not as a professional historian but as an essayist and critic for such journals as the *New York Review of Books* and the *New York Times Book Review*.

His book *American Counterpoint* is a collection of ten of these more popular essays (three have not been published before) and a preface that amounts to another. It opens with two fascinating historiographi-cal reviews, "The Southern Ethic in a Puritan World," which examines the origins of the laziness-leisure (take your pick) component of the "Southern way of life," and "Protestant Slavery in a Catholic World," which examines the uneasy coexistence in the South of northern Euro-pean culture and a Latin labor system. In a third essay, a demographic tour de force results when Woodward asks the question why, when most New World slave societies showed long-term decreases in their slave populations, the United States freed ten times as many blacks as were ever imported.

Three other essays dissect the thought of three quite different Southerners. "A Southern War Against Capitalism" looks at the life and work of George Fitzhugh, an able pre-Civil War propagandist for slavery. One of Fitzhugh's arguments was that laissez-faire capitalism was only an experiment, and he drew on many of the same sources as Karl Marx to show that the experiment was not working. "A Southern Brief for Racial Equality" treats Lewis Harvie Blair, whose "Prosperity of the South Dependent on the Elevation of the Negro" (1889) was an uncompromising attack on white supremacy. (Blair later recanted.) The last essay of the volume, "The Elusive Mind of the South," is a critical examination of W. J. Cash's *The Mind of the South* (1941), a haunting masterpiece which has acquired a considerable reputation, partly as a work of history. Woodward gives it high marks for style, but thinks the content leaves something to be desired—which, come to think of it, is one thing Cash was saying about the South. In a few places, Woodward is severe (he scoffs, kindly) with those who let sentimentality cloud their reading of historical evidence. Cash, writing of the continuity of Southern culture, speaks of the new Southern skyscrapers and asks: "Softly: do you not hear behind that the gallop of Jeb Stuart's cavalry-men?" Woodward replied, after consideration, "The answer is 'No!' Not one ghostly echo of a gallop. And neither did Jack Cash. He only thought he did when he was bemused."

Ironically, Woodward himself may once have been guilty of the fault he finds in Cash. In his well-known book *The Strange Career of Jim Crow* he attempted to show that segregation was a relatively late development in the South, and hence might perhaps be more easily uprooted. The past was speaking to the present again: This book was published in 1955. Some historians have argued that Woodward's desire to place segregation outside the "authentic" Southern tradition led him to overlook evidence of its early practice. In "The Strange Career of a Historical Controversy" Woodward answers his critics, with a model of what scholarly controversy should be but too seldom is.

This volume offers the general reader a good introduction to the historiography of the American South. It offers an even better intro-duction to the thought and style of its leading interpreter.

Eugene D. Genovese

I first met Gene Genovese when he rented the apartment over our garage (we used to get notes from him dated from "The Quarters"). Our sometime tenant and his wife, Elizabeth Fox-Genovese, have become dear friends of ours, a fact that may cloud his judgment of my work, but not, I think, mine of his. If I had to, I would probably lie for Gene, but in this review I didn't have to. (By the way, he is—not surprisingly—no longer an atheist.).

Eugene Genovese is, of course, the foremost living historian of the Old South's slave society—and maybe the "living" is not needed. He has also been for many years an exemplary "public intellectual," bringing his formidable intelligence and analytic skills to bear on issues of the day in a variety of forums. What he has to say on almost any subject is worth hearing—not because he has always (or perhaps even usually) been right, but because what he has to say is invariably *interesting*, and because he says it so well. So I started with a strong prejudice in favor of *The Southern Front: History and Politics in the Cultural War*. And I was not disappointed. This collection of essays and reviews ranges over most of his recent interests, and it is a pleasure to watch his mind at work on them (especially when he offers a generous assessment of my own work). As Genovese says, commenting on someone else's collection, such compilations are inevitably uneven, and this one is no exception. But the individual chapters do add up to a remarkably coherent whole, complementing and reinforcing one another in a variety of surprising ways.

The book begins with three biographical reflections on what Genovese calls, somewhat misleadingly, "Representative Carolinians." (Would that James Johnston Pettigrew and James Henley Thornwell had been "representative"—what a society that would have been!) Two of these pieces began as admiring reviews of books I have read, and they are good books, but I can honestly say that the reviews make even better reading. Taken together, these three essays quickly establish a number of features that mark the entire book: Genovese's admiration for what he sees as worthy and unjustly neglected aspects of the Southern tradition; his impatience with cant (especially politically correct cant); his generous sympathy with men of integrity, intellect, and courage committed to lost (even rightly lost) causes; his learning, tough-mindedness, and wit.

I won't summarize the seventeen chapters that follow—five dealing with slave society, five with religion, and seven with current cultural and political questions—but Genovese has read widely and reflected well. If the book has a central theme, it probably has to do with Genovese's alarm at the excesses of unchecked individualism, and his search for a corrective. He once found that in Marxism (perhaps still does, with some major, rueful reservations), but he argues that similar themes can be found in the Southern conservative tradition that originated in the defense of slavery, traced into this century through the Vanderbilt Agrarians and Richard Weaver to M. E. Bradford and other, lesser lights. Not all of the essays address this theme explicitly, but it does recur in a great many of them, is useful background for nearly all, and links the antebellum material to the more contemporary matters treated toward the end of the book.

Obviously those who share Genovese's views, at least in some respects, will take the most satisfaction from seeing them so well argued. But even readers who disagree with his prescription, or who don't see the problem in the first place, will find much of profit here. There is, in the first place, simply a wealth of little-known *fact*. It is good to learn about Pettigrew and Thornwell and M. E. Bradford and Eugene Rivers—all are fascinating men, who should be better known than they are.

In addition, though, it is a pleasure to learn more about Eugene Genovese, who is at least as interesting as the people he writes about. For starters, the persona revealed in these essays is an amusing and perceptive companion. There is something gallant about his defense of unfashionable scholars who he believes have been ignored or treated shabbily by the academy, and he has a remarkable talent for unearthing such folk and celebrating their contributions (thereby, if you will, "expanding the canon"). For instance, he must be one of a very few who have read the major works of both the Communist historian Herbert Aptheker and the (Pat) Buchananite journalist Samuel Francis—and he is probably unique in admiring them both.

It is piquantly ironic that this professed atheist should show a more penetrating understanding of Christian theology and the life of faith than most seminary professors of my acquaintance, an understanding perhaps acquired by entering into the minds of his antebellum subjects. And Genovese may have picked up his splendid manners from the same place. Again and again, he calls for civil discourse, with all points of view freely expressed and evaluated on their intellectual merits; again and again, he illustrates how courteous and principled disagreement is expressed, and he disarmingly seeks (and often finds) common ground with many who would be only too glad to treat him as an adversary.

Genovese can wield a stiletto, though, and when he smells cowardice or bad faith, a truncheon. That truncheon is freely employed in his epilogue, where he assails some of his fellow leftists less for their complicity in the crimes of Stalinism than for their lack of candor about it. This is a powerful piece, and he was wise to put it last: anything after it would have been anticlimax.

M. E. Bradford

This review of Mel Bradford's last book suggests why this Texas-sized man and personality should be better known—and perhaps why he is not. I have appended a memoir written when he died, far too young, at age fifty-eight.

In his last book, *Against the Barbarians and Other Reflections on Familiar Themes*, the late M. E. ("Mel") Bradford, longtime professor of English at the University of Dallas, returns to topics that engaged his attention for decades, among them the nature and necessity of tradition, American regional literatures, the thought of the founding fathers, and the iniquity of centralizing politicians. For those who know Bradford's work, the themes treated in these twenty-five essays will indeed be familiar ones, and most will be glad to see them addressed with his accustomed vigor and discernment. Those who do not know Bradford's work probably should, and this volume can serve as an introduction to this independent and engaging thinker.

Bradford's title essay defends the traditional view of literary study against its contemporary adversaries, but Bradford was not simply opposed to change. Subsequent essays make it clear that, like his friend Elizabeth Fox-Genovese, he believed that we need a literary canon but would positively have welcomed an expansion of it—in his case, to include more literature from the American South and West. At the time of his death, he was working on a biography of his teacher, the Agrarian poet and essayist Donald Davidson: an essay treating Davidson's poem "Woodlands, 1956–1960" (occasioned by a series of visits to the home of William Gilmore Simms) gives us a taste of what might have been.

The book's centerpiece turns to another familiar theme, giving us a lengthy reading of the debates on the ratification of the Constitution of the United States, followed by sketches of fourteen men who framed it or engaged in those debates, both well-known (e.g., Patrick Henry) and obscure (e.g., Eliphalet Dyer of Connecticut). Bradford gives particular attention to the losing, anti-federalist side, and his indictment of latter-day political discourse is no less powerful for being left implicit. His sketches make it perfectly clear how far we have come from our republican origins, and how relatively negligible is the thought of most public figures these days.

Perhaps my favorite essay here is "A Long Farewell to Union: The Southern Valedictories of 1860–1861," in which Bradford examines the moving rhetoric of Southern senators as they left Washington to join their states in secession. Like his sketches of the founders, this simply presents a point of view and caste of mind that must strike most modern readers as antique, not to say alien, but that was, in fact, pretty much Bradford's own. Once again, we are reminded of what we have lost.

Ironically, given the profusion and diversity of his scholarship, Bradford may have been best known for his criticism of Abraham Lincoln—criticism that may have cost him the chairmanship of the National Endowment for the Humanities in the early 1980s when he was assailed for it by a number of people who would later be conspicuous in the attack on "political correctness." Bradford's admirers would be disappointed if there were nothing in this book on Lincoln, and he was always too much the gentleman to disappoint us: "Lincoln and the Language of Hate and Fear" is the book's concluding essay.

Bradford's essays on the literature of the American West and on Lyndon Johnson (who almost makes Lincoln look good) will have special resonance for his fellow Texans. But they are not the only readers who should make or renew their acquaintance with one of the most interesting thinkers the Lone Star State has ever nurtured.

*   *   *

Others will remember Mel Bradford for his formidable scholarship or his dashing polemical works, and I will, too. But what I will miss most is the presence of the man himself: his conversation, his humor and his courtliness, his gift for friendly argumentation, his startling mix of erudition and folksiness. In *Why the South Will Survive*, Mel wrote about a gathering in someone's hotel room after a scholarly conference:

> Most of the participants in the evening's celebration were Southern scholars, some of them well acquainted and some new to many of the group. They were of both sexes and three generations. The common denominator of our discourse was the business of the day. Yet we

spoke of much else besides: of friends and mentors and the rumors of both—their fortunes and misfortunes, their origins and our own; of illustrative stories, many of them drawn from outside the narrow confines of the academy; of adversaries, ancient and modern; of our delight in the progress of one another's work, and reports of our personal lives; and most particularly in the rehearsal of common bonds antecedent to our professional identities, visible as much in the manner of our speaking as in its content—in idiom, in humor, in certain hyperbolic gestures, verging on swagger, panache, and familiarity. The round robin of the talk was intense and friendly, serious and droll, carried on as if all present feared that it would be some time before they would all be together again and were determined to hear and say it all.

All in all, a non-Southern visitor told Mel, it was "more like a family reunion than the usual polite and professional alcoholic postmortem to a long day's session." Mel believed that Southerners, even Southern academics, are like that. Certainly he was, and he brought it out in others.

As it happens, I met Mel for the first time in very similar circumstances, in a hotel room after a conference—in Columbia that time. But he and I were on some of the same lecture and conference circuits, so that was just the first of many such evenings we spent together. In Nashville and Dallas and Atlanta, in Chapel Hill and (not long before his untimely death) back in Columbia, often with Marie and my wife Dale, each time the good talk simply picked up where it left off, as if we had been apart only a few hours, not months, or years. I want to believe that right now Mel and his old friends are passing the Jack Daniel's around, gossiping about the rest of us, mixing high ideas and low humor, telling stories and lies. I hope to join them someday.

IV

What They Say About Dixie

Of Collard Greens and Kings

To my delight, when my godson graduated from a Chicago high school, he wanted to go to a Southern college. Unfortunately he picked Duke, which means that his idea of the South has no doubt come to include things like the rice diet, Mercedes Marxism, and holistic therapy with crystals (or "voodoo rocks," as my buddy Fetzer calls them). Everything's up-to-date at Buck Duke's place, alas.

Nevertheless, the lad was moving in the right geographical direction, and since he would be physically present in Durham for the next four years, I hoped he might also discover things like Levi Garrett and Shirley Caesar's gospel music and the Durham Bulls (not entirely destroyed by the success of the movie about them). So for a graduation present I gave him a copy of the *Encyclopedia of Southern Culture*, produced by a team at the Center for the Study of Southern Culture at the University of Mississippi. "Here are a few things you ought to know," I told him.

About thirteen hundred things, as a matter of fact, that being the number of entries, written by nearly eight hundred authors, spread over 1,634 pages, and ranging alphabetically from Aaron (Hank) to Zydeco. The time has come, apparently, to talk of many things—of gays and grits and shotgun shacks, of collard greens and Kings (Martin Luther and Elvis). This book doesn't cost a great deal more than a good country ham these days; weighing in at nine and a half pounds on my bathroom scale, it is cheaper by weight than rib eye. A while back, a review in the *New York Times* said that the new *Oxford English Dictionary* is a bargain at eleven cents a page: well, this sucker will cost you nearer to three.

Of course, the book is so cheap (relatively speaking) because it has been heavily subsidized, especially by the National Endowment for the Humanities. In other words, it's your tax dollars at work again, and I know nobody asked you. But consider the alternatives. It beats a congressional pay raise, doesn't it? If extortion is inevitable, relax and enjoy it—and there is a lot to enjoy here, by no means exclusively for Southerners. One of the pleasures of the book is browsing for odd juxtapositions. In the catch-all "History and Manners" section, for instance, a charming sequence of entries goes:

Gardner, Dave
Gays
Goo Goo Clusters
Grits
Hammond, James Henry

Southerners my age will remember Brother Dave Gardner as the off-the-wall white Southern comedian who greeted the news of *Brown v. Board of Education* by saying: "Let 'em go to school, beloved. We went, and we didn't learn nothin." Grand Ole Opry fans and candy lovers will know Goo Goo Clusters. Hammond was the politician, libertine, and proslavery theorist who announced that cotton was king and no one would dare make war on it (a slight miscalculation). Grits I presume you know about, and gays, too: Southerners are more likely than other Americans to like one, but not the other.

This is mostly good reading and good fun. There are the makings of a fine board game here. But the encyclopedia has a problem, and it is one that, in its own little way, reflects a broader problem for the South and the nation. The editors—I am sure with the best of liberal intentions—have set aside separate sections on "Black Life" and "Women's Life." (There are, of course, no sections on "White Life" or "Men's Life.") The result is shabby treatment of some Southern blacks and women who deserve better, and maybe better treatment for others than they deserve. Whites who fought segregation, or defended it, for example, are treated under "Law" or "Politics" or "Violence"; most blacks who fought it are consigned to the ghetto of "Black Life."

Offensive as this Jim Crow organization may be, at least it is not followed consistently. Jean Toomer is under "Black Life," but Ralph Ellison, thank goodness, is found under "Literature." Julia Peterkin is in "Women's Life," but Flannery O'Connor is in "Literature" with the real writers, where she belongs. The principle of organization eludes me. Could it be that the "Black Life" and "Women's Life" sections are just reservations for the second-rate? No, here is Loretta Lynn in "Women's Life": surely she belongs in "Music" every bit as much as Charlie Daniels. Does black trump female? No, writer Margaret Walker is in "Black Life," but Maggie Lena Walker, founder of the oldest black bank in the United States, winds up in "Women's Life." (Alice Walker is inexplicably in "Literature.")

I give up. All I can suggest is that liberal piety now dictates that books have sections explicitly devoted to blacks and women. For my part, I don't think it is worth a klutzy organizational scheme that makes it impossible to predict where a particular entry will be found. To be sure, the book has an index, but flipping back and forth through sixteen hundred pages is no fun. A straightforward A-to-Z listing would have been better than this.

Whatever my misgivings about the book's flagrant tokenism, though, I think it is a major achievement. Having said that (and with the examples of Southerners like Jim Wright and Newt Gingrich before me), I should probably declare an interest. I wrote a couple of the entries, and I was supposed to line up contributors for the "Recreation" section. However, one of the editors, Charles Wilson (known to some of us as "the Diderot of Dixie"), wound up doing much of that work—and not just for me. Eventually, Wilson had to write seventy of the entries himself and he is now an authority on some of the *strangest* things. Tying up those loose ends took a while: Wilson jokes that the encyclopedia paints a comprehensive portrait of Southern culture five years before it was published.

Anyway, since I didn't do much, and I got my little share of your tax dollars up front, I see no real conflict of interest in my plugging this book. Besides, if I don't do it, who will? Almost everyone who has written about Southern culture at all contributed to it.

One of the most interesting things about this book is that it has become something of a cultural event in its own right. Its publication was widely noted, but the most affecting notice I ran across was when I heard coeditor Bill Ferris on a Charlotte radio call-in talk show. Ferris would talk awhile about some entry from the encyclopedia; then the phone lines would light up like a Christmas tree as listeners from all over the South called in to say "Yes! That's the way we used to do it!" or "I remember when my daddy. . . ."

I couldn't help noticing the elegiac tone of many of these testimonials, a sense of old ways slipping away. One of my friends suggests that the encyclopedia is the equivalent for the South of reviewing one's life in the course of drowning—drowning, he adds, in the mainstream. Another friend sees it as a product of what he calls the Postmortem South, a region that exists mostly in and on nostalgia. But both of these pessimists are professional historians, and so are most of the contributors to this encyclopedia; especially given that fact, I am struck by how many of the regional icons and attributes it treats are of quite recent provenance.

If you will forgive a homely simile that I have used elsewhere, the South strikes me as like an old pair of blue jeans. It has shrunk a bit, faded some; it has a few holes in it. There is always the possibility that it will split at the seams. But it's more comfortable than it used to be, and I think there's still a lot of wear in it. Consult this remarkable book and see if you don't agree.

Red and Yellow,
Black and White

In *An Asian Anthropologist in the South*, Professor Choong Soon Kim of the University of Tennessee at Martin brings, to say the least, an unusual perspective to his studies of the South, and the result is often a startling sort of objectivity. Kim's dispassion is fortified not only by the norms of his profession, but by his non-Western background. By his own admission, when he came to do graduate work in Georgia, he knew almost nothing about the South, and most of what he thought he knew was wrong. This absence of preconceptions, coupled with his obvious "foreignness," turned out to be an advantage: he could study the folkways of the Southern tribes without having to take sides in their continuing intertribal struggles. This may well be the first time the South has been studied by someone with so little in the way of ax to grind.

Kim's brushes with (black and white) ethnocentrism are disturbing, at least to those of us who value the South's reputation for hospitality, but I must say that there are some pleasant ironies here. While Kim recognizes that the natives can be dangerous (he received anonymous threats and once had a rattlesnake thrown at him—dead, as it happens, but he didn't know), I sense that he found our ethnocentric pretensions more amusing than otherwise. In Korea, it turns out, his family was of considerable consequence, apparently a noble one—in any case, one that once owned a paper mill to turn out paper for its own use. This may account for Kim's commendable self-esteem, which remained unthreatened by the exigencies of field work. (He discovered, for example, that he got better cooperation by adopting the role of the "humble Asian": polite, smiling, helpless, harmless. Although it is clear that he is neither helpless nor—in a pinch—harmless, he did what worked best, and allows that it helped him to understand black "Uncle Tomming" better.) His background also led him not to take it personally when crowds of children gathered to stare at him: he remembered doing the same thing to the first Westerner he ever saw. And when people avoided physical contact with him, he recalled a train ride when he and other Koreans stood for hours, rather than sit next to an American.

One of Kim's biggest problems was adjusting to the strange native diet. His first week in Georgia, he accidentally bought several cans of dog food at the grocery store, since it hadn't occurred to him that the same store might stock food for both dogs and humans. For that matter, as he observes, a Korean store might well stock dog *meat*, a different matter altogether. Sweetened ice tea was also a problem for someone whose idea of tea was quite different, and he drew undesired attention to himself in a Georgia motel restaurant by declining the salad and dessert that came with the steak he had ordered. ("Salads look to me like a vegetable garden come to the table," he tells us.) Fortunately he soon discovered that vegetable soup was edible and got on with his work.

Kim quickly identified the significant symbols and totems of the native culture and used them to advantage. When he found a key informant's office decked with University of Georgia football pennants, he knew that as a student at the university, he was in good shape. Before Kim had left the office, the man had arranged a series of meetings with town leaders through his civic club, inquired about a Korean boy he had known during the war, given Kim access to all aspects of his lumbering operation, and signed him up for the country club.

Even when people were helpful and friendly, though (and that was not always the case), it was *because* Kim was "different"—and the more different the better. As long as he was clearly a foreigner most Southerners were friendly, sometimes overwhelmingly so. Once his English improved, though, once he was no longer a student but a professor, once it looked as if he might stay—well, then he didn't get any special breaks (indeed, sometimes the contrary).

Loneliness is an experience common to first-generation immigrants and to anthropologists in the field, and it may be the keynote of this book. There are poignant scenes like the one where Kim has gone into the woods to study a lumbering crew and the men simply ignore him. No one will speak to him or even acknowledge his presence. "Sitting there in the woods," Kim writes, "I began to ask myself why I was dedicating a part of my life to study the wood workers' cause and wondered what on earth I was doing all alone in the middle of the luxuriant Southern forest."

Perhaps partly as a result of his own marginality, Kim attracted and was attracted to others who didn't quite fit in to the South's social structure. There were some other Asians: a war-bride (whose husband surprised Kim with his condescending views of blacks); a Korean orphan raised in Georgia from infancy (whose racial views also surprised Kim, and who was Korean only in physical appearance); and a third-generation Japanese traveling chicken-sexer (who had some wise things to say about Southerners' respect for competence). But there were other marginal folks as well, like a black logging entrepreneur, who lived in a house shabby and unpainted on the outside, but paneled, carpeted, and impeccable inside. Kim learned that he was the first guest—black, white, or yellow—to set foot in the remodeled house, and the man and his wife explained: whites wouldn't come in anyway, and they wouldn't like what they saw if they did; blacks, seeing the signs of affluence, would have tried to borrow money. They had left the outside unpainted on purpose, and, in their way, were as lonesome as Kim.

The second half of the book describes Kim's studies of another marginal group, the Choctaw Indians of Mississippi and west Tennessee. Although some of the traditional ways remain, these Indians have been pretty well acculturated to the culture of the rural South—to the point where a visiting Plains Indian sneered that they were not redskins at all, just rednecks. But, for all that, like the Mississippi Chinese that James Loewen studied in a book with that title, like Kim himself, they do not entirely wish, nor are they entirely allowed, simply to pass into the South's biracial society. Add this similarity to the physical and (to some extent) cultural similarity between the Choctaws and Professor Kim, and it is not surprising that they seem for the most part to have been delighted to find one another.

The story of how different Southerners reacted to an unusual stimulus—that is, to Professor Kim—is often fascinating, informative, and (he will know I do not intend the word to be patronizing) charming. Kim's low-key sense of humor pervades the account, and he is every bit as aware as his readers of the ironies of the situation.

In the end, his reflections are modest. He does not pretend to have understood the South. "The harder I have tried," he says, "the more confused I have become." Part of the problem is that Southerners "tend to be very diplomatic when they speak. They avoid any straightforward expressions if possible." He finds us, in a word, inscrutable.

Telling about the South

American Southerners have always been acutely concerned with what has been said about their region (indeed, they have said a great deal of it themselves), but only recently has the content of this discourse become grist for the academic mill. It was only a couple of decades ago that the historian George Tindall suggested in two influential essays that, whatever else it may be, the South is undeniably an idea, which can be studied as such.

Perhaps coincidentally, Tindall's suggestion was followed in short order by a number of remarkable books that, more or less, did just that. Notable among them were Jack Temple Kirby's *Media-Made Dixie*, Michael O'Brien's *The Idea of the American South*, Richard H. King's *A Southern Renaissance*, Daniel Joseph Singal's *The War Within*, and Fred C. Hobson's *Tell About the South*. James C. Cobb's *The Selling of the South* came at the same subject from a slightly different angle—as, for that matter, did my own *Southern Folk, Plain and Fancy*. In other words, lately it seems that looking at what has been said about the South has become about as common as looking at the region itself. Richard Gray's prize-winning *Writing the South: Ideas of an American Region* offers an English literary scholar's contribution to that undertaking.

Gray asserts that "as good a way as any of portraying and exploring things . . . is on the level of the individual sensibility, in the imaginative details of particular works," and certainly that is an appropriate way for students of literature to explore things. So long as they do not cut themselves off from other ways of knowing, their approach can complement, correct, and flesh out conclusions arrived at by quite other means. Gray, whose reading has ranged widely into history and the social sciences, is a model in this regard. He examines selected specimens from the several generations of Southern writers who have "been engaged not so much in writing about the South as in writing the South," men and women who "have, whether they have known it or not (and, as a matter of fact, many have known it) been busy re-imagining and remaking their place in the act of seeing and describing it."

But he is not content just to recount what these writers have had to say about their region. Like most of the non-Southern contributors to this enterprise, he has a thesis—a couple of them, in fact. (It may say something about Southern culture that most of the Southerners' work has been largely descriptive—at its most ambitious, taxonomic. King's is an exception, but he teaches at Nottingham.) Like W. J. Cash in *The Mind of the South*, Gray insists on the coherence and continuity of the old code of the white South, and he concludes that Southern writers of the latest, postmodern generation "are finishing a story that began four hundred years ago; they are composing an epitaph—and a not entirely affectionate one, at that—for the idea and arguments of the South."

I am not entirely persuaded on either of these scores, but Gray's book is valuable nevertheless. Most of it is devoted to tracing the idea of the South from its seventeenth-century origins through its two lines, patrician and plebeian (or paternalist and populist), down to our own time. Gray begins with an account of the construction of the idea of Virginia, examining early pamphleteers, the colony's first families, and some members of the great Revolutionary generation—Jefferson, Taylor, and Randolph. For the antebellum period, he turns to Calhoun, the novelist William Gilmore Simms, and the humorists of the southwestern frontier; for the period after the Civil War (known elsewhere as the Gilded Age) to the plantation novelists and to Mark Twain. In the twentieth century, by Gray's account, the Southern story was taken up by the Nashville Agrarians and by William Faulkner, until it finally collapsed, exhausted, within the last thirty years. (Gray's last substantive chapter looks at Eudora Welty and Walker Percy.)

Gray's assessment of the writers he examines is judicious and often illuminating; in particular, his lengthy chapter on William Faulkner will reward even those students of literature with no particular interest in the South. But I find most provocative his argument that the South is almost over, a conclusion that follows, he argues, from the assumption that "the South is primarily a concept, a matter of knowing even more than being." If this is so, the South ceases to exist if people stop thinking about it.

Gray thinks that time is upon us. In the works of recent Southern writers, particularly those of Walker Percy, he claims to find "the feeling of everything running down," and "the sense of waiting for the end." Percy is a treacherous fulcrum on which to rest a conclusion that the idea of the South has had its day (he is after all just one of today's Southern writers, and a master of irony at that); still, Gray is probably correct that the South "has changed beyond recognition, and so the codes used to understand it, the vocabulary required to name and know it, will have to undergo a similar change."

But to change—even "beyond recognition"—is not necessarily to die. George Orwell once wrote of his native land that great changes would come to pass, but that "England will still be England, an everlasting animal stretching into the future and the past, and like all living things, having the power to change out of recognition and yet remain the same." Gray is certainly correct that the old myth has lost its near-monopoly, the coercive character that allowed those who did not serve it to be defined as not "real" Southerners. He is right, too, that the anomaly of the old code's persistence in radically altered material circumstances has made many Southerners, in his happy phrase, "amphibious creatures." Mythic confusion—no doubt evident longer and more clearly in the work of the South's literary artists—has characterized Southern culture at large since the 1960s, as Stephen A. Smith has pointed out in an unjustly neglected monograph, *Myth, Media, and the Southern Mind.*

But recognizing this is far from admitting that there will soon be no idea of the South, or that the new one will have nothing to do with the old. To the passage quoted above Orwell added that "It needs some very great disaster, such as prolonged subjugation by a foreign enemy, to destroy a national culture." By one reckoning, of course, that is exactly what the American South has experienced since 1865, so Gray could be right about the impending end. I doubt it, but we shall see soon enough.

The Imagined South

There has been no shortage of Southerners ready to tell one another and any Yankee who would listen what the South is all about. In his fascinating *Myth, Media, and the Southern Mind* Stephen Smith, one-time aide to Arkansas governor Bill Clinton and now professor of communication at the University of Arkansas, looks at what they have had to say, and concludes that it has changed, lately.

He argues that there was a remarkable continuity from the early 1800s until quite recently in the myths of the South, the shared images (not wholly false, necessarily) of what the region had been, was, and could be. The myth of the Old South was developed in the antebellum period as a defense of the South's beleaguered society. Its elements included white supremacy, paternalism, and the chivalric tradition—and they should be familiar to any modern viewer of TV miniseries. "Of all the mind-pictures created by the romantic Southerner," wrote historian T. Harry Williams, "the greatest, the most appealing, and the most enduring is the legend of the Old South." (As a student of rhetoric, Smith is adept at quotation. This one, like those below, is from the book.)

The Old South myth became even more important after the Civil War, serving to explain what the Lost Cause was all about. Even exponents of the first "New South" in the 1880s had no quarrel with the old myths: they didn't want to alter the South's social patterns in any fundamental way, only to transpose them from agriculture to industry. "There is, in very fact, no Old South and no New. There is only The South. Fundamentally, as it was in the beginning it is now, and, if God please, it shall be evermore." (Thus a writer in the *Journal of Southern History*, in 1949. "Next to fried foods," according to Walter Hines Page, "the South has suffered most from oratory.") By the 1950s the old myths were looking a little threadbare, but they were dusted off to serve one last time in the defense of the indefensible, in Jim Crow's Last Stand. If nothing else, Jefferson Davis's thoughts in Ross Barnett's words served to illustrate Marx's maxim about history's repeating itself, first as tragedy, then as farce.

But sometime between the New Deal and the Voting Rights Act of 1965, Smith believes, the strain between myth and reality finally became too great. The old myth simply lost its credibility, its compelling power. A "period of mythic confusion"—sort of a regional identity crisis—ensued in the late 1960s, as the South's cultural myth-makers struggled to catch up with the latest New South which had more or less emerged in fact. By the 1970s, Smith argues, they had succeeded. The backbone of the book is his analysis of what he believes is now "the predominant and most successful mythic vision" of the South, a radical departure from the Old South/Lost Cause/New South myths that had "controlled Southern culture and Southern rhetoric for one hundred fifty years."

Smith makes it clear that the new myth, like the old ones, was created and propagated by an elite. Members of what we might call the South's New Class, "an imaginative, well-educated, vocal, literate, and enthusiastic cadre of middle- and upper-middle-class Southern professionals," forged it in the smithies of their souls, and by the sort of informal collaboration that affluence and modern technology make possible. Reading each others' articles, flying around the South to conferences, quoting and promoting each other, they came together to form a critical mass (in every sense of that phrase). Smith doesn't say it, but the increasing numbers and influence of such Southerners—artists, scholars, journalists, politicians, preachers, both black and white—may have had as much to do with the emergence of the new myth as did the exhaustion of the old ones.

The new myth they constructed may have reached its apogee— certainly it was most noisily voiced about—during and immediately after the 1976 presidential campaign, when interpreters of the South found the Yankee media prepared not only to listen but to *pay*. Poking through these interpreters' accounts, through the speeches of politicians, the lyrics of country music, and the pages of magazines ranging from *Southern Exposure* to *Southern Living*, Smith finds three principal "mythic themes" echoing and re-echoing.

What Smith calls the theme of *equality* (although "interracial civility" might be a better label) was epitomized by the moment at the Democratic convention in 1976 when "Daddy" King, Jimmy Carter, Andrew Young, and even George Wallace came together to the strains of "We Shall Overcome." A variety of Southerners, including a number of impressive new politicians and some old ones, too, began in the early 1970s to suggest that the South might have something to offer the nation as a model for race relations. Southern whites have been known to say as much ever since the slavery era, of course, but the fact that some black Southerners were saying it as well really was something new. Whether celebrated as an accomplished fact or merely held out as a possibility, this must be the most striking departure from the old myths. Smith's discussion of this theme offers, among other things, an illuminating dramaturgical analysis of the civil rights movement.

Smith's second theme is that of *distinctiveness*. Southerners' belief that they have things in common that set them off from other Americans is nothing new. That belief persists, Smith shows, even as some of the most obvious differences are disappearing. What the important differences are seen to be has changed, but the belief that there are important differences has not. Smith writes about the South's new "electronic folklore," about its distinctive manners, music, and speech-ways, about its food and buildings and sports.

Finally, Smith identifies the theme of *place and community*. "The Southern sense of place" is a phrase now so hackneyed that it has become a cliché to call it a cliché. Smith documents the obvious fact that many have talked about this, and the less obvious fact that nearly everyone sees it as something worthwhile (something very similar was once known as parochialism). The value placed on community would seem to conflict in some obvious ways with growth and what used to be known as "progress," and Smith goes beyond his data to guarded optimism about the future.

Smith doesn't claim that these themes describe what the South is, or even what it is becoming. They just summarize what many now *say* the South is, and a concluding chapter on "The Meaning of Myth" says why that is worth knowing. He notes, and it should be emphasized, that all three themes are inclusive ones. Unlike the themes of the older myths, these can be shared in and celebrated by all Southerners, black and white, native and newcomer.

Smith seems confident that there will continue to be *some* myth of the South, that it will not become simply the label for a piece of territory with what he calls (in a rare lapse) a "dysfunctional amythic culture." I share that confidence, not just because a lot of us mythmongers have an investment in the South, but because it really *is* different from the rest of the United States. Personally, I think Smith may underrate the vitality, and the flexibility, and the staying power of the old myths; in any case, I believe that he understates the continuity between them and the new one he has explored here. But that is the kind of argument I would like to pursue with him over some Jack Daniels—maybe at the next symposium on the future of the South.

V

Six Southerners

Lady Propagandist
of the Old South

Louisa S. McCord wrote and published dozens of poems, incisive essays on the major questions of her day, a five-act tragedy based on the story of the Gracchi, and innumerable reviews, memoirs, and reminiscences, as well as a translation of the work of the French political economist Claude-Frédéric Bastiat. As historian Michael O'Brien observes in his introduction to the two volumes of her collected works, "No other woman [of her time and place] wrote with more force, across such a range of genres, or participated so influentially in social and political discourse." Very few men did so. Yet probably not one reader in a hundred—nay, one in a thousand—has ever heard of Mrs. McCord. Why is this?

The answer surely lies in the fact that she deployed her talents in the antebellum American South, and, as a conservative Southerner, wound up on the losing side of nearly every argument she entered, notably those about women's rights and slavery. Her considerable reputation went down to ashes with the civilization she defended so ably but so futilely, and today many of her opinions are (to put it no more strongly) decidedly unfashionable. Only recently have a few intellectual historians begun to see her as not just an Old South oddball, but (in O'Brien's words) "one of the leading conservatives in American thought."

All of her published writings and what remains of her private correspondence are collected in these two impeccably edited volumes. Although few will want to read them straight through (in particular, a little of her sentimental poetry goes a long way, and her edifying drama will not be to everyone's taste), it is good to have these materials collected for scholars, and many general readers will find a dip bracing.

Her forthright defense of Southern slavery makes the most startling reading. Her devotion to the South's peculiar institution seems sometimes to have amused even her proslavery friends, one of whom (the president of the University of South Carolina) summarized her letters to him from an English trip, thus: "it is all vanity and vexation of spirits. The garden culture of England has not enough green to show it off[;] Poets Corner at Westminster is a dirty hole—how can England do any thing having no negro slavery[?]"

But in her view slavery was indeed prerequisite for civilized white society. It was also best for the enslaved. As she wrote to one critic of the system, "You believe the negro to be an oppressed race, while we believe him to be a protected one. You assume the ground that we are committing a constant injustice towards him, while we are convinced that we are his only safeguard from extermination, at least in this country." She denied that she intended any "personal disrespect," but suggested that "when you remember that this subject is one with which, nationally, as well as individually, our every interest—life, fortune, and fame—is inseparably linked, you will scarcely be surprised that we should be sensitive on the subject."

She responded tirelessly to slavery's opponents, both in print and in private correspondence, accusing them of ignorance and of condemning slavery "from theory, not insight." When the Duchess of Sutherland's efforts led to "The Affectionate and Christian Address of Many Thousands of the Women of England to Their Sisters, the Women of the United States of America," calling for abolition, McCord replied with an open letter offering to free her 160 slaves and place them in the duchess's hands for "any experiments to which they shall not themselves object," provided "that your Grace shall bind yourself, out of the income of your immense property, to preserve from the abject want which is, in my opinion, likely to ensue from your experiment, these helpless creatures, whom I am (supposing always that they are consenting to the change) ready to transfer to you." (She estimated that "one fifteenth part of one year's income" would suffice, but apparently the duchess did not respond.) Privately she groused that the duchess "understands as little of negroes as of cotton-planting" and complained of her "mis-chievous interference in a subject of which she is as professedly ignorant, as, in all probability she is of Greek and Hebrew."

It is often interesting, as here, to compare McCord's letters and her essays. In her letters she sometimes dropped the rhetorical hauteur of her essays and went for the jugular. In a lengthy review of *Uncle Tom's Cabin*, for instance, she showed conclusively that Harriet Beecher Stowe was a lousy ethnographer—for whatever that may be worth—but to a Philadelphia cousin she wrote that "that abominable woman's abominable book" was "one mass of fanatical bitterness and foul misrepresentation wrapped in the garb of Christian charity," "as malicious and gross an abolitionist production (though I confess a cunning one) as ever dis-graced the press," adding that Mrs. Stowe "has certainly never been in any Southern State further than across the Kentucky line at most, and there in very doubtful society. All her Southern ladies and gentlemen talk coarse Yankee."

In her own case, incidentally, McCord's claim that slavery put masters under obligation seems genuine enough. When her father's estate was being settled, she begged not to be given any slaves, as she already had enough to care for. There is little in here of the darker side of slavery, only some mysterious references in her letters to a house servant named June, who tried to inveigle his freedom from McCord's senile father and was sold out of state for his troublemaking.

McCord's views on the Woman Question were of a piece with her position on slavery. Like Frederick Douglass and the Grimké sisters, she saw an analogy between the position of women and that of slaves. Unlike those abolitionists, however, she defended the existing distinctions, arguing that they were both inevitable and valuable. A sample of her thought (and her verse):

> And shall our daughters cast their woman robes,
> A useless cumbrance, aside, to seize
> Some freer imitation of the man,
> Whose lordly strut and dashing stride attract
> Their envious love for notoriety?

More prosaically: "She [Woman] has no right to bury her talent beneath silks or ribands, frippery or flowers; nor yet has she the right, because she fancies not her task, to grasp at another's, which is, or which she imagines is, easier."

McCord's arguments were not unusual. Other Southerners supported slavery in similar terms, and the idea that the sexes should have separate spheres was widespread—and not just in the South. But the learning, clarity, and force with which she expressed them were unusual indeed, especially for a woman; among upper-class Southern women she was virtually unique. It is ironic that this defender of traditional femininity was credited again and again with "masculine intellect," "masculine vigor," "masculine energy," "masculine strength," or "masculine force of character" (all quotations from her reviewers, usually—but not always—meant as compliments). Who was this unladylike lady?

Asked once for a biographical notice, Mrs. McCord replied, "I am flattered by the compliment, but know nothing about myself, except that I am my father's daughter, born Dec[ember], 1810, married May, 1840, and am not dead yet." Although she was following the conventions of her time and place, this response was not exactly self-effacing: her father was a former speaker of the US House of Representatives and president of the Bank of the United States. The covers of these two volumes are also instructive. The first is a photograph in profile of a homely Victorian lady with a double chin and what just might be a wry expression. The second shows a noble bust in classical attire, in the style of Hiram Powers—not surprising, because it was in fact sculpted by Powers.

Louisa McCord was born to a distinguished South Carolina family and was raised in that state and in Philadelphia, where her father's career took him. Her intellectual interests were evident early, and she was always an avid reader, in several languages. She married late, raised three children, and began to write prolifically in the 1840s. As she put it (characteristically), "An effortless life is, to a restless mind, a weary fate to be doomed to; and as no other door is open to me, I may as well push on at this. Should I fail, the very effort will have given an object to many an otherwise dissatisfied hour, and although I shall have gazed at the sun in vain, it will at least have been a comfort to dream that I could reach him." In the 1850s her domestic situation turned truly dreary—a senile father, irresponsible brothers, failing eyesight, and poor health all around—and she found Columbia, South Carolina, a "horrid little place," enlivened too rarely by events like the tournament in which her nephew participated, sporting an ostrich plume she had given him.

When South Carolina's secession came in 1860, she greeted it with enthusiasm, writing to Hiram Powers, "Our spirited little State has declared its independence." She suspected (correctly) that the expatriate Powers would "sympathize not greatly with the throbbing spirit of our now fully roused country," because "loud mouthed fanaticism has so cried down our institutions, and pretended philanthropy so covered us with slander and falsehood." Still, she wrote, "I am sure if this little sheet had room enough for all I want to say, I could make a good South Carolinian of you. I see it in your eye." She promptly assumed the presidencies of the Soldiers' Relief Association and the Soldiers' Clothing Association, and put her money where her secesh mouth was by outfitting a company of Zouaves to serve under her son's command. (Her friends and relations saluted her fondly as "mother of the Gracchi!")

After the early, heady days of Southern independence, however, things went steadily downhill. Her beloved son was killed in battle. When her house was seized and looted by Union troops, her library was destroyed, and McCord herself was throttled and relieved of her father's pocket watch. After the collapse of the Confederacy, she spent the fourteen years until her death largely as a sort of refugee, staying with various relations in South Carolina and Canada. And she never surrendered. After the US centennial celebration in 1876, she wrote a cousin that she was so "utterly demoralized" by "the jollification, and fraternizing, and gush of loyalty and love;—and the burying of hatchets; and dancing in chains;—that, as I could not kneel down and shout 'glory! glory!'—nor find my way to the 'love, peace, and charity' frame of mind,—I have been trying to keep very quiet and very stupid, hemning [sic], in good-woman style, pocket handkerchiefs, and so forth."

Not likely.

The Man from New Orleans

In the Birmingham Museum of Art a few years ago I came across a stunning tea service, made (the label said) by William Spratling, an Alabamian who had revitalized the silver industry in Taxco, Mexico. I had never heard of him, but soon after that, at a party in Washington, an up-scale Georgetown antiques dealer peered intently at my wife's throat and said "I hope you've got that necklace insured." The necklace, which I'd bought in an east Tennessee junk shop just because I liked its looks, turned out to be by an early student of Spratling's. (It wasn't insured—but it is now.) Since then, Mexican silver has become something of an obsession, and I jumped at the chance to tell the Oxford American's *readers about the Southern connection.*

When Warner Brothers made a movie in 1948 about the life of William Spratling, they called it "The Man from New Orleans," and Spratling liked that label. (He certainly liked it better than "Silver Bill," which is what *Reader's Digest* called him; he threatened to sue Warner Brothers if they called it that.) In fact, Spratling was not really from New Orleans; he had only lived there for a few years before moving to Mexico. But he was at least a Southerner, an Auburn graduate who sometimes affected the molasses accent and courtly style of a Southern gent. Writer, architect, artist, pilot, yachtsman, adventurer, horticulturist, entrepreneur, friend of the rich and famous, connoisseur of pre-Columbian art, inventor of the margarita (he said), and one of the world's finest designers of silver jewelry and silverware, he was not your average Auburn man—but, then, Bill Spratling wasn't average by any standard.

The son of an Alabama-bred father and a New England mother, he was born in 1900 in upstate New York, where his father ran a hospital for epileptics. But the family didn't stay there long. Both parents were in poor health and apparently unstable, and they were often separated. Before Billy was a teenager, his mother had died of tuberculosis, and his father had suffered a "nervous breakdown" and gone off to Florida (where he died a few years later in what was said to be a hunting accident, possibly a suicide). The Spratling children were parceled out to various relatives; Billy was passed around among his father's people in Atlanta and east Alabama. The nearest thing he had to a home was the family farm near Auburn, where he went to high school and then to college.

The boy had demonstrated an early talent for drawing, and at Auburn he developed it to the point that he found himself lecturing as an undergraduate in courses in the architecture department. In 1921 he left Auburn (without a degree) and shortly afterward took a teaching position in architecture at Tulane. He rented an apartment in the French Quarter and acquired a roommate from Mississippi, an aspiring writer named Faulkner. The two Bills quickly became part of New Orleans's surprisingly vibrant literary and artistic scene, drinking with the likes of writers Lyle Saxon, Hamilton Basso, and Sherwood Anderson; artists Caroline Durieux and Ellsworth Woodward; and the circle around the little magazine, *The Double Dealer*. Visitors like John Dos Passos and Anita Loos dropped in from time to time.

Spratling supplemented his Tulane salary by selling articles and drawings to a variety of architectural and travel magazines, and he illustrated several books by his writer friends: *Picturesque New Orleans*, with Lyle Saxon; *The Wrought Iron Work of Old New Orleans*, with his Tulane colleague and fellow architect Nathaniel Curtis; and *Plantation Houses of Louisiana*, with a redoubtable woman named Natalie Scott. He and Faulkner collaborated on *Sherwood Anderson and Other Famous Creoles*, a droll collection of satirical sketches of New Orleans personalities, including themselves. (The title is a play on Miguel Covarrubias's *The Prince of Wales and Other Famous Americans*. Maybe you had to be there.)

Spratling also sketched his way around Europe twice (once with Faulkner), and he spent three summers in the late 1920s drawing and writing about colonial architecture in Mexico, where he befriended leading figures in that country's post-revolutionary artistic renaissance, among them Covarrubias, Diego Rivera, and David Siqueiros. In 1929, abruptly and rather mysteriously, he quit his job at Tulane and moved to Taxco, a picturesque village in the mountains south of Mexico City that had once been a thriving center of silver-mining.

He hoped to make a living writing about Mexico for American audiences (his book *Little Mexico* was published in 1932, with an appreciative foreword by Rivera), but that proved more difficult than he had foreseen. To supplement his income he began to design furniture and tinware, then—perhaps at the suggestion of his friend Dwight Morrow, the American ambassador—branched out into silver, commissioning goldsmiths from a nearby village to produce jewelry and tableware from his designs.

The rest, as they say, is history. Soon Spratling had established the "Taller de las Delicias" (later Spratling y Artesanos) and was producing objects in tin, copper, leather, and fabrics, as well as silver. Within a few years, he was the town's leading businessman, with a workshop employing scores of artisans and an elaborate apprenticeship system for training local boys in silversmithing.

From the outset, Spratling's designs were characterized by a clean, architectural quality, often employing pre-Columbian motifs. (He was rapidly educating himself on that subject.) He worked either in plain silver or in silver combined with wood, tortoise shell, or semiprecious stones from the immediate vicinity. "I've always had the conviction," he wrote, "that certain materials have the right to be worked in a given community because they are native to that area and that the work of the designer is to utilize these materials and to dignify them."

Many of the young men who trained with Spratling started their own workshops, and they were joined by American and European designers attracted by the town's cheap living, cheap labor, and good company. At one point it was estimated that there were two thousand silversmiths working in the town—with, it must be said, varying degrees of artistry. (Some simply copied Spratling's designs: he complained once that it took less than a month for one of his new designs to start appearing in other shops.)

But there was plenty of business to go around. After the completion of the highway from Mexico City to Acapulco in the mid-1930s Taxco became a regular stop on the touristic itinerary, and when World War II cut off the supply of jewelry from Europe, Montgomery Ward and other American retailers placed large orders. By the end of the war, Taxco had become a sort of combination artists' colony and tourist trap, largely through Spratling's doing, if not at all to his satisfaction.

Spratling had always had a knack for befriending influential and celebrated people (as well as a coterie of older women, two of whom—Natalie Scott and Sherwood Anderson's ex-wife Elizabeth—moved to Taxco to be with him), but he had now become a celebrity in his own right, hobnobbing with movie stars and politicians. His friends and visitors included Errol Flynn, Lyndon Johnson, Hart Crane, Leon

Trotsky, Clare Booth Luce, Bette Davis, Richard Nixon, John Huston, Katherine Anne Porter, and Orson Wells. Georgia O'Keefe, who rarely wore jewelry, was photographed wearing a Spratling pin.

But pride goeth before a fall. After the war, American demand for Mexican silver fell off, and some disastrous business decisions put Spratling y Artesanos out of business. Spratling moved to a ranch south of Taxco and continued his silver business, but on a greatly reduced scale.

He also continued to pursue his archeological interests and remained heavily involved in the sometimes shady world of artifact trading, for which he atoned by donating important collections to the National University of Mexico and the National Museum of Anthropology in Mexico City. In 1960 he published *More Human than Divine* (dedicated to Covarrubias), largely photographs of his collection of pre-Columbian sculpture.

The most engaging account of Spratling's remarkable life is his auto-biographical *File on Spratling*, published shortly after his 1967 death in a car wreck (driving too fast, as usual). But it has long been out of print, and it is also, shall we say . . . not always reliable. Even the brooding Siqueiros portrait on its dust jacket—a bare-chested young man with large dark eyes, a neat mustache, and an unsmiling mouth—gives fair warning that this book is an artful rendering, touched up a bit for effect.

In fact, Spratling told a lot of little fibs about himself and implied a good many more. His autobiography is as much an artifice as any of his silver designs, with a great deal of omission, misdirection, and creative rearrangement. Being "the man from New Orleans" was the least of it.

Two biographies issued to mark the centenary of Spratling's birth have tried to sort fact from fiction. Their covers, like the books themselves, are less romantic than Spratling's. Both are illustrated by remarkably similar black-and-white photographs of Spratling (fully clothed) standing in profile, hand in pocket, leg cocked. *The Color of Silver*, by Auburn professor Taylor Littleton, shows us a young man in his French Quarter apartment in the 1920s, his right arm resting on an untidy bookcase, and Littleton's book, published in LSU's Southern Biography Series, is especially informative on Spratling's time in Dixie: growing up in Georgia and Alabama, college days at Auburn, living *la vie bohème* in New Orleans. The cover photograph of *The Silver Gringo*, by Joan Mark of Harvard's Peabody Museum, taken some twenty years after Littleton's, shows an accomplished, self-confident, graying man of affairs in his Mexican ranch house, right arm resting on the mantle of an adobe fireplace—and Mark concentrates on Spratling's life in Taxco (he moves there on page fifteen).

The two books differ in other ways as well. Littleton relies much more on letters, family papers, and interviews with Spratling's relatives. Mark has more interviews with Spratling's *Tasqueño* neighbors, and she is more ready to repeat their small-town gossip and speculation. In particular, she offers some dish on the subject of Spratling's homosexuality. Littleton, perhaps out of deference to the family, perhaps because there is little to go on in the written record, is very circumspect on the matter—but so was Spratling.

Mark's book is the livelier of the two, but at more than twice the length, Littleton's is far more thorough, and some of what Mark omits is important. When Mark doesn't mention Spratling's 1962 honorary degree from Auburn and Littleton treats it as an important emotional homecoming, for example, one is tempted to suspect the Auburn professor of home-team exaggeration—until he quotes a letter in which Spratling tells a friend that the degree was "a sort of vindication of my life objectives and a deep satisfaction to me after all these years."

Littleton's book is also at least occasionally more accurate. Mark misdates her cover photograph by fifteen years or so, for instance, while Littleton gets another from the same sitting right. More importantly, Mark says that Spratling's mother died after his father abandoned his family; Littleton says correctly that the elder Spratling's collapse and flight to Florida came after his wife's death. (It does make a difference in how one thinks of the man.)

But these are minor points. Mark's book is a splendid introduction for readers who have no idea who Bill Spratling was or why they should care. After you've read it, I'll wager you will want to know more, and Littleton is your man for that.

Both books—Mark's especially—indicate that Spratling turned cranky toward the end of his life (alcohol may have been a factor) and suggest that he was well on his way to becoming a grouchy old man when he died. But I prefer to think of him earlier, shooting pedestrians from his French Quarter window with the BB gun he and Faulkner kept for that purpose (the highest score was for hitting a Negro nun), skinny-dipping with visitors to his ranch, or hiring a boy to set off a stink bomb in the noisy whorehouse across the street from his house in Taxco. Picture him nearly drowning while sailing alone (with no previous experience) from Santa Monica to Acapulco, or flying blind through foul weather and mountain passes to Alaska to teach Eskimos how to make jewelry, at the invitation of his friend, Governor Ernest Greuning.

And there is always that marvelous silver. You can get some idea of what the excitement was all about from the half-tones in the two biographies, but far better—indeed, the next best thing to actually seeing and handling the objects themselves (and much cheaper than buying them)—is to pick up a copy of *Spratling Silver*, a tribute by Sandraline Cederwall and Hal Riney, with gorgeous full-page photographs of over seventy pieces, plus pictures of Spratling at work and play.

"The true color of silver is white," Spratling wrote once (giving Littleton the title for his biography), "the same color as extreme heat and extreme cold. It is also the same color as the first food received by an infant and it is the color of light. Its very malleability is an invitation to work it." And he did, with genius.

The World's Best-Selling Novelist

Surely most readers past their youth remember Erskine Caldwell—if not as the youthful peer of Faulkner and Wolfe, at least as the author of vaguely smutty drugstore paperbacks with lurid covers. But when Caldwell died in 1987, I suspect many were surprised to hear that he had lived that long, and for younger folk the one-time "World's Best-Selling Author!" seems to have dropped completely off the screen. Dan Miller, for instance, begins *Erskine Caldwell: The Journey from Tobacco Road* with the startling admission that "I first heard of Erskine Caldwell in 1989. . . . His name did not ring a bell."

Perhaps this is fitting. Caldwell was a regular literary Vesuvius, spewing out more than a hundred short stories, twenty novels, and ten works of nonfiction in his career, but his flashes of literary talent were few and far between. He was, moreover, a pure-tee scoundrel: an egotist, a liar, a cheat, a coward, a tightwad, a poseur, an opportunist, and (when it suited him) a fellow-travelling propagandist. Miller says Caldwell's typical male character—Jeeter Lester, say, or Ty Ty Walden—is "shiftless, conscienceless, incorrigibly lecherous, and possessed of a childlike innocence that blinds him to the ramifications of even his most hideous behavior," and much the same could be said of their creator. No, all in all, this sounds like someone who deserves to be neglected.

So why this biography? Not just to show that Caldwell had an unhappy childhood (that is no excuse unless you live in California and have a high-priced lawyer). Not to argue that he was actually a great writer (Miller doesn't really try). But there is an interesting study here in the sociology of literary reputation. Why was the young Caldwell so overpraised? And why are his modest but undeniable accomplishments now so ignored? Miller demonstrates the truth of both premises and addresses these questions, although he can't really answer them.

Miller ably recounts the facts of Caldwell's youth (what cheap psychologizing he can't resist is mostly in endnotes, often misnumbered), but his story really begins when this Georgia boy, the only child of a socially conscious Protestant minister and a genteel Virginia-bred schoolteacher, burst on the literary scene with two shocking novels about depraved Southern rural families, *Tobacco Road* in 1932 and *God's Little Acre* the next year, starring Jeeter and Ty Ty, respectively. Nobody knew quite what to make of what one editor called Caldwell's "grotesque overrealism," but whatever it was, it was quite different from the genteel stuff entombed in Joel Chandler Harris's Library of Southern Literature. "There has already been too much of 'romance,' of 'magnolia blossoms,' of 'Negro dialect,'" Caldwell solemnly announced. "It is time someone really wrote about 'life.'" But when one Southern lady summarized modern Southern literature as "On the night the hogs ate Willie, Mama died when she heard what Daddy did to Sister" she surely had Caldwell in mind: in his story "Kneel to the Rising Sun" a character *is* eaten by hogs.

Many Southerners responded predictably to Caldwell's obvious dislike for the South, even though it was nothing special (he didn't like New England or California either). "Understand this you SON-OF-A-BITCH," one anonymous letter warned. "Write and talk fast, for when the time comes only the one you doubt will be able to save you." (Caldwell overcame his left-wing prejudices long enough to ask the FBI to investigate that one.) Some "progressive" Southerners were also predictable. A Raleigh newspaperman called *God's Little Acre* "one of the finest studies of the Southern poor white that has ever come into our literature," and a Richmond reviewer saw *Tobacco Road* as a "compelling argument for diversified farming."

Caldwell himself believed that he was crusading for social justice and sexual liberation, and he bitterly resented reviewers who saw him in the tradition of eye-gouging antebellum southwestern humor ("tall yarns," one wrote, spun with "a sunny humor"). He claimed to be a "proletarian writer," and in 1932 even endorsed the Communist ticket in the presidential election. Impressed by Caldwell's (inflated) working-class credentials, the literary left tried hard to believe him when he said that the Lesters were merely "a Georgia Family . . . starving of malnutrition and pellagra because the absentee landlord has stopped giving them credit for food and seed." The *New Republic*, for instance, applauded him for documenting "the scant hopes and the ineluctable vassalage of these poor whites." But there was a problem: As a reviewer in the

Daily Worker observed, Caldwell's characters are so disgusting that they "lose the power to compel either pity or indignation."

All these varied reactions make some sort of sense. What is harder to understand is the extravagant praise of literati like Lewis Mumford, Malcolm Cowley, and Ezra Pound for Caldwell's artistic achievement. He was compared to Twain, Dickens, and Balzac; soon he would be ranked with Faulkner and Wolfe as a leading figure in the Southern Renaissance, with Steinbeck as a chronicler of the rural poor, and with Hemingway as a stylistic innovator. But, overpraised or not, *God's Little Acre* would mark the high point of Caldwell's literary reputation.

This was not immediately obvious. Caldwell turned for a while to documentary journalism, reporting on the American poor and our heroic Soviet allies, often working with the glamorous photographer Margaret Bourke-White, who became his second wife (of four). Meanwhile, work in Hollywood (which he despised), the stage adaptation of *Tobacco Road* (which set Broadway records), and the new market for paperback books (six million copies of *God's Little Acre* sold in five years) were making Caldwell a rich man.

But a steady decline in critical regard accompanied the rise in his paperback sales. Every year or two he wrote a new, bad book or recycled an old one, and he kept writing short stories, but by the 1950s—widely regarded as a Communist, a pornographer, and a has-been—he was no longer publishing them in reputable places. Two well-reviewed nonfiction books in the 1960s did nothing to revive critical interest in him, but in the 1970s he began to receive some recognition—most of it, ironically, from his native region. A couple of Southern universities honored him, and a Southern president invited him to the White House. Eventually the daily two packs of cigarettes and fifth of bourbon took their toll on his health, but he stubbornly hung on and kept writing. His last book was published a month before his death at age eighty-four.

It should be said that some think more highly of Caldwell than most American English professors do. He ranks with Jerry Lewis in the French cultural pantheon, for instance. And many of his fellow writers admire him: in 1984 he was even elected to the American Academy of Arts and Letters. William Faulkner said, "I think that the first books, *God's Little Acre* and the short stories, that's enough for any man." I hesitate to disagree with Faulkner. Still, the picture that emerges from this book is pretty much that of a thoroughgoing hack. It rings true when Caldwell says that writing, to him, was "like digging ditches or anything else. . . . You know you have to make a living. . . . It's the only job I've got and I have to work at it full time." Writing supported him well. As the royalties rolled in he grew less annoyed by misunderstandings of his work, became an avid investor in the stock market, and appeared as a "Man of Distinction" in a Calvert Whiskey advertisement.

But if Caldwell was a hack, he was a dedicated one. The man rarely wrote well, but by God he *wrote*. He sacrificed his family, his friendships, his health, finally even his literary reputation to keep that stream flowing. In an interview Miller doesn't quote, Caldwell remarked, "I'd hate to have to read my own biography [because] my life is really rather dull. . . . I'm a writer, and the only thing I like to do in life is write." But Miller's account is not dull at all: if nothing else there is a morbid fascination in watching Caldwell deceive himself and betray nearly everyone who was ever decent to him, all in the service of his craft. In the end, you feel something like admiration for his sheer perseverance and indomitable spirit. It's just like Jeeter and Ty Ty.

Mover and Shaker

Governor John Connally of Texas died in 1993 from pneumonia, complicated by a lung condition believed to be related to the wound he received from Lee Harvey Oswald. His seventy-six years in many ways recapitulated the history of the twentieth-century South, from humble agrarian origins, early New Deal loyalties, and military valor, to political and economic success (with an occasional whiff of corruption), finally switching political allegiance to an ambivalent Republican Party, but always with the nagging sense that he never got his just desserts from the Eastern Establishment.

Like most Southerners of his generation, Connally was not born to prosperity. His father was successively a tenant farmer, a bricklayer, a barber, a butcher, and finally a bus owner/driver and local politician. The young Connally wore kneepads cut from old tires to pick cotton. (Later he did not talk much about these inelegant origins—not that he was ashamed of them, he says.) At sixteen, he went off to the state university, where he was active in a drama club that during the 1930s produced Eli Wallach, Zachary Scott, Allen Ludden, and television actress Betty White. (Walter Cronkite was on the publicity committee.) In Austin he was elected president of the student assembly, and he made friends that lasted him for life: future businessmen, politicians and political lawyers, among them Robert Strauss and Congressman Jake Pickle. He acquired a law degree and got his first taste of statewide politics working for a business-backed gubernatorial candidate who lost to the inimitable W. Lee ("Pass the biscuits, Pappy") O'Daniel of the musical group Light Crust Doughboys. Fatefully, he came to the notice of an ambitious young New Dealer named Lyndon Johnson, whom he served as factotum and advisor off and on for the next thirty years.

After Navy service in World War II—which gave him a Bronze Star, the Legion of Merit, and a taste for the recordings of Enrico Caruso—his fortunes rose with those of his patron and his state. As he moved back and forth between Washington and Texas, from government to business and back again, his talents and connections made him a wealthy man by non-Texas standards, a prominent figure in the conservative wing of the Texas Democratic Party, and eventually a popular and successful three-term governor, elected to his last term with 72 percent of the vote.

When Johnson became president, he often sought Connally's advice (Connally says), but he didn't always take it. Connally says that he disagreed with his mentor about three things: he wanted to threaten Hanoi with nuclear attack, he disapproved of the volume and speed (but not the aims) of Johnson's social legislation, and he thought Johnson suffered a "failure of nerve" in not replacing Kennedy's cabinet—including Robert Kennedy—with his own men.

After 1968 the McGovernite handwriting was on the wall for conservative Democrats, and Connally, like many other Southerners, changed first his vote and then his party. Approached by Billy Graham (of all people) about Gergenizing the Nixon cabinet as Secretary of Defense or the Treasury, Connally took Treasury. "State has the glamour, Defense has the toys, but Treasury is and always has been the most powerful job in the cabinet," he observes. He says he was always "a conservative who believed in an active government," and he certainly backed a good many statist measures as Secretary of the Treasury, notably a 10 percent import "surcharge" to "correct unfair trade balances," the Lockheed loan guarantee, and Nixon's ill-fated wage and price controls. (This last is one of the two mistakes he acknowledges in this book, the other being the real estate investments that bankrupted him in 1987.) He left Treasury, just in time to avoid Watergate, over a dispute about his prerogatives as Secretary (an undersecretary was reporting directly to the White House staff).

After that the story is all anticlimax: a trial on bribery charges, a humiliating unsuccessful run for president, a Republican White House that seemed happy to leave him practicing law in Texas, personal bankruptcy, the election of his bitter enemy George Bush. Of course, Alexander Hamilton's career topped out at Secretary of the Treasury, too, but Connally was no Alexander Hamilton. Sure, he says things like "I never planned, or sought, or wanted a long career in politics," or "I never felt afflicted with Potomac fever," or "I could have spent my whole life happily as a pretty fair cattleman, or even as a corporate lawyer." But he was obviously consumed by the what-ifs. He believed he could have had the Democratic nomination for president in 1968, if Kennedy had not been shot. Nixon would have delivered him the Republican nomination in 1976, if it had not been for Watergate.

And then there was his actual, if short-lived, presidential campaign in 1980. Clearly this was a man who very much wanted the brass ring of American politics, and it plainly grieved him that bad luck and other people's blunders and malice kept him from getting it.

This book's last chapters are largely about those blunders and that malice. But what is an autobiography for if not to settle old scores and to give one's own side of ancient disputes? Connally was a good hater, and he is charmingly forthright in his self-service. His book is full of innuendo, hints of plots, and implied skullduggery on the part of everyone from the young man who eloped with his daughter (who subsequently killed herself) to every politician who ever crossed him, of whom there were many. As for giving the author's side of things—well, Connally does have a lot of explaining to do.

Start with the 1948 Senate election that gave LBJ the nickname (which he hated) "Landslide Lyndon." According to Connally, who was Johnson's campaign manager, "There has been so much pure drivel written about the Senate election of '48 that it has driven out the impure drivel." Connally says that he was determined to avoid a repeat of 1941 when Johnson had a Senate seat stolen from him by a group of operators that included Coke Stevenson, his 1948 opponent. So Johnson's workers were told to report low vote totals initially so the other side would underestimate how many votes they had to steal to win. Then, when Johnson's totals mysteriously increased, see, it just *looked* as if new votes were being generated. It was really just that the actual totals were being reported for the first time. "There may have been invalid votes that were cast for Lyndon Johnson," Connally allows. "But they were not bought and they were not stolen."

Or consider the 1955 bill to end natural gas price controls that was derailed when Senator Case of South Dakota rose to report on the Senate floor that he had been given an envelope full of hundred dollar bills by a lobbyist. "My personal conviction," says Connally, "was that no attempt had been made to bribe anyone. A contribution that would have been given routinely was handled clumsily, with atrocious timing."

And of course there was the Kennedy assassination. The book's publicist says that Connally "will be most vividly remembered as the man who rode in front of Kennedy in the Dallas motorcade." If so, that's ironic, because it is hard to imagine Connally playing second-fiddle to anyone (except possibly LBJ, and that only in his youth). Connally reports that the Kennedy visit was forced on him by the president, who wanted to meet and mend fences with big-money Texans. Ticket sales for the fundraisers were weak, he says, until he worked the phones for two nights and personally sold $50,000 worth (a lot of money in those days). He tried to talk the president out of having a motorcade, but the president's advance men insisted on it. They are the ones who released the route to the press, too. Connally even repeats Marina Oswald's speculation that Oswald was actually gunning for him, not the president; he is convinced, he says, that at the very least Oswald wanted to kill them both. His account of the assassination makes you want to refurbish an old joke to make the punch line read: "Who's that man with Governor Connally?" Other than believing that a separate bullet was intended for him, however, Connally accepted the Warren Commission report. He quotes Earl Warren: "What possible set of circumstances could get me and Dick Russell to conspire on *anything*?"

The longest explanation—it gets a full chapter—has to do with Connally's indictment and trial in the 1974 Milk Fund scandal. Jake Jacobsen, an Austin lawyer and lobbyist for the milk producers, a man with "the personality of an eel, but a friendly eel," plea-bargained his way out of a prison term by agreeing to testify that he had delivered $10,000 to Connally in 1971 for advising President Nixon to raise milk price supports. Then and later, Connally denied the charge indignantly: "I would not have condoned for one minute anything of questionable character, much less anything illegal." While he denies that he could be bought, he also adduces what could be called the Rostenkowski defense: It is ridiculous to think that he could be bought for a lousy ten grand. Connally claims his prosecution was politically inspired, and among the conspirators he names Jim Wright and Watergate special prosecutor Leon Jaworski (who worked for a rival Houston law firm), as well as Dick Cheney and most of Gerald Ford's cabinet, who wanted to keep him off the 1976 Republican ticket. At the trial, Connally's character witnesses included Robert McNamara, Dean Rusk, Barbara Jordan, Lady Bird Johnson, and the ubiquitous Billy Graham, and much of the government's case came down to whether he had said "oil in Texas" or "all the taxes" on one of the Watergate tapes. In the end, he was acquitted, but the episode haunted his political career thereafter.

But there was more to Connally's stalled career than the incompetence and conniving of others. The political skills he picked up from mentors like Sam Rayburn and Lyndon Johnson served him well in the intrigues of state government, and they made him an effective power broker, advisor, and confidante for presidents. But the style that served him so well in Texas electoral politics was like a rare wine that doesn't travel well. Elsewhere, this can-do wheeler-dealer came across as something like J. R. Ewing of "Dallas," a Huey Long in tailored suits, a suaver version of Lyndon Johnson—indeed, the very personification of the "Rimster Cowboy" that gave Kirkpatrick Sale bad dreams in his 1975 book, *Power Shift: The Rise of the Southern Rim and Its Challenge to the Eastern Establishment*. But it was not just the Eastern Establishment who didn't cotton to the Connally style. In the 1980 South Carolina Republican primary, Ronald Reagan cleaned his clock: a $12 million campaign netted Connally exactly one delegate to the Republican convention.

Connally had the virtues as well as the defects of his type. Reagan's election left him free to pursue a short, disastrous career in Texas real estate development, and his ensuing bankruptcy showed him at his best. Although he claims that "the failure of the loan was not the result of mismanagement but of circumstances in the general economy" and argues that the government should have intervened to tide embarrassed real estate investors over (it did it for Lockheed, after all), when his position finally collapsed, he took it like a man. He and his wife could have sold their belongings privately, to a dealer, but they decided that a public auction, however painful, would bring a higher price and let him to do better by his creditors. And the Connallys were there, at the sale, to explain to buyers the history and provenance of their art and other effects. The scene is actually moving, lessened only slightly by the fact that Connally knew that it was.

A first-person account like this is probably not the best way to get the flavor of the sort of politics Connally practiced. The tendency to straighten one's tie and pose for posterity seems to be irresistible. And presumably we have Mickey Herskowitz (previously the coauthor of Bette Davis's and Dan Rather's "autobiographies") to thank for the occasional attempts at vivid prose, most of which could have been omitted. (For instance, "Rangeland has a character all its own: hard and open, begging to be ridden, but unsparing to those who do." Or, "Texas always was, and is today, a hardscrabble land that has to be broken and held by the pure strength of man and woman. It was on that strength always that it was made to produce and prosper, never on the bounty of its own natural endowment"—which is, incidentally, a monumentally dumb thing to say in a book largely about oil money.)

Still, Connally does tell some nice stories. Some of the best are about his big-oil friends. When oil millionaire Sid Richardson (Connally's sometime employer) bought the New York Central railroad, for instance, he discovered that his part of the price was $5 million more than he had thought. His only question was "What was the name of that railroad again?" Another oil man, Oscar Wyatt, went with Connally on a mission to Baghdad just before the Gulf War—unapproved and in fact discouraged by the Bush administration—to meet with Saddam Hussein and bring out some of the American hostages. Like Wyatt, Connally opposed the war, partly because he saw it as a gimmick to restore the despised Bush's popularity, partly because (as Wyatt put it), "In nineteen years of trading with the Arabs, the one and only thing I've learned is to stay out of their chickenshit conflicts."

Not surprisingly, many of Connally's best stories are about Lyndon Johnson. For example, Johnson was given to calling people at 5:30 AM and asking "What are you doing?"—to which Wayne Hays once replied, "Well, Mr. President, I've been lying here hoping you would call." Connally shared Bill Moyers's admiration for LBJ's "moral imagination," and he seems to have been genuinely fond of the man, but he had few illusions about Johnson's devious intelligence and bulldozer tactics. He applauds the few—among them, Sheldon Cohen of the Internal Revenue Service and Joe Barr, undersecretary of the treasury—who stood up to Johnson successfully.

Oddly, two of the stories in this book are about the unlikely subject of Russian women. One concerns Lyndon Johnson's first meeting with Franklin Roosevelt. The young congressman went to the White House to seek a favor for his district. After listening patiently for a few minutes, Roosevelt asked him, out of the blue, "Did you ever see a Russian woman naked?" It seems that Harry Hopkins had visited the Soviet Union and brought back the intelligence that heavy labor had made the New Soviet Woman differently constructed from the American model, information FDR apparently found bemusing.

It is possible that Hopkins didn't meet a representative sample. Forty years later, Richard Nixon told Connally about the parade of Aeroflot stewardesses to the bedroom of the visiting Leonid Brezhnev. According to the president, those Russian women were quite fetching. Just like the Russkies to keep the best for themselves.

Connally's book concludes with a hodgepodge of policy recommendations—national service, a value-added tax, term limits, a ten dollar a barrel tax on imported oil, federal standards for public school curricula, and (this one piquant, given the source) the restriction or elimination of plea-bargaining—that, if nothing else, suggest why neither major party was ever really comfortable with this it's-broke-let's-fix-it Texan. Sound familiar?

Let me refresh your memory. Picture John Connally, not as a bitter has-been offering advice no one wants, but in his prime, in 1972, a fifty-three-year-old mover and shaker bringing President Nixon to his ranch to eat barbecue and corn on the cob with the other movers and shakers of Texas. Here he is, tall and handsome, laughing and shaking hands, the gracious host. Here is Alan Shivers, a former governor, and Miss Ima Hogg, daughter of another. There is Anne Armstrong, over yonder are Bunker Hunt, Perry Bass, the Murchison brothers . . . and an interesting young newcomer named H. Ross Perot.

Hardy Perennial

The poet and critic Allen Tate once began to write a biography of Robert E. Lee, but abandoned it when he decided that Lee was not complicated enough to sustain his interest. With Lee, Tate concluded, what you saw was what you got: a man of duty, untroubled by doubt and apparently by temptation. Nadine Cohodas's *Strom Thurmond and the Politics of Southern Change* presents another sort of marble man, embodying principles, winning elections, and representing his constituents without reflection or second thoughts. The man portrayed in this book has no discernible interior life at all and not even a private life apart from politics. He is not just a marble man, but a hollow one.

That may be accurate. In fact, I suspect it is. But Cohodas's Thurmond doesn't even have any real peculiarities. For a successful mid-century Southern politician, he is strangely colorless. This book is an admirable transcript of the words of Southern politics, but the music is heard only rarely. Cohodas just doesn't seem to be particularly interested in the man himself—either that, or she wasn't tuning the right frequencies. True, Thurmond is no Edwin Edwards or George Wallace, but there are these *stories* about him.

Early on, for instance, Cohodas quotes the Clemson college year-book's assessment of the young Thurmond as a "ladies' man of the 'first water,'" but she doesn't mention that that reputation, mutatis mutandis, has followed him ever since. (At the time of the Clarence Thomas hearings we were told that Thurmond, among other white male senators, "just doesn't get it." Maybe not, but apparently he still tries.) Cohodas does record Thurmond's penchant for taking young beauty queens to wife (his first young enough to be his daughter; his second young enough to be his *grand* daughter), and she reproduces a famous LIFE photograph captioned "VIRILE GOVERNOR demonstrates his prowess in the mansion yard day before wedding" (he was standing on his head). But she simply deposits these data with us and moves on briskly to more dignified matters, not pausing to ask whether Thurmond's amorous impulses are the most spontaneous and human thing about the old goat, evidence that he is interested in *something* besides politics, or just another good career move. It is true that Thurmond's tastes have given rise to a good deal of bawdy humor in these parts, but, as another Southern pol once observed, they do love a *man* in the country.

Similarly, the late Lee Atwater told one of his former teachers (a friend of mine) that Thurmond has almost no sense of humor. According to Atwater, though, the senator loves to hear stories of political dirty tricks—the same ones, over and over. He laughs and laughs. This sort of thing makes the man more interesting, if not more sympathetic, but it is absent from this book.

To say that Cohodas's sketch is one-dimensional, however, is not to say that her account of Thurmond's public life will interest only political junkies. The man has been involved in some of the great events of our time, and his career provides much food for thought—usually depressing thought—about ends and means, motives and unanticipated consequences. Even if that thought is usually left as an exercise for the reader, Cohodas has done us a service by assembling the raw materials. She gives us one of the best summaries available of the legal and legislative struggle for the civil rights of black Southerners, a struggle from which Thurmond emerged by virtue of his electoral popularity, political agility, and sheer longevity as one of the few survivors on the losing side.

Until 1948, Thurmond's story was one of monotonous political success, with no more than the usual treachery and double-dealing (in fact, probably less than usual). Born into the segregated South of 1902, he went to college at Clemson, where he was an athlete and BMOC. He served briefly as a high-school teacher and coach until, at the age of twenty-six, he was elected county school superintendent. Three years later (having, on the side, studied privately for the bar, passed it, and begun a law practice) he ran successfully for the state senate. After five years in that body, he was elected to a state judgeship. World War II interrupted this steady progression, but within six months of returning to South Carolina, Thurmond announced that he was running for governor. He was forty-four years old when he took office in 1947, with less than half his life and not much more than a quarter of his career behind him.

Some of Thurmond's most striking attributes were evident from the first. He has always been an indefatigable and incessant campaigner, never missing a chance to shake hands, learning and remembering every name, spending his spare moments writing notes of sympathy and congratulation to constituents. Also consistently evident was his physical and political courage. As a judge he once faced down an armed householder. He was wounded and won a Bronze Star while landing in France on D-Day with the Eighty-Second Airborne. As governor he took firm action against a lynch mob (and won the plaudits of a number of people, black and white, who would later see him as a hopeless reactionary: it was not his fault that a jury later acquitted the lynchers).

Ironically, for a South Carolina Democrat in the 1940s, the young Thurmond was something of a progressive. Listen to him, in 1947: "We who believe in a liberal political philosophy, in the importance of human rights as well as property rights, in the preservation and strengthening of the economic and social gains brought about by the efforts of the Democratic Party . . . will vote for the election of Harry Truman." But, of course, that was not to be. A year later Thurmond was running against Truman himself, as the candidate of the National States' Rights Democratic Party, the "Dixiecrats."

Like George Wallace twenty years later, Thurmond ran in opposition to the interventionist liberalism of the national Democratic Party, claiming to stand for limited (federal) government and strict construction of the (federal) Constitution, especially but not exclusively in matters having to do with states' powers to order race relations. Cohodas carefully examines the evidence, and essentially accepts Thurmond's account of his motives. She concludes that he was acting as a genuine conservative, consistently (for a politician) opposed to the extension of federal power into matters reserved by the Constitution to the states. In 1948, of course, many other Southern politicians had no interest in limited government except in defense of white supremacy, but Thurmond has always denied that he was ever a racist and, in a narrow sense, he is apparently correct. As a South Carolina NAACP official put it, "I never thought Strom Thurmond actually hated black people. He just never really needed them."

Whatever his motives, his act of disloyalty put Thurmond in the national Democrats' doghouse for good. Although he ran successfully to fill a vacant Senate seat in 1954 (beating the state organization's handpicked candidate, and becoming the first person ever elected to the Senate by a write-in vote), he was doomed by the times and his principles to a stance of perpetual opposition, whatever party was in power. When one of his staffers during the Kennedy-Johnson years was asked if he worked for the government, he replied, "No, I work against the government." Thurmond's career had seemingly topped out at leader of the Southern diehards. No influential assignments, cabinet posts, or vice-presidential nominations for him.

But the man had moves in reserve that no one had suspected. After Lyndon Johnson pushed through the Civil Rights Act of 1964, Thurmond changed parties, in what was seen at the time as an act of daring. Campaigning for his friend and political ally Barry Goldwater, he explained that if Lyndon Johnson was reelected "freedom as we have known it in this country is doomed, and individuals will be destined to lives of regulation, control, coercion, intimidation, and subservience to a power elite who shall rule from Washington." (He got that right, anyway.) Goldwater lost big, of course, and Democrats sneered about rats swimming to a sinking ship, but four years later the election of Richard Nixon began an era of Republican dominance of the White House, and got Thurmond inside the tent. So many of his friends and advisors were in the Nixon administration that some called the White House "Uncle Strom's cabin." The Reagan landslide of 1980 installed Thurmond as chairman of the Senate Judiciary Committee, replacing none other than Ted Kennedy, to the dismay of right-thinking liberals everywhere.

That didn't last, but he is still in the Senate, and still campaigning. (He shook my hand at a stock car race not long ago.) Now in his nineties, he is certainly entitled to rest on his laurels, but he just keeps going, and going. One has to suspect that he doesn't know how to do anything else. Cohodas's portrait of the old man is almost sad. Unintentionally, I suspect, she portrays him as a goofy old duffer handled by savvy staffers who recognize that their jobs and influence depend on his popularity back in the sticks, but who labor mightily to keep him from weird acts of self-expression while he is in Washington. Republicans, meanwhile, not knowing what else to do with him, have begun to treat him as a venerable elder statesman. The waning days of the hapless Bush administration saw many strange sights, but none stranger than Thurmond's being awarded the Presidential Medal of Freedom, the first (and presumably the last) segregationist champion to be so honored.

Cohodas is fascinated by the fact that this former Dixiecrat has come to terms with some of the changes he so stoutly opposed, fashioning an accommodation with the new electorate created by the Voting Rights Act of 1965. In this, he is like the latter-day George Wallace. During Wallace's last gubernatorial campaign, a knowledgeable friend explained to me why the polls showed Wallace with a substantial minority of the black vote. "There are going to be a lot of black mosquito-control inspectors in Alabama," he said. Thurmond, too, has brought home the bacon for his black constituents. (The man may have principles, but he's no fool: he has always been happy to take federal money for South Carolina.)

He has also become responsive to black voters' opinions on other matters. He would not put it this way, but he now treats them as a component of the concurrent majority, at least on issues that directly affect their racial interests. He appointed a black staff member even before more liberal Southern senators did so, he eventually voted for the Voting Rights Act of 1982 (after laboring mightily to amend some of its more obnoxious features), and he has sponsored legislation to set up National Historically Black Colleges Week (although I observed at the time that the senator has always been in favor of separate black colleges).

Unlike Wallace, however, Thurmond has never admitted that he ever did anything wrong. Forced to look back on his defense of segregation, he now says, "The reason I took the position I did was, one, that was the law of South Carolina, the law of my state, and next, it was the thinking of the people I represented." In his mind, he is now defending a different law and representing a more inclusive electorate, that's all.

One consistent thread does link the 1940s to the 1990s. Thurmond continues to oppose federal intervention and activism in most matters. The story is told (not in this book) that once, when Thurmond was explicating the Tenth Amendment during a Southern filibuster, his South Carolina colleague Olin Johnston turned to another Southern senator and said, "Listen to old Strom. You know, he really believes that shit." Say this for Thurmond: apparently he really did, and does.

And Thurmond's principles are not bad ones; the Tenth Amendment is one of my favorites, too. But he did our principles a disservice—in fact, may have dealt them a death blow. State governments that failed to protect the persons and property of black citizens, that even used state power to hold them in subordination, invited the growth of countervailing legislative, bureaucratic, and judicial power at the federal level. Thurmond was a stalwart opponent of that growth, but he has never acknowledged the abuse and neglect that made it almost inevitable. By their doomed defense of segregation and white supremacy, Thurmond and his allies gave states' rights a bad name that lingers to this day, alienated many who should have joined them in the cause of limited government, and forced men and women who sought only simple justice to expedients that some may live to regret. That is some of that food for depressing thought I mentioned earlier.

The Southern Elvis

When Vernon Chadwick organized the First International Elvis Confer-
ence at the University of Mississippi in 1995, people like the chancellor
of the university and the mayor of Oxford were very nervous, suspect-
ing (correctly) that various sophisticates would sneer at them. Later
conferences were downsized and moved to the more hospitable setting
of Memphis, but I am proud to have shared the limelight at the first
one with a stellar cast of Elvisians including Elvis's cook and El Vez,
the Mexican Elvis. I gave the lead-off paper, which means I got on the
network evening news (the camera crews didn't stick around).

It is an honor to kick off this historic conference, and I thought
I would start with some appropriately modest summary of my qualifications for the job. How about these?

Elvis and I have the same birthday.

I, too, was a teenager in Tennessee.

My grandparents, like his, were cousins.

Somehow I doubt that you're impressed, and you probably shouldn't
be. The part of east Tennessee I come from is closer to the Canadian
border than it is to Memphis, more Appalachia than Deep South. My
January 8 birthday came a crucial seven years after his: I don't remember the Depression, FDR, or much of World War II, and I was just a
thirteen-year-old paperboy when Elvis played the Civic Auditorium
in Kingsport—too young to go hear him, too young even to want to.
Which leaves us only with those grandparents, and I don't know what
can be made of that.

So I can't speak about Elvis with the kind of authority that impresses
Southerners. I never even met the man. My knowledge, such as it is,
is all second-hand—book-learning, not from experience or intuition.
And even my book-learning is severely limited. Getting ready for this,
I checked out what we academic types call "the literature" on Elvis,
and I'm here to tell you there is a hunka hunka literature out there.

Elvis can't quite match the Civil War (which I am told has generated an average of a book a day since Appomattox), but in the last quarter-century the Library of Congress has catalogued over three hundred books about him, in at least nine languages. One magazine and journal database includes over two hundred articles in just the last seven years with the word "Elvis" in the title. You will find them in publications ranging from the *Journal of Philately* to *Christianity and Crisis*, *Ladies' Home Journal* to the *UCLA Law Review*, *Bon Appétit* to *Cultural Studies*. There is an article in *Florists' Review* on how to have an "Elvis wedding," while *Studies in Popular Culture* offers a treatise on "Elvis and the Aesthetics of Post-Modernism." Of course, these databases are not infallible. One article I turned up had the fascinating title, "Surgical Management of Collapsed Elvis in a Jaguar," which sounds like the title of a piece of visionary art. But actually it appeared in the *Journal of the American Veterinary Medical Association* and "Elvis" was just a typo for "Pelvis"—not the first time those two words have been associated.

And when we turn from magazines to newspapers things get *really* out of hand: between 1989 and 1995 alone nearly fourteen hundred stories in major newspapers referred to Elvis. One example from the *Boston Globe* was "Pocahontas: The Elvis Connection," about Wayne Newton's announcement that he is descended from Pocahontas and his belief that Elvis is reaching out to him from beyond. And this is the more or less *respectable* press: *Weekly World News* and other purveyors of stories like "Statue of Elvis Found on Mars" are not indexed.

After all this, I quickly gave up any thoughts I had of mastering what has already been written about Elvis. It probably can't be done. Certainly not if you are going to do anything else. Can anything possibly remain to be said?

Clearly the boy has made a name for himself. Long ago Elvis became one of those figures like Scarlett or Sherlock, on a first-name basis with the world. (Of course it helped that his first name wasn't, say, Robert.) "Elvis" has even become a common noun, as in one news story I found about a guy known as "the Elvis of bowling."

How did this happen? The sociology of genius is an interesting study, and every bit as important as the genetics and psychology of it. Elvis had an extraordinary talent, but he also had the great good fortune to be in the right place at the right time for that talent to be recognized and acclaimed. His flower didn't bloom unseen or waste its sweetness very long on the desert air of the First Assembly of God. Whatever the balance of individual genius and social readiness to nurture and to reward it, the combination has clearly made him a figure of unique cultural importance. But everyone knows that.

So I am going to discuss how Elvis was *not* unique—how he was, in many ways, quite ordinary. None of what I'm going to say here is new. It is ground that has been covered by Vaughan Grisham, Elaine Dundy, Peter Guralnik, and others to whom I'm indebted for it. What they have written makes it clear that, in most respects that would interest a sociologist, Elvis was from an ordinary Southern white family, and he was born and raised in an ordinary Southern town. You could even say that the Presleys and Tupelo were extraordinarily ordinary—not just typical but exemplary. The histories of the Presleys and of Tupelo illustrate much broader themes in Southern history; one way or another they illustrate important trends from the collapse of cotton tenancy to the rise of Pentecostalism, and involve high-profile Southern institutions from Parchman penitentiary to the Tennessee Valley Authority.

It is worth emphasizing Elvis's ordinariness, I think, because that is part of his fascination and his appeal. Although he became a remarkable cultural phenomenon, his background and first nineteen years were, in broad outline, much the same as those of hundreds of thousands of other Southern white boys. To understand how he was unique, we have to start by understanding how he was not. To understand him, you have understand where he came from. You can't stop there, but that is where you have to start.

He was born, of course, in 1935, in Tupelo, the son of Vernon Presley and the former Gladys Smith, and, as Elaine Dundy's genealogical research makes clear, even his ancestry was typical for a Southern white boy. His ancestors, like those of most white Southerners, were mostly British. The Smiths, his mother's family, were of English descent, moving west from South Carolina after the Civil War, but most of the rest were Celtic rather than Anglo-Saxon. The Presley name came to America with Scots who settled in North Carolina in the eighteenth century, then moved south and west over the years. Most of Elvis's other ancestors were Scotch-Irish, part of the great wave of migration from Scotland to Ulster to Pennsylvania, then down the Shenandoah Valley to settle the Southern interior from southwest Virginia to Texas.

The story of Elvis's forebears, like those of many white Southerners, was one of restless mobility: settling, then moving on, settling again for a generation or two, then moving on again, escaping problems or seeking opportunity or both, looking for a fresh start somewhere else.

Most of them were farmers—after the early 1800s *cotton* farmers—and most were yeomen of the sort Daniel Hundley described in 1860: "Nearly always poor, at least so far as this world's goods are to be taken into the account," Hundley wrote, their only "inheritance [was] the ability and the will to earn an honest livelihood . . . by the toilsome sweat of their own brows." Hundley adds that the yeoman exhibited "a manly independence of character"; that he would not "under any circumstances humiliate himself to curry favor with the rich or those in authority"; that he was courageous, never wounded from behind. But he was not all tedious Jeffersonian nobility: Hundley added that he was fond of turkey shoots, frolics, barbecues, and—true to his Scotch-Irish heritage—the drinking of home-brewed spirits. (We will come back to those spirits in a moment, because they figure in Elvis's story.)

Most of the two-thirds of Southern white families who didn't own slaves in 1860 were yeomen. The Southern yeoman was only rarely a slaveholder (he couldn't afford it), but when he was, he worked alongside his slaves. Culturally if not politically these people were the backbone of the Old South, as Frank Owsley showed some time ago in his pathbreaking *Plain Folk of the Old South*. They furnished the foot soldiers of the Confederate army.

But not all of them stood up for Dixie in 1861. Gladys's father was named *Robert Lee* Smith—hard to get more Confederate than that—but one of Elvis's great-great-grandfathers appears to have been a Confederate deserter (twice), and a collateral relative was a North Alabama Unionist who named a son "Grant," *after* the Civil War. This record of mixed, or shifting, or nonexistent Confederate loyalties is far more common in Southern genealogies than the mythology of the Lost Cause allowed, and probably not many latter-day Southerners have ancestry that would stand up to the kind of scrutiny that Elvis's has received.

You may recall the "American Trilogy," the medley that Elvis often used for his Las Vegas finale, which mixed up "Dixie" and "The Battle Hymn of the Republic" and threw in the Negro spiritual "All My Trials" for good measure. He came by the mixture of Union and Confederate honestly. It has not been established that any of his forebears were African American, but there was a great-great-great-grandfather who first fought the Indians with Andy Jackson and then married one, a woman named Morning Dove White who gave Elvis the Cherokee great-great-great-grandmother that almost every Southerner claims to have. (She's not Pocahontas, but she will do.)

Anyway, by the beginning of the twentieth century, many of the South's white yeomen had lost their land and had joined the great majority of Southern blacks as sharecroppers and tenant farmers. Half the South's farmers—two-thirds of all cotton farmers—didn't own the land they farmed, and half of the South's tenants and sharecroppers were white. Among them were both of Elvis's grandfathers.

Vernon Presley's father, J. D., was one of ten children (by unknown fathers) of what is known these days as a "single mother." She supported her family by farming on shares, and her son followed in her footsteps. Gladys Presley's father, Bob Smith, was a sharecropper, too, but soon after he married his first cousin Doll, she went to bed with the tuberculosis that was endemic in the rural South and spent the rest of her surprisingly lengthy life as that classic Southern figure, the "shut-in." Bob Smith found it necessary to augment his family's meager farming income by distilling and selling illegal whiskey.

When Vernon Presley and Gladys Smith moved to East Tupelo, they were among the first of their families to leave the land: Gladys to run a sewing machine in the Garment Factory for two dollars a day, Vernon to pursue a string of odd, but definitely urban jobs: milkman, cabinetmaker, lumberyard worker, delivery-truck driver (delivering wholesale groceries and also, it appears, bootleg liquor).

Incidentally, Gladys was not unusual in being a working woman. In this century, Southern women have actually been more likely than women elsewhere to work outside their homes. Many of them—and probably most of their men—would have preferred it otherwise, but economic circumstances made it necessary. This was certainly true for the Presleys. Whenever the family could afford it, Gladys left the labor force. But they could seldom afford it. She worked for the Garment Factory before and during her pregnancy. She picked cotton with the young Elvis sitting on her picking sack. She worked at the Mid-South Laundry. After the family moved to Memphis, she found work immediately as a seamstress for Fashion Curtains. Later she worked in a cafeteria, then as a nurse's aide.

In moving to Tupelo the Presleys were a small part of a great demographic trend that moved rural Southerners into towns, farmers into industrial and service occupations. When Elvis was born, two-thirds of all Southerners lived in the countryside and half the South's labor force were farmers; by the time of his death, two-thirds were urban and suburban folk, fewer than 5 percent were farmers, and the sharecropper was an endangered species. Vernon and Gladys were only a generation ahead of the Hale County, Alabama, families portrayed by James Agee and Walker Evans in *Let Us Now Praise Famous Men*. Those families were still sharecropping when Agee and Evans paid their famous visit in the late 1930s; forty years later their children had made the same transition Vernon and Gladys made: both men and women were working in service and industrial occupations: welder, meatpacker, nursing-home attendant, and so forth. Economically, they were still near the bottom, but the bottom was not nearly as low as it had been in the 1930s.

What kind of place was Tupelo when the young Presley family lived there? Well, it was very different from the town one sees today. And it was part of a state and a region that were very different from what *they* are today.

L. P. Hartley's remark that "the past is a foreign country; they do things differently there" has become almost a cliché, but certainly it is true for the American South. In my experience as a teacher, I have found it almost impossible for young people today really to understand what it meant to live in the South of the 1930s. What it meant to live with the day-to-day constraints and indignities of Jim Crow—not just to live with them, but to take them for granted as simply *how things are*. What it meant to live in a region as poor as the South, a region with an economy uncomfortably like that of today's Third World. But we need to recognize that those among us who, like the Presleys, grew up in that foreign country of the past made a transition in their lifetimes as dramatic and sometimes as wrenching as emigration.

In the 1930s the research of Howard Odum and his colleagues at North Carolina, Charles Johnson at Fisk, and other sociologists documented the South's problems of poverty, dependence, ignorance, disease, malnutrition, inadequate housing, and environmental degradation, and showed that they were concentrated in the old cotton belt of the Deep South, that long arc from eastern North Carolina to East Texas, where the shadow of the plantation still lingered. In this respect as in many others, Mississippi was the most Southern of the Southern states. In 1931 H. L. Mencken had put together indicators of health, literacy, economic well-being, and so forth, to show readers of *The American Mercury* that what he called "the level of civilization" was lower in the former Confederate states than anywhere else in the country. And by these measures, Mencken announced, "the worst American state" was Mississippi.

In the year of Elvis's birth, Tupelo was home to some seven thousand souls, and it served another thirty thousand residents of Lee

County as a market, banking, and shopping center. Two-thirds of the county's residents were white; only a couple of dozen were foreign-born. Outside Tupelo, four out of five Lee Countians lived on farms, most of them growing cotton, many—like Elvis's grandparents—as tenants or sharecroppers. Vaughan Grisham calculates that in 1930 the cash income of the average Lee County cotton-farmer had fallen to something on the order of two hundred dollars, *before* paying loan interest, fertilizer bills, etc.

Tupelo was in many respects a typical cotton-belt county seat, and to the considerable extent that its prosperity was tied up with the cotton economy, the town was in serious trouble—like the South as a whole. But in some ways the town was unusual, certainly for Mississippi. It had hedged its economic bets, and it pointed the way to the South's future.

Tupelo had come into being in 1859 when the Mobile & Ohio Railroad was built to pass near a pond lined with tupelo gum trees. Folks from a nearby village bypassed by the railroad moved to the new settlement, which they first called Gum Pond, then Tupelo. Within a year they had built a railroad station, a store, and two saloons. The new town played a modest role in the Civil War—Forrest and Beauregard both headquartered there at one time or another—but the period that interests us begins in the 1880s. It was then that Tupelo beat out its rivals for the Saint Louis-San Francisco Railroad, persuading the railroad to deviate from a more direct route by offering what one historian discreetly calls "liberal inducements"—a practice that would come to full flower fifty years later, and one that is not unknown even today.

Once it had become the junction-point for two railroad lines, Tupelo was set to emerge in the twentieth century as a go-getting, industrial town of a sort more common in north Alabama, Georgia, or the Carolina Piedmont than in Mississippi. In 1938 the three-year-old Elvis lived in what the WPA state guide said was "perhaps Mississippi's best example of what contemporary commentators call the 'New South'— industry rising in the midst of agriculture and agricultural customs." The year Elvis was born, Mississippi elected as its governor Hugh White, who instituted a program he called BAWI—"Balance Agriculture with Industry." Tupelo had been trying for decades, with some success, to do just that.

It is easy to make fun of the kind of relentless New South boosters who could write brochures like this early twentieth-century one, quoted by Elaine Dundy:

Wanted! Five thousand enthusiastic, thrifty, loyal people to move to Tupelo and Lee County within the next five years and make this their home. Brilliant opportunities loom for people who come to Lee County which promises to be the greatest and the best county in Mississippi.

A pamphlet from the 1920s called "Tupelo, Premier City of Northeast Mississippi" extolled the city's virtues. Dundy says it was "distributed throughout the South boasting of [the town's] excellent schools, government fish hatchery, Tupelo cotton mills, fertilizer factory, fire and sewage system, its handsome courthouse, its beautiful post office, sixteen passenger trains daily, a beautiful Confederate monument, the annual Mississippi-Alabama State Fair [important, as you will recall, in Elvis's story]; two railroad systems, a cotton market, a well-organized police station, an ice factory, a creamery, the mills, a hospital, and a Coca-Cola bottling plant." The pamphlet added: "In the city of 6,000, 5,999 are boosters in every sense of the word." And I would not have cared to be the one who wasn't.

As I say, it is easy to make fun of this mentality, and W. J. Cash did it, savagely, in *The Mind of the South*. But the efforts of Tupelo's boosters had paid off. It is instructive to look at the "points of interest" that 1938 guide lists for Tupelo. There was that fish hatchery, obtained for the town by an influential congressman. And there was a boulder erected by the Colonial Dames to commemorate DeSoto's expedition. Otherwise, however, every single point of interest mentioned was a factory or a mill firmly anchored on the products of local agriculture.

One of them, significantly, was *not* based on cotton. Following the lead of the *Progressive Farmer* magazine and papers like the Memphis *Commercial Appeal*, Tupelo's boosters had long been active in the Southern campaign for agricultural diversification. The railroads had urged farmers to grow strawberries and tomatoes; the town's newspaper and its forward-looking business community had given away packaged home orchards and held lotteries with Jersey cattle as the prize. Although diversification was a tricky proposition, by the 1930s the Tupelo area had enough dairying operations that Carnation Milk had found it worthwhile to open a condensing plant in the town. By 1938 it was producing thirty million cans of condensed milk a year, much of it no doubt destined for those graham-cracker-crust pies that had already become a staple of the Southern table.

Aside from the condensory, however, all of Tupelo's industry depended on the products of those cotton fields. The Tupelo Cotton

Mill, one of the largest in the South, produced "more than 25 miles of cloth a day." The factory where Gladys ran a sewing machine took that cloth and turned it into shirts. Reed's Manufacturing employed six hundred women to make work dresses, smocks, and aprons. Milam Manufacturing used the same cotton fabric to make children's clothes. These plants relied on the surrounding countryside for much of their labor, as well as for their raw materials. Gladys was actually unusual in living in town: 85 percent of the twelve hundred women who worked in Tupelo's garment factories lived outside of town and rode special school buses to work.

Mississippi's combination of economic distress and reliable Democratic voting meant that the New Deal was very much a presence in the state. The WPA provided at least two of Vernon's many jobs: one in the 1930s when he worked briefly on the expansion of the Biloxi shipyard, another during the war when he helped to build "Japtown," a POW camp near Como. Right outside of Tupelo was the Tupelo Homestead Resettlement Project, built by the federal Resettlement Administration. But the most significant New Deal program for Tupelo was the Tennessee Valley Authority. Thanks to its long-time Congressman, John Elliott Rankin, the chief promoter of lost-cost power in Congress, Tupelo was named America's "First TVA City," and when Gladys was seven months pregnant, Franklin Roosevelt came to town, the most exciting event in Lee County since Machine Gun Kelly robbed the bank in 1932. A crowd of seventy-five thousand turned out to greet the president, and thereafter TVA supplied the power for everything from the Carnation condensory to the movie projector at the Strand Theater (which the young Elvis preferred, rats and all, to the Lyric, because admission was only a dime).

Even more electrifying was an event that took place a little over a year after Elvis's birth. At 9:04 on the evening of April 5, 1936, a tornado hit the town. In thirty-three seconds it leveled forty-eight blocks, nine hundred homes, and scores of other buildings, including the Methodist church across the street from the Presleys' house. It killed over two hundred people—twice as many as Hurricane Camille killed in the entire state—and estimates of the number injured range up to two thousand. This in a town of seven thousand inhabitants. The birth of heroes is often marked with signs and portents, but this was something else.

Tupelo had often referred to itself as "the city beautiful." This designation did not apply to the mill housing of South Tupelo, or to East Tupelo, on the "wrong side of the tracks" (where Vernon built the house where

Elvis was born), or to black neighborhoods like Shakerag, next door to where the Presleys moved after East Tupelo. But the town had taken great pride in its broad streets and lofty trees. Vaughan Grisham points out that the tornado's devastation apparently put an end to that proud self-designation. The town bounced back with remarkable resilience, but it never again called itself "the city beautiful."

The next year saw another blow to the town's self-image as the labor unrest that had troubled the South's textile industry elsewhere finally arrived in northeast Mississippi. Gladys's two-dollar-a-day wage at the Garment Plant was standard. That worked out to about five hundred dollars a year, and it may have looked good to a cotton cropper whose last crop paid him two hundred. But it was pretty far from a comfortable living, and in 1937 workers at the textile mill staged a sit-down strike, demanding a 15 percent raise and a forty-hour rather than a forty-six-hour week. Soon after, an organizer from the ILGWU appeared in town and began to talk to Gladys's former coworkers at the Garment Plant.

Vaughan Grisham reports that the town's newspaper covered the dispute objectively and even sympathetically, but most of Tupelo's business leaders moved quickly to oppose the strike and the unionizing drive. Low wages were, after all, one of Southern industry's few competitive advantages. The National Guard engaged in "artillery practice" next to the mill. After two weeks the strike folded, after a rumor circulated that the mill-owners planned to burn the mill and blame the strikers. Jimmy Cox, a leader of the strike, was grabbed on the street and taken for a ride. A rope was put around his neck and tied to a car axle, but his abductors finally settled for a savage beating. Twenty women at the Garment Plant who had joined the ILGWU were fired, and the organizer was threatened and driven from town. Ruthless opposition was effective, as it had been elsewhere in the South. No more was heard about unionization, and Tupelo's competitive advantage remained intact.

Another aspect of Tupelo that its boosters didn't emphasize was its pattern of race relations. Day to day, the races rubbed along together, but they did it within the usual Southern framework of black disfranchisement, segregation of public facilities and much of private life, petty harassment and occasionally brutal intimidation. Grisham recounts, for example, the routine humiliations black Tupeloans experienced at the hands of the police. Many responded by joining the Great Migration that took millions of Southern blacks from the rural and small-town South to Southern cities and beyond, to the cities of the Northeast and Midwest.

Tupelo's congressman John Rankin was, as I mentioned, a great champion of TVA. But he was better known throughout the nation as a race-baiting Southern demagogue. His political career began after World War I when he founded a racist newspaper called *New Era*. Grisham summarizes what that paper was all about: "The favorite themes were the defense of lynchings, pleas for the repudiation of the Fifteenth Amendment and alterations of the Fourteenth Amendment of the Constitution, and general assaults on 'do-good troublemakers.'" Rankin used this platform to get elected to Congress in 1920. A black leader commented later, "Thank God Mr. Rankin got himself sent to Washington or I suppose all of us colored people would have had to leave Tupelo." When Elvis was ten years old, his congressman was still running against "interests outside the state who literally hate the white people of the South and want to destroy everything for which we stand."

But it tells us something about Tupelo that Rankin was finally unseated in 1952, when his rhetoric came to be seen as an impediment to industrialization. Although being black in Tupelo was no picnic, the town's boosterism spared it the worst excesses of Jim Crow's death throes. Grisham tells a revealing story. He spoke to a segregationist who had sworn to kill anyone advocating desegregation, and asked him about the editor of the *Tupelo Daily Journal*, who had been a moderate, even liberal, voice in race relations. The man replied, "I just knew that George McLean [the editor] was a God-damned Communist, but he was the man who was bringing jobs into the area and if anything happened to him we would have all been sunk." All in all, it seems Tupelo was something of a vest-pocket, Mississippi version of Atlanta, the "city too busy to hate."

I have been talking about the town's economic and political institutions, and they are certainly much of what made Tupelo, Tupelo. But it would be wrong not to mention some other institutions that were equally important in shaping the life of the town. Although the WPA guide didn't mention it, Tupelo, like almost every other Southern town, was a city of churches—dozens of them in the town and the nearby countryside, ranging from the big Baptist and Methodist establishments downtown to the more modest churches and tabernacles serving the white millworkers and common folk of East and South Tupelo and the black residents of Tupelo's three Negro sections. Two Tupelo churches figure prominently in Elvis's story.

One, of course, is the Assembly of God in East Tupelo, the church the Presleys attended. It was built by the Reverend Gains Mansell, Gladys's uncle, and after World War II Vernon himself became a deacon. The denomination was a new one—founded in Hot Springs, Arkansas, in 1914, it was a mere twenty years old when Elvis was born—but it was one of the fastest growing of the great family of Pentecostal and Holiness groups that trace their origins to what some have called the "Third Great Awakening" at the turn of the century. Some of those groups are black, some are white, a few are strikingly both, but all believe in such gifts of the Holy Spirit as speaking in tongues; most practice faith-healing, foot-washing, and other activities found in scripture; nearly all have traditions of lively and powerful gospel music; and none has ever gotten much respect from uptown Christians, much less from secular humanists.

The other Tupelo church that figures in our story is the Sanctified Church, which met in a permanent tent in the black neighborhood of Shakerag. After the Presleys moved from East Tupelo into town, they lived on the edge of Shakerag, and much speculation has centered on how much exposure the young Elvis had to the black gospel music being performed down the street from his house. (After he moved to Memphis, of course, we don't have to speculate.)

Anyway, this was the town in which Elvis was born and in which he spent his first thirteen years. During the 1930s and 1940s, Tupelo's population was growing, slowly, and the rural population of Lee County was declining, as country folk like Vernon and Gladys moved to town to escape the precarious life of tenant farming for the steady, if underpaid, discipline of the factory. Tornadoes, strikes, presidential visits. and bank robberies were the exception, not the rule. For all that Tupelo would have liked to bustle, it was basically a quiet, country sort of place, like scores if not hundreds of others, a county seat existing in symbiosis with its surrounding countryside.

But it is a mistake to think of Tupelo as an isolated backwater. A backwater it may have been, but hardly isolated. Remember those sixteen passenger trains every day. And almost exactly a hundred miles to the northeast was the big city of Memphis. It *was* a big city, with a population of over three hundred thousand—a railroad center, home to cotton brokers, a major mule market, and the annual Cotton Carnival—and it served a substantial hinterland. The Peabody Hotel was the haunt of white cotton buyers, planters, and debutantes, and Beale Street provided shopping and nightlife not just for Negro Memphis (40 percent of the city's population) but for black folk from miles around.

Memphis did not play the same role for northeast Mississippi that it did for the Delta, but it was always there, just over the horizon. Elvis's great-uncle, the mayor of East Tupelo, used to take the town's school-children on a bus for excursions to the Memphis Zoo, and it was a great day when the East Tupelo Consolidated School's band was invited to play for the Cotton Carnival.

When Vernon lost his truck-driving job in 1948, it was time to move on, time for another fresh start, and Memphis must have been an appealing choice. From time to time Vernon had joined the army of Southern men who worked essentially as what the Germans call *Gastarbeiter*—guest workers—leaving their families to do factory work in one big city or another. During the war he had worked for a while in Memphis, and he knew his way around.

When the Presleys left Tupelo for the big city, once again they were a typical part of a larger picture. Vaughan Grisham reports that 20 percent of Mississippi's population left the state during the 1950s, the culmination of an historic mass migration from the rural and small town South. In 1960 ten million Americans born in the South were living outside the region altogether, mostly in Northern cities. We hear a lot about the Great Migration of blacks, but two-thirds of that ten million were white.

The Supreme Court handed down its decision in *Brown* v. *Board of Education* on May 17, 1954, a day that came to be known in some white Southern circles as "Black Monday." It marked the beginning of the end of Jim Crow, of *de jure* racial segregation in the South. Seven weeks later to the day, on another Monday, July 5, Elvis recorded a country-flavored version of the rhythm-and-blues hit "That's All Right, Mama," an act of *musical* integration that set the stage for rock and roll. And he knew what he was doing. He said, "The colored folk been singin' it and playin' it just the way I'm doin' now, man, for more years than I know. Nobody paid it no mind 'til I goosed it up." That spring of 1954 Elvis, like the South as a whole, took a big step into the unknown, and neither would ever be the same.

But I heard a story the other day that reminded me of Elvis. It's about an old boy who was out fishing on one of our power-company lakes in North Carolina when he caught an enormous catfish. He hauled it up on the dock and cut it open, and this genie appeared. "I am the genie of the catfish," it said, "and you can have one wish."

The old boy was startled, but he pulled himself together and looked hard at the genie. "Let me get this straight," he said. "You mean I can have anything I want?"

"That's right," said the genie. "Anything you want."

The fellow looked at his boat, and his dock, and the lake, and scratched his head and said, "I believe I'd like a cold beer."

As I say, that story reminded me of Elvis. Here was a Southern boy who had success beyond measure and wealth beyond imagining. He could have had anything he wanted, but, in effect, he looked around, scratched his head, and said, "I believe I'd like a peanut butter and banana sandwich."

Elvis became a pop-culture icon and—never forget—a phenomenal musical influence. As Bruce Springsteen has said, "It was like he came along and whispered some dream in everybody's ear, and somehow we all dreamed it." Eventually, like all too many other Southern musicians, he became the classic hero-victim, doomed by his own excesses. But my point is that he remained to a remarkable extent what he was raised to be in the Tupelo years: a polite and humble gospel-singing Southern boy, who loved his mama, greasy food, and hanging out with the boys. As we say in the South, he didn't get above his raising—which is why so many of us who never met him feel as if we have known him all our lives.

The End of Elvis

So Elvis gets two chapters. His later years are another story.

In my paper "The Problem of Periodization in Elvis Studies" (forthcoming), I point out that most Elvisians have long accepted a tripartite division of the King's career, a simple trichotomy apparently first broached by the musical revue *Elvis*, which opened in London's West End within months of Elvis's death (and which, unlike its subject, was successfully revived twenty years later). Represented in the revue by three different actors, the periods are basically just Early Elvis, Middle Elvis, and Late Elvis, corresponding roughly to 1950s/1960s/1970s, to Memphis/Hollywood-Hawaii/Las Vegas, to ducktail haircut/gold-lamé jacket/white fringed jumpsuit, to soulful rockabilly/trivial pop/wretched excess. (In his 1991 study of the posthumous career, Greil Marcus suggests a fourth period, "Dead Elvis," but that's another story.)

Almost everyone agrees that Middle Elvis was a low point. When the Post Office asked which Elvis should appear on a postage stamp, it simply ignored that possibility. Opinions differ, however, about the relative merits of the other two. Although Americans voted overwhelmingly to put Early Elvis on the stamp, Late Elvis partisans are fiercely devoted and can be prodigiously learned. (I once overheard a couple of them earnestly discussing exactly when Elvis changed his cape length.) But the fact that so many of them are Elvis impersonators or English professors should give us pause. (By the way, that first sentence above is a *joke*.) An entertainer as easy to caricature or to deconstruct as Late Elvis verges on what might be called Liberaceism. Say what you will about Early Elvis—the hillbilly cat, the Tupelo Flash—he wasn't *ridiculous*.

No, like most normal Americans, I prefer the Elvis that lit up the fifties to the one that flamed out in the seventies. I see the boy as something like Coca-Cola, another Southern-American product that taught the world to sing, but lost its regional savor in the process (although Coke took the dope *out*). In *Last Train to Memphis*, Peter Guralnick

169

did a great job on the first Elvis, so I was prepared to slog through the 670 pages (plus notes and index) of Guralnik's *Careless Love* to see what he had to say about the later two, but largely as a matter of duty—and because the *Oxford American* was willing to pay me. I wasn't looking forward to it.

But it turns out that *Careless Love* tells a compelling story. Anyone who cares about Elvis needs to read it. (Anyone who doesn't care needs to read *Last Train to Memphis*). Guralnik rightly sees it as "the story of Elvis' inexorable decline—what could almost be called the *vanishing* of Elvis Presley," and if it's a stretch to compare it to the stories of Job and Oedipus Rex (as Guralnik does, in a rare lapse), it is something more than just a tale of galloping weirdness like that of Howard Hughes, or Doris Duke. I kept being reminded of another poor-white momma's boy, a man who grew up a mere 170 miles from Memphis with some-thing like the same insecurities, impulsiveness, and bad taste, the same winning charm, the same ability to be whatever others want, the same nonchalance about truth and falsehood, the same sexual appetites and odd scruples, the same self-destructive streak. (Hint: His Secret Service codename was "Elvis.")

But enough about that.

The broad outlines of Guralnik's story are well-known to anyone likely to care. In 1960 Elvis came back from the army, where he'd been introduced to pep pills and karate, and soon went to California where he was introduced to mind-altering drugs and New Age Spirituality. Under the influence of the mysterious "Colonel" Parker, he made a string of increasingly perfunctory movies and recorded mostly negli-gible songs from the movie soundtracks. (Speaking of tragic waste, it's painful to watch Guralnik, the author of *Lost Highway* and *Sweet Soul Music*, have to deal with this dreck, although he does so briskly, not-ing for instance that *Girls! Girls! Girls!* was "a decided step backwards artistically . . . even from *Blue Hawaii*.")

At first, fans didn't seem to care (by 1964, Elvis was the highest paid star in Hollywood), but what passed for Elvis's "private life" was falling apart, as unbridled self-indulgence began to take its toll on his psyche and physique. (Once, on the road to Flagstaff, he saw a cloud turn into the face of Joseph Stalin, and briefly determined to become a monk.) Marriage to his ex-nymphette girlfriend didn't help at all; in fact, it spoiled their somewhat kinky romance. Meanwhile, as the movies went from bad to worse and what we might call the *cultural* sixties got seri-ous, all except the truly hard-core fans deserted him. The soundtrack album from *Easy Come, Easy Go* (1967—with songs like "Yoga Is as Yoga Does") sold only thirty-six thousand copies, and the low point was probably the day in 1968 when Elvis stood on Sunset Boulevard and nobody even recognized him.

But this nadir set the stage for the triumphant 1968 television special that marked the transition to Late Elvis. Despite "tasteless" production numbers and "cheesy" orchestrated medleys (Guralnick's aesthetic judgments are unerring), Elvis "shrugged off the lethargic blandness" that had come to characterize his work. Excited by this success, he went back on the road with a series of great live shows, notably in Las Vegas the next year. (His first Vegas appearance was such a musical and commercial success that it even moved the Colonel to tears.)

Soon, though, these shows subsided into routine, or worse. Fans still loved them, but critics began to notice that they were often "sloppy, hurriedly rehearsed, mundanely lit, poorly amplified, occasionally monotonous, often silly, and haphazardly coordinated," that Elvis was "drawn, tired, and noticeably heavier," "indifferent, uninterested, and unappealing," just "going through the motions" (all quotes from reviews). Spectacle became grandiosity became self-parody—as when Elvis ended his shows, arms outstretched, "somewhere between a demigod and a giant bat."

His wife left him. He got into weapons in a big way and prescription medication in a bigger way. He added cocaine to his regimen, and he started shooting televisions and commodes and other irritants. He began ranting in private about the Beatles and hippies and patriotism, and he offered his services as a special drug-enforcement agent to President Nixon. (He seems to have wanted the badge for his collection.) His expenses got completely out of hand—to the point where he had to borrow money against his beloved Graceland. This downward spiral ended only with his squalid death, from "polypharmacy," in 1977.

The story, as I said, is well-known, and Guralnick's major contribution is to flesh it out with shovels-full—no, wheelbarrows-full—shoot, *dumptrucks*-full of details. His eighty-plus pages of notes and bibliography aren't just for show. He has read everything and talked to everyone, he knows as much as it's humanly possible to know, and what he doesn't tell us seems to be only what Little, Brown's lawyers won't let him (for instance, I'll bet, about those "vitamin shots"). It's not a criticism to say that, for the most part, Guralnick's details reinforce the accepted picture—it is, after all, a picture he helped to shape in his earlier work.

But almost as valuable as the details Guralnick offers are his informed judgments. He documents, for example, the astounding range of music that Elvis listened to and admired, showing how the man was a voracious and indiscriminate absorber of influences. But he also pretty obviously believes that Elvis was almost always at his best when closest to his roots in rhythm and blues, Southern gospel, and country music. This opinion was shared by Sam Phillips, Elvis's old Sun Records buddy. Here is Phillips on the first, electrifying Vegas show (edited for family consumption): "I never heard a better rhythm section in my life. There was some raunchy-[expletive] [expletive]. I told him that. I said, 'Elvis, man, that was fabulous, but, you know, that song "Memories" has got to go!' I said, "[Expletive], didn't that [expletive] bog down the [expletive] show?' And he said, 'Mr. Phillips, I just love that song.' And of course, he kept on singing it ever since."

As Guralnick shows, if anyone doubted it, Elvis did some excruciatingly bad stuff. Some of it he liked (no one ever said his taste was infallible), but what's puzzling is that he did so much stuff he *knew* was bad. Before he became hopelessly drug-addled, he usually did know the difference between good and bad music (although he did have those lapses). Sometimes, though, he just didn't care. Once he asked one of the Jordanaires, "Man, what do we do with a piece of shit like this?"—but recorded it anyway.

And consider his movies. Elvis talked often about how he really and truly wanted to be a better actor, and on Guralnick's evidence, he knew a lot about movies. (He once explained why *To Kill a Mockingbird* was better than *Lawrence of Arabia*, but would get beat out at the Academy Awards, and he recognized that *King Creole* was the best of his own movies.) That Elvis's acting got worse with time, not better, is usually attributed to the malign influence of Colonel Parker and the Hollywood star system. But Guralnick quotes director Gene Nelson who believes that Elvis "didn't really want to learn," and characterizes Elvis's expressed desire to "prove myself as an actor" as, by 1967, a "slightly shopworn mantra." It very much looks as if he was as good as he really wanted to be.

No, like his pal Sinatra, Elvis pretty much Did It His Way, in his career as in his life. At his best he was great. The tragedy is that he could have been consistently great, and just didn't care enough to do it. It was too easy, too profitable, just to be "Elvis." The rewards for doing anything more were merely intrinsic.

And this points to an unavoidable shortcoming of this book—and probably of any book about Elvis. The man himself remains elusive.

Was he so arrogant that he didn't have to prove anything to himself? Or was he so insecure that he *couldn't* prove anything to himself? That you can write it either way reflects one secret of Elvis's appeal. As his friend Marion Keisker, Sam Phillips's assistant at Sun Records, put it, "He was like a mirror. Whatever you were looking for, you were going to find in him. . . . He had all the intricacy of the very simple."

VI

Southern Culture, High and Low

Southern Laughter

When I taught at Millsaps College one semester, I put together a sym-posium that brought some smart and funny people to Jackson to talk about Southern humor. A few years later, I reassembled the same cast to entertain a meeting of Southern college and university presidents in Miami. The first time, I got away with being master of ceremonies, but in Miami I had to say something myself.

One Sunday a while back I happened to read a *New York Times Book Review* in which one of the books reviewed was described as "full of brash, irreverent, New York–style one-liners." Just a few pages later, another review referred to "the deft, rapier wit of the British." I got to thinking about those phrases. Do we ever hear about "brash irreverent Mississippi-style one-liners," or "the deft rapier wit of Tennesseans"? I don't think so.

But some of the funniest people I know are Southerners. Lots of Southerners have even made their livings by being funny: Bill Arp, Mark Twain, Stepin Fetchit, Pigmeat Markham, Junior Samples, Brett Butler, George Wallace (the black comedian, not the white governor)—these folks and many, many others. And if some of those names make you uncomfortable—well, we'll get to that.

Think about country music. I won't start reciting funny titles for you—you can find lists of them on the internet—but Ray Stevens is just one of many songwriters who has specialized in writing funny lyrics. (OK, one title: "Take Your Tongue out of My Mouth, I'm Kissing You Goodbye.") Even many more or less serious songs have funny lines; in "Betty's Being Bad," for example, Marshall Chapman wrote one of the all-time great country lyrics: ".45's quicker than 409 / Betty cleaned house for the very last time." (Save that thought.) Even the blues can be funny, although it usually depends on context and is hard to excerpt. But how about when B. B. King moans that nobody loves him except his mother, "And she could be jivin' too." (That is the very first entry, by the way, in the indispensable *Roy Blount's Book of Southern Humor*, a book that should be in every Southern household.)

On radio, in the movies, on television, funny Southerners have been a staple for almost as long as those mediums have been around. From Andy Brown to Andy Taylor (on "Amos 'n' Andy" and "The Andy Griffith Show," respectively), from the white-face minstrel show of "Hee Haw" to the *Southern Living* world of "Designing Women," Americans have been bombarded with a great many different versions of the amusing South, some more amusing than others.

When it comes to Southern politics, the old style at least—well, "Marse Henry" Watterson, the turn-of-the-century editor of the Louisville *Courier-Journal*, sure was understating it when he wrote that "humor has played no small part in our politics." We have seen an astounding array of office-holding scoundrels and wags in the South, a great many of whom have been at least intermittently funny, often on purpose. Southern political humor has filled several books, but let me tell one story that was a favorite of "Fiddling Bob" Taylor of Tennessee.

Governor Taylor liked to tell about the man who wanted to predict his son's future. He put a Bible, a silver dollar, and a bottle of whiskey on a table and hid to see which the boy would choose. He figured that if the boy took the Bible, he would be a preacher; if he took the dollar, he would be a businessman; and if he took the bottle, he would be a drunkard. Well, the little boy came into the room, put the dollar in his pocket, took a swig from the bottle, and picked up the Bible. "My God!" said the father. "He's going to be a *politician!*" (I also like Bob Taylor's description of the Mason-Dixon Line as "a great crimson scar of politics across the face of the grandest country God ever made. There it is," he said, "and there it will remain, the dividing line between cold bread and hot biscuits.")

And it's not just professional and semiprofessional humorists like entertainers and politicians who have been funny. As Roy Blount observed: "Being humorous in the South is like being motorized in Los Angeles or argumentative in New York—humorous is not generally a whole calling in and of itself, it's just something that you're in trouble if you aren't."

Southerners of all kinds have shown a gift for joking, in all sorts of settings. At the Southern Baptist Theological Seminary in Louisville not long ago, for instance, I heard why, if you're going fishing with a Baptist, you had better take two. (If you only take one, he'll drink all your beer.)

Southerners have even been humorous in *battle*. In 1878, in an article called "Johnny Reb at Play," one veteran observed that "there could be no greater mistake" than to view the Confederate soldier as a "melodramatic, [or] tragic, character" because "he was in the largest sense a humorist." Many reminiscences of the War are spiced with tales of practical jokes, snipe hunts, louse races, and songs about goober peas and Yellow Rose. Confederates joked about inflation: One army surgeon reported that he "made $2000 on a barrel of peach brandy after drinking off of it a week." They even joked about killing: Private Sam Watkins noticed that his company's officers took the braid off their uniforms before battle, so Yankee riflemen would not recognize them as officers. Watkins said he thought this was a mistake. He said he always shot at privates, because they were the ones who were trying to kill him. He said he always thought of officers as "harmless personages."

Eighty years later, in another war, on another continent, Ernie Pyle wrote about the men in a South Carolina artillery unit: "Practically everybody had a nickname—such odd ones as 'Rabbit' and 'Wartime' and 'Tamper' and 'Mote'. . . . Most of them had little education, and their grammar was atrocious, but . . . they accepted their hardships with a sense of gaiety and good humor that is seldom found in Army outfits."

Humor is not the only thing that has permeated Southern life, but it has been one of the things. So, despite Roy Blount's warning about the "fundamental truth: that nothing is less humorous, or less Southern, than making a genuine, good-faith effort to define and explain humor, particularly Southern humor," I want to explore the question of what is Southern about Southern humor.

Blount says that when he is being interviewed about being a Southern humorist, if he's lucky, he gets asked whether Southerners laugh at different things than Northerners do.

"Yes," he says. "Northerners."

That's a little Southern joke. But if we take the question seriously, humor does seem to be one of what Edgar Thompson called the "idiomatic imponderables" that make up a culture. Like wine, it doesn't always travel well, and Americans from different regions sometimes don't appreciate one another's vintages.

You probably know "Car Talk," that NPR program where two brothers give automotive advice, one-up each other, and put down cars and people they don't like. Now, I have lived in Boston. I can tell you that, aside from being smarter than average, Tom and Ray Magliozzi are utterly typical Boston-Italian wise guys. Their aggressive conversational style is completely unremarkable where they come from. But for Southerners the constant interrupting and needling takes some getting used to. Apparently so many listeners complained about how *rude* the Magliozzis were that South Carolina Public Radio dropped "Car Talk" for a while. (Although I gather it is back now, which speaks either to South Carolinians' growing tolerance for northeastern modes of discourse or to the growing number of Yankee migrants in the Palmetto State.)

Of course Northerners don't always get Southern jokes, either. Sometimes the jokes have to be explained, which is death to any sort of humor. In the musical comedy based on Doug Marlette's comic strip "Kudzu," for example, the Reverend Will B. Dunn complains that his town of Bypass, North Carolina, is "so backward even the Episcopalians handle snakes." My wife and I were watching the musical with a woman from Massachusetts—an intelligent, well-educated, with-it woman— who just didn't get it. At intermission she asked why the audience had cracked up. I did my best to tell her, but by the time I finished even *I* didn't think it was funny anymore.

The South Carolina journalist Ben Robertson had a similar experience when he told a general in the Polish army that the Polish boys who played football for Fordham were puzzled when University of Georgia players called them "damn Yankees." After all, they were Dodgers fans. When the general didn't understand why that was funny, Robertson tried to explain, but got hopelessly tangled up in the many meanings of "Yankee" and gave it up as a bad business.

Jerry Clower or the Reverend Grady Nutt—not to mention Moms Mabley or Brother Dave Gardner—really requires some background to appreciate properly, or sometimes even at all. Jeff Foxworthy's line about how "You might be a redneck if you've ever been too drunk to fish" is understood differently by those of us who have relatives like that—not to mention those of us who have been too drunk to fish. Roy Blount and Molly Ivins are both successful outside the Southern context, but when they are working Southern audiences both their material and their delivery are different. It's like hearing Sam Cooke's steamy performances on the chitlin circuit rather than his innocuous hit records.

This business of humor getting lost or mangled in translation happens in another, very important circumstance. We are told that the *past* is a foreign country, that they do things differently there. It's true that we can only be tourists in the past—at best, naturalized citizens—and we often don't speak the language, don't understand what is going on. One of the things they do differently in the past is that they laugh at different things.

Consider "southwestern humor," a species that came out of the Southern frontier in the antebellum period. It was written by folks like Augustus Baldwin Longstreet, Johnson J. Hooper, George Washington Harris, Joseph B. Baldwin, and a few dozen lesser lights. (Mark Twain came out of this school, but transcended it.) You can find the antecedents of southwestern humor over a century earlier in the Virginia aristocrat William Byrd's description of North Carolina white trash (that is to say, as he saw it, North Carolinians in general). Byrd wrote that Tar Heels did not distinguish Sunday from any other day, which would be an advantage if they were hard-working, but "they keep so many Sabbaths every week that their disregard of the seventh day has no manner of cruelty in it either to servants or cattle."

That sort of set the tone. But this kind of humor reached its full flowering in the antebellum period. Indeed, one student of southwestern humor tells us that by then it "had no counterpart in the humor of any other section of the United States. It was distinctly and peculiarly Southern; and it was provincial, wholly local." There is something puzzling about southwestern humor, though: It's not funny. Not only that, it's hard to believe most of it ever *was* funny. But it apparently was. Why doesn't it translate into modern Southern?

A valuable book by Wade Hall, *The Smiling Phoenix*, identifies four defining features of the genre. First, southwestern humor was violent. It was all about pain. It is hard to parody, but in 1850 the Galveston *Weekly Journal* did it:

> They fit and fit,
> And gouged and bit,
> And struggled in the mud
> Until the ground
> For miles around
> Was kivered with their blood
> And a pile of noses, ears, and eyes,
> Large and massive reached the skies.

Could almost be a country song, couldn't it?

A second characteristic of southwestern humor, also illustrated by that poem, is *exaggeration*, and a third characteristic is that the subject is always *poor whites*. (I started to say that Southern whites have not found violent black folks amusing, but then I recalled a number of razor-totin' exceptions who came along later. That is a subject for another day—and probably another analyst.)

Violence still figures in Southern humor. Some will recall Brother Dave Gardner's story about turning Miss Baby's head around. (It can't be summarized.) Hank Williams Jr. sings about giving his brother-in-law an "attitude adjustment" with a tire-iron. And the group Confederate Railroad has a song about a dumped girlfriend who gets violent, called "She Took It Like a Man."

Southerners still find exaggeration funny, too. Many of Jerry Clower's stories rely on it. Lewis Grizzard used to joke about his checkered marital history: he said he had seen bumper stickers in Atlanta that said "Honk if you've been married to Lewis Grizzard." Moms Mabley has a great line: "Old man say to me: 'When I was a boy, I used to live in the country.' Damn, when you was a boy, *everybody* lived in the country!"

And Lord knows common Southern white folks can still be funny: That is what "Hee Haw" was all about, and those country songs, and Jeff Foxworthy.

So if violence, exaggeration, and poor whites can still be funny, what is the problem with southwestern humor? The problem, I think, is not with who is talked about or what is said about them, but with *who says it, to whom.*

The fourth characteristic of southwestern humor, according to Wade Hall, is that it was almost always written by educated—indeed professional—men for educated (and often non-Southern) audiences. Almost all the southwestern humorists were politically conservative, too, but that is not the problem. I would argue that most humorists are conservative, at some level. What *is* a problem is smugness. In that book of his that I keep quoting, Roy Blount observes that "what surely leads to spoilage in Southern or any other humor is condescension." And southwestern humor is tainted with a sort of Whiggish amusement at the antics of the lower orders.

Obviously, the same is true of a lot of racist humor. In both cases the use of dialect is a giveaway. When speech is rendered sort of pseudo-phonetically, with all manner of supposedly comic misspellings thrown in, it not only makes this stuff hard to read, it emphasizes the social gulf between the subjects of the account and the gentleman-narrator (who of course speaks and spells correctly).

After the Civil War, for the white South, condescension toward the comical poor white was largely replaced by condescension toward the comical Negro, who became the principal butt of white Southern humor during Reconstruction and for decades afterward. (The social and political functions of that change are too obvious to fool with. Let's just say that Uncle Remus was the best of a very bad lot.) To the extent that poor white folks were still around in Southern literary humor, they became kinder and gentler. The eye-gougers and gander-pullers and sharpsters of southwestern humor were largely replaced by the rustic philosophers and village swains of sentimental local color.

Wade Hall suggests, or at least implies, some possible reasons for that change, among them that the War had made violence less funny, that white Southerners wanted to present a united front and had to soften the class distinctions of antebellum days to do it, and that post-War Southern humor was more often written by women. Could be. Certainly, for whatever reason, there seems to have been a general triumph of Victorian—one could almost say Methodist—gentility in white Southern humor, at least of the literary sort. As Opie Read wrote in 1885, in the *Arkansaw Traveler*, "The days of vulgar humor are over in this country. . . . The reading public is becoming more refined. . . . The humorist of the future must be chaste and truthful."

Well, Read was too optimistic: Some years later the Lester family of *Tobacco Road* breathed new life into the classic white trash formula and, as I said, violence, exaggeration, and poor white characters still play a prominent part in Southern humor. But with a difference: the judgmental gentleman-observer is gone.

Think about the stories of the late Jerry Clower, for example. At first glance the capers of the Ledbetter family might seem to be straight out of A. B. Longstreet's *Georgia Scenes*: You have Tater Ledbetter, a part-time veterinarian, who examines a cat and bills the owner a few dollars for medicine and five hundred for the "cat-scan." Odell Ledbetter proves he's not dumb by working a jigsaw puzzle in two weeks that says on the box, "4 to 7 years." Clower even tells some stories about "ring-tail roarers" that look a lot like A. B. Longstreet's Ransy Sniffle.

But there is a difference. It *matters* that Longstreet was a graduate of Yale, while Jerry Clower went to Mississippi State on a football scholarship. It matters that Longstreet was writing books for a refined, literate, and largely non-Southern audience, while Clower was working the Grand Ole Opry, Dollywood, and Christian radio. It matters that Longstreet was a Methodist minister and a college president, while

Clower had worked as a fertilizer salesman. Well, maybe not that much difference there. Anyway, Clower never set himself up to be better than the people he was joking about. His humor was Jacksonian, not Whiggish, more like Davy Crockett than like A. B. Longstreet. He was *entitled*.

Southwestern humor, like the racist humor that largely replaced it, was based on prejudice. Clower's humor was rooted in sympathetic understanding. It will wear better, I suspect. I don't deny that humor based on prejudice can be funny—but only if you share the humorist's prejudices. When times and prejudices change, it becomes mystifying at best, offensive at worst. I think that is what happened to southwestern humor, and perhaps to white racist humor as well. (I don't hear many racist jokes these days, do you?)

Let me close by mentioning another kind of Southern humor, one that I find deeply attractive, perhaps the limiting case of humor based on sympathetic understanding. This is humor based on one's *own* shortcomings and misfortunes. This strain may always have been present in the humor of ordinary Southerners—I suspect it has been—but it is certainly rare in the written record. I am happy to say that there seems to be a lot more of it these days, perhaps just because we are hearing more from ordinary Southerners than we used to. There is plenty of it in country music, for instance, where a lot of the funny songs about violence involve the singer's getting beaten up. Remember the B. B. King lyric about how nobody loves him. And even Lewis Grizzard, who certainly had a mean streak, could make a good, wry joke at his own expense. He said once, for example, that he didn't think he would marry again—"I'll just find a woman who hates me and buy her a house."

Southerners don't have a monopoly on this sort of self-deprecating humor (just think of Woody Allen), but we seem to do it well, and in our own way, with our own material. And it certainly beats some of the alternatives.

A Cokelorist at Work

"Southerners need carbonation," according to a character in one of Nancy Lemann's novels. Certainly the South's hot climate, its religious strictures on alcohol, and perhaps a regional tendency to hypochondria combined in the late nineteenth century to make it the principal font of the modern soft drink, and Southerners still lead the nation in soda pop consumption. In one recent year, North Carolina's per capita consumption was 55.4 gallons—enough, I am told, to leach the calcium from many Tar Heel bones and make stress fractures a minor public health problem.

Like Carolina's Pepsi and Dr Pepper (from Texas), Georgia's Coca-Cola began as a patent medicine. John Pemberton, a Confederate veteran who had moved to Atlanta to seek his fortune, was one of many Southern pharmacists who saw the commercial opportunities offered by the newly popular soda fountain in a setting characterized by widespread neurasthenia among Southern ladies (who were supposed to be high-strung) and depression, alcoholism, and drug addiction among Confederate veterans (Pemberton was himself a morphine addict). An early version of what became Coke was marketed as especially valuable for "ladies, and all whose sedentary employment causes nervous prostration, irregularities of the stomach, bowels and kidneys, who require a nerve tonic and a pure, delightful diffusible stimulant." Moreover, all three principal ingredients were believed to be aphrodisiacs.

When Atlanta went dry in 1886, Pemberton was ready with a "temperance drink" that he called Coca-Cola, after the coca leaf and the kola nut used in its production. Yes, despite what the guides at Coke's Atlanta museum have been told to say and the company's president's insistence in a 1959 statement that Coca-Cola was a "meaningless but fanciful and alliterative name," the *real* Classic Coke did contain cocaine. By 1902, however, the dope had been removed, under pressure from ministers and from public opinion alarmed by the specter of Negro coke fiends. By then the marketing genius of Frank Robinson, a native of Maine and a *Union* army veteran, had transformed the product from a nostrum to a soft drink, and this Southern gift to civilization soon escaped its native habitat. Fifty years after its invention Coca-Cola had become as much a symbol of America as the Statue of Liberty, which shared its birth year, "a sublimated essence of all that America stands for," in the words of William Allen White. By its centenary Coke had transcended mere nationality and its advertising was teaching the world to sing in over 135 countries in over sixty languages. Today three-quarters of the company's profits come from overseas sales and Iceland (of all places) leads the world in per capita consumption. In its first fifty years, the company sold nearly a billion gallons of syrup; in the next decade it sold a billion more. A two-hundred-dollar share of 1892 stock, with dividends reinvested, would be worth $500 million today.

Mark Pendergrast is an Atlantan on both sides of his family, and his interest in Coke is practically congenital. (Coke president Robert Woodruff proposed, unsuccessfully, to Pendergrast's grandmother). He tells this commercial success story well, tracing the ins and outs of ownership and management struggles, examining the tensions between the company and its independent bottlers, and sketching profiles of the powerful and often unpleasant characters who built and managed the company. Along the way he looks at Coke's deft dealings with an array of critics at home and abroad, from the US Bureau of Chemistry in 1902, through the WCTU, the Nazi Health Ministry, and Mao Tse Tung (who denounced Coke as "the opiate of the running dogs of revanchist capitalism"), to Jesse Jackson.

The key to the Coca-Cola story lies in the enormous profits to be made by selling colored and flavored water. At the turn of the century a gallon of syrup that cost a dollar to produce yielded $6.40 at the fountain, enough for everyone involved to make money (often a great deal of it), while leaving enough for marketing to guarantee that nobody could escape the product, its spokesmen, or its advertising. (The company now spends $4 billion a year on marketing.) The result, as Pendergrast amply documents, has been a sort of cultural ubiquity; as one company man put it, not exaggerating at all, Coke has "entered the lives of more people . . . than any other product or ideology, including the Christian religion."

Coca-Cola has, after all, affected everything from urban mythology (the Coke and aspirin high) to Cold War mixology (the Cuba Libre). It has inspired country songs ("Coca-Cola Cowboy") and rock lyrics ("Coca-Cola Douche"). In the movies, Coke containers have dropped from the Kalahari sky in *The Gods Must Be Crazy* and tapped an end-of-the-world radio key in *On The Beach*; in real life they have figured in allegations of sexual misbehavior against Fatty Arbuckle and Clarence Thomas. The iconic beverage has longstanding ties to such other American icons as McDonald's and Disneyland, and mythic figures from Uncle Sam (as early as 1907) to Santa Claus and Mickey Mouse have been appropriated for its ads.

In fact, nearly everyone this side of Mother Teresa seems to have had a Coke connection. Seemingly every American sports and entertainment hero except Elvis has appeared in its commercials: Ty Cobb, Jesse Owens, Ozzie and Harriet, Eddie Fisher, Anita Bryant, Floyd Patterson, Ray Charles (who later defected to Pepsi), Neil Diamond, Bill Cosby, and literally scores of others. Hitler reportedly quaffed the drink while watching *Gone with the Wind* in his private theater. In post-war Germany Marshal Zhukov couldn't be seen drinking imperialist brew, so Mark Clark provided him with Coke specially made to be colorless. Desmond Tutu defused a protest over Coke's half-hearted disinvestment policy by appearing in a smiling picture with the company's president. Adolfo Calero was a Coca-Cola bottler until the Sandinistas grabbed his plant. Even the young Hillary Rodham makes an appearance in this book, denouncing Joseph Califano as a "sell-out" and a "shit" for representing a Coca-Cola executive before a Senate subcommittee investigating conditions for migrant workers in the company's Florida citrus groves.

It is all here: everything you ever wanted to know about Coca-Cola (including the secret formula), and probably much else besides. One chapter, for instance, examines how American fighting men in World War II completed the identification of Coke and country. Pendergrast offers a barrage of such interesting Coke facts as the price of a wartime black-market bottle (generally five to forty dollars, but one brought $4,000 at auction in Italy) and the battle password for crossing the Rhine (guess what). The author of *God Is My Co-Pilot* was not the only American who believed himself to be fighting for "America, Democracy, and Coca-Cola"; Pemberton quotes extensively from other GIs' letters home to prove the point. So important was Coke to the war effort ("the cause that refreshes," as one wag put it) that the company was exempted from sugar rationing, and German and Japanese POWs were assigned to work in bottling plants.

Ironically, just as European intellectuals began to complain about the "coca-colonization"—meaning Americanization—of the post-war world, the company began its transformation (as one executive put it) from "an American company with branches abroad [to] a multi-national business," overcoming such obstacles as the Arab Boycott and the fact that the Chinese characters closest to the sound of Coca-Cola mean "Bite the wax tadpole." The company's internationalization increasingly illustrates Jefferson's observation that the merchant has no country; it offers something to offend everyone, whether third-party supply arrangements with Communist China during the Cold War, lingering acquiescence in *apartheid*, or the replacement of Norman Rockwell by "I'd Like to Teach the World to Sing."

Pendergrast also examines Coke's changing responses to the Pepsi challenge. For decades Big Red could simply ignore its competitor. In a 1948 poll of veterans, two-thirds identified Coke as their favorite soft drink; only 8 percent chose Pepsi. True, Pepsi offered more soft drink for the consumer's nickel, but it was widely viewed as "over-sweet bellywash for kids and poor people," and, in the South, as a Negro drink. Coke's often radical marketing innovations had been coupled with extreme conservatism with respect to its very successful product. The company's logo dated from 1887, its formula essentially from the turn of the century, its six-ounce "Mae West" bottle from 1914. But during the 1950s and 1960s Pepsi slowly gained ground, and by the late 1970s it actually surpassed Coke in supermarket sales and advertising dollars. The company's executives responded reluctantly, first, in 1955, with "King Size Coke"; then with competitive advertising, implicitly recognizing that Pepsi existed; finally, in 1985, with the sweeter, more Pepsi-like "New Coke."

I believe my favorite of the many delightful stories in this book has to do with the reception that innovation received. Despite its superiority in "scientific," blind taste-tests, the new product was rejected by American consumers as inferior in every way (even, according to a Harvard Medical School study, in its spermicidal properties). Interviewed at a supermarket, one elderly Atlanta lady said, "To use the vernacular of the teenagers, it sucks." The company received over forty thousand letters of protest and as many as eight thousand irate phone calls a day. "There are only two things in my life: God and Coca-Cola," one customer wrote. "Now you have taken one of those things away from me." Another complained that "I don't think I would be more upset if you were to burn the flag on our front yard."

During the furor the company's president joked that "I'm sleeping like a baby. I wake up crying every hour." Although he continued to insist that the new formulation was superior, Coca-Cola (unlike, say, the Episcopal Church or the US Government) knows how and when to cut its losses when it has a product nobody wants. When the restoration of "Classic Coke" was greeted with hosannas, ironically turning the greatest marketing blunder of all time into a commercial triumph for the company, one executive commented: "Some critics will say Coca-Cola made a marketing mistake. Some cynics will say we planned the whole thing. The truth is we are not that dumb and we are not that smart." (The company's president still doggedly drinks New Coke, now relabeled "Coke II." When it was renamed, the *Atlanta Journal-Constitution*'s readers suggested such slogans as "Coke II: The embarrassment continues" and "Coke II: It's not like we spilled it in Prince George Sound.")

I could go on. The book is full of wonderful stories and tidbits like these. Pendergrast's asides on world and national politics are generally banal, and his efforts at anthropological analysis often have an earnest, term-paper quality about them ("As a sacred symbol, Coca-Cola induces varying 'worshipful' moods, ranging from exaltation to pensive solitude, from near-orgasmic togetherness to playful games of chase"); but when he simply sticks to reporting the Cokelore he has gathered so assiduously, he is superb.

The National Magazine of the South

Founded practically on the centenary of Appomattox, *Southern Living* magazine is now approaching middle age with something like three million subscribers and fourteen million "readers" (I employ quotation marks as one myself), which makes it not just America's most successful regional magazine but one of its most successful magazines, period. And it has generated a great many lucrative spinoffs: we are told that *Southern Living Annual Recipes*, for example, is "the single most valuable book title in American publishing," selling over a million copies a year.

In *Life at Southern Living*, two old-timers at the magazine treat us to some reminiscences. Reading it is like standing around the water cooler, listening to company gossip. Or maybe standing around the Waterford crystal punchbowl (the authors want us to understand that this is a classy operation). Much of it is of the "you had to be there" variety, but there are some good stories here. *Southern Living* itself, of course, is "simple, square, and straightforward," as long-time editor Gary McCalla puts it, but McCalla's sidekick John Logue claims that "the *exact opposite* [is true] of the people who wrote it, designed it, photographed it, and sold it." Certainly this staid "shelter" magazine has sheltered some hard-drinking practical jokers, with a penchant for memorable misbehavior at sales conferences.

So how did these wild and crazy guys produce such an anodyne publication, and make so much money doing it? McCalla and Logue are refreshingly candid about *Southern Living*'s formula for success, and if the tone of their account is somewhat smug—well, they have a lot to be smug about.

"The South's own magazine" began to make serious money only when it figured out what it was doing—and not doing. *Southern Living* sprang from the old *Progressive Farmer*, which was run, we are told, by

191

a bunch of old-timers who did tacky things like belonging to the Lions Club, driving pickup trucks, volunteering as deputy sheriffs, and not accepting whiskey ads. They had long crusaded "for better schools, better roads, rural electricity, and better lives for farm families," and they wanted their new magazine to crusade, as well: in particular, to explain the virtues of farm life to an increasingly urban South and to defend racial segregation. (They offered the cover of the first issue to Lurleen Wallace.) Otherwise, they didn't have much idea of what the magazine should be. Early issues had articles like "Teenage Drivers a Problem?" and the head of the New York sales office complained that the magazine was full of "religious columns and little women with these skirts made out of material like little kitty cats sewed on them and beehive hairdos."

Emory Cunningham, a young advertising sales executive, had a different idea. As he saw it, in the 1960s "everybody was running down the South" and "Southern people were thirsting for something to make them feel good about themselves." A magazine that offered that could reach affluent Southerners and attract lucrative consumer advertising. (Cunningham eventually became president of the organization.) In 1968 McCalla and Logue wrote a "White Paper" that proposed what *Southern Living* subsequently became: "a seriously departmentalized magazine: Travel, Homes, Food, and Gardening, with features and people mixed in when worthy." A crucial ingredient was that "*stories will not deal with civic problems, socio-economic issues, or politics*" (their emphasis). When McCalla took over as editor he decreed that the magazine "should publish on subjects it understood, and on subjects that were positive, and let everybody else take care of the negative, which plenty of people were doing." An audience that felt neglected and misunderstood also appreciated the fact that each issue had "something in it from within a few miles of your home."

It is hard to say whether *Southern Living* was really something new or merely a variation on classic New South boosterism, but, reading between the lines, the organization seems to have been undeniably in one Southern tradition: Cunningham apparently ran it like an old-style Southern textile mill, complete with paternalism and a cheap and docile labor force (editorial costs were half the national average). Another key to the magazine's profitability is that the editorial and advertising departments have always been intimately, not to say incestuously, related—no "firewall" here—and there is no question which partner runs the show. Logue and McCalla tell of tending bar at a travel organization convention and note proudly that "Time, Inc., editors would have conceded a year's salary before they would have served drinks at an advertising hospitality suite." And which magazine, they ask, has more travel ads?

There have been setbacks, of course. The "Southern Living Homemakers' Cookbook Library," packaged by Millard Fuller (founder of Habitat for Humanity) and Morris Dees (now of the Southern Poverty Law Center), was a catastrophe, perhaps because none of the recipes had actually been tested. *Southpoint*, a magazine for Southern yuppies, lasted only five issues and lost $5 million. The corporation's book-publishing arm, Oxmoor House, lost another million on costly coffee-table books (many of them excellent), until Don Logan took over, saying it would work "if you thought of yourself more in the direct-marketing business, as opposed to being a book publisher"—a strategy that led to such gems as *How to Cook for Your Man and Still Want to Look at Him Naked*. (Logan went on to become president and CEO of Time, Inc., after it bought *Southern Living* in 1985.)

Over the years critics have sniped at *Southern Living* for its unclouded picture of the sunny South. At the margin, however, it has helped to make the South a better place, with healthier and more interesting food on its tables, more varied and appropriate plants in its gardens, and more comfortable and attractive homes (most of them, to be sure, in the style known in-house at the magazine as "Junior League Georgian"). It has also published some good writing about the South, much of it by the magazine's own staff, and it has honored some admirable people who have done admirable things in their communities. It has even crusaded a little bit, in its way, especially for wilderness areas and (under design editor Philip Morris) for historic preservation and downtown revitalization.

A new generation of management has introduced a few cautious changes. There are more black faces in the magazine now, for instance, which makes sense. (The South's black middle class is a growing market, and last time I looked one *Southern Living* reader in eight was African American.) But do not look for any major departure from the *Southern Living* formula. You don't hitch a cash cow to a plow.

Carolina Couch Crime

In the small-town American South porch-sitting was once a nearly universal pastime. As a place for sipping tea or Co' Cola, smoking or dipping, telling stories, courting, and watching lightning bugs, the front porch was unsurpassed. Southern porches have been celebrated in song ("Swinging'" and "My Tennessee Mountain Home," to name just two country-music examples) and story (Zora Neale Hurston: "It was the time for sitting on porches beside the road. It was the time to hear things and talk."). James Agee wrote about a porch in *A Death in the Family* (Samuel Barber set his words to music in "Knoxville: Summer of 1915"), and who can forget Faulkner's Greek chorus of neighborhood men, sitting on the Bundrens' porch in *As I Lay Dying*? A recent book on black Southern storytelling is fittingly entitled *The Power of the Porch*.

Sure, the actual activity of porch-sitting (if "activity" is the word for it) has largely succumbed to the assaults of air-conditioning, cable television, and migrants from places with cold evenings. Many new Southern homes substitute a solipsistic deck out back for the traditional outward-looking front porch. But Southerners are still nostalgically attached to porches as icons of old-timey leisure and sociability, and they crop up in unlikely places. Durham's alternative newspaper, for instance, heavily into things like healing crystals, opens each issue with a section called "The Front Porch." One of the Charlotte airport's interminable corridors offers a display of photographs of Charlotteans sitting on their porches. And new, planned, neo-traditionalist developments like north Florida's Seaside have reintroduced porches in a hopeful attempt to build community.

Yes, we take our porches seriously down here. So when the Appearance Commission of the eastern North Carolina town of Wilson decided to do something about how the town looked, it was no surprise that they started with Wilson's front porches. It was no surprise either that when they proposed a ban on upholstered furniture they ran into some resistance from folks who like their porches just the way they are.

The commission came up with some lame excuses about eliminating breeding places for rats and fleas, but the real objection was that the stuff just looks so *trashy*. As Commissioner Sarah Rasino told the *Charlotte Observer*, "Upholstered furniture exposed to the elements becomes waterlogged, deteriorates, and the stuffing falls out. Homes that have upholstered surfaces on porches tend to have trash in the yard, too. It goes hand in hand."

There is a social-class angle to this, of course. Like much of the South's traditional culture, porch-sitting survives in its least self-conscious form among poor and working-class folk, black and white. It is not the country-club set, after all, who enjoy waving as the cars go by. Moreover, these are the same folks who often can't afford air-conditioning or cable TV. The problem, as the Appearance Commission sees it, is that they often can't afford decent-looking porch furniture either—or at least that they see no reason why they shouldn't furnish their porches with beat-up old sofas or recliners that have outlived their usefulness in the living room.

To Wilson's embarrassment, the smart-ass metropolitan newspapers had a lot of fun with this story, and some of my academic colleagues played along. Emory University historian Dan Carter lamented in the *New York Times* what he saw as "the ultimate yuppiefication of the South," adding tongue-in-cheek that "there's nothing more inviting than an old front seat from a 1957 Chevrolet sitting on a front porch." Charles Reagan Wilson of the University of Mississippi told the *Charlotte Observer* that the proposal was "an outrage," a violation of the Southern "idea of the outdoors as a livable space." He invoked Dolly Parton and the memory of Elvis Presley, and groused that "Next thing, they'll ban pink flamingos in front yards."

But for all the talk of ratty porch furniture as an regional tradition, what the Appearance Commission really threatens is a different Southern tradition altogether, one that W. J. Cash wrote about in *The Mind of the South* nearly sixty years ago, the region's "intense individualism." The "ruling element" in this tradition, according to Cash, was "an intense distrust of, and, indeed, downright aversion to, any actual exercise of authority beyond the barest minimum essential to the existence of the social organism," and this down-home libertarianism is still with us, celebrated in dozens of country songs by singers like Hank Williams Jr., Charlie Daniels, Bobby Bare, Merle Haggard, and David Allan Coe. In 1976 Roy Reed described it for readers of the *New York Times*. The South, he wrote, is given [its] dominant tone by men—and women who acquiesce in this matter—who carry in their hearts or genes or livers or lights an ancient, God-credited belief that a man has a right to do as he pleases. A right to be let alone in whatever plain of triumph he has staked out and won for his own. A right to go to hell or climb to the stars or sit still and do nothing, just as he damn well pleases, without restraint from anybody else and most assuredly without interference from any government anywhere. . . . It is no accident that the most determined holdouts against land-use legislation in the United States are country people from the South. They will take care of their own land, and let the next man take care of his. If the next man puts in a rendering plant or a junkyard, that is his business.

Reed argued that this is another Lost Cause, lost "about the time [a man] lost the irretrievable right to take a leak off his own front porch" (a front porch activity I forgot to mention). But, he wrote, "they have not yet taken [Southerners'] right to curse and defy."

And that's about the size of it in Wilson. Last I heard there was a whole lot of cursing and defying going on, but the Appearance commissars seemed determined to stick to their guns. And that is a shame. Although I actually sympathize with their motives (I live in a neighborhood full of university students), something more important than appearances is at stake here. If a man can't choose his own damn *porch furniture*, what the hell can he choose?

I say they can have my La-Z-Boy when they pry it from my cold dead fingers.

VII

Southern Lit (and One Movie)

Taking a Stand

When the book review editor of the Raleigh News and Observer *asked several Tar Heels to write about books that had "changed their lives" I jumped at the chance.*

The old rap on Southerners is that more of us write books than read them, and for a century or so after Appomattox it was certainly true that the South was not much of a literary market. But that doesn't mean that we haven't taken books seriously down here. In fact, we may even have taken them more seriously than other Americans. Would antebellum whites have passed laws forbidding slaves to read if they thought it didn't matter? Would the Gideons (headquarters: Nashville, Tennessee) do what they do if they didn't believe in the transforming power of the Word? Don't the episodes of book banning that periodically embarrass enlightened Southern opinion speak to a belief that reading can change people's lives? When New York mayor Jimmy Walker remarked that no girl was ever ruined by a book he revealed his contempt for books, or possibly for girls. Anyway, most Southerners—even those who think putting up with obscenity and blasphemy is the price of freedom—know better.

I can write with some conviction about the power of books, because three or four have surely changed my life, for better or for worse. One of them is a peculiar volume called *I'll Take My Stand*, a stirring defense of the South by twelve young men, most of them associated with Vanderbilt University. That book was originally published in 1930, but I didn't encounter it until 1963, when I was an undergraduate at the Massachusetts Institute of Technology.

In those early days of the civil rights movement, Southerners in New England were constantly being called on to explain the South, challenged to defend it or (more often) simply denounced for their association with it. I got my share of this, but why did I respond? Why did I care? The South had not really meant much to me when I was growing up in Tennessee. But living in Massachusetts had taught me that there were many Southern things worth defending. How to defend them, though, without defending those things that, even then, were plainly indefensible? Not easy questions, not even for a college junior who thought he knew just about everything.

I had been brooding about them one day when I came across a new Harper paperback edition of *I'll Take My Stand* at the MIT bookstore. The title sounded interesting and I recognized Robert Penn Warren's name, although I had never heard of the other authors, or the book itself. (A nice Southern touch: among the names I didn't recognize was John Donald Wade, who turned out to be a cousin of the Duke student I was dating, and later married.) Out of curiosity, I bought the volume (books were cheaper then), took it back to my room and read it straight through.

It was a revelation. Thanks to the Dayton Monkey Trial and other events of the 1920s, these young Southerners had written at a time when the South's reputation was just about as unsavory as in the early 1960s, but they, too, believed there was another side to the story, and they had set out to tell it. It is true that the South they were defending—an overwhelmingly rural region of small, independent farmers—didn't look much like the South I knew, thirty years later. In fact, I came to learn in time, some critics said it didn't look much like the South of 1930. Never mind. These Vanderbilt Agrarians valued many of the same aspects of the South that I had come to appreciate, after leaving it: manners, religion, tradition, community feeling. And, unlike the most conspicuous defenders of the "Southern way of life" in 1963, they were eloquent, learned, and humane.

That book demonstrated to me some things I should have known, but didn't: that a Southerner doesn't have to spit on his ancestors' graves to write about the South, that you can acknowledge the South's faults but love it for its virtues, that "conservative Southern intellectual" is not a contradiction in terms. I was ready to sign up.

Of course, my response to this book had as much to do with where and when I read it as with what it said. Later I learned that some other Southerners my age responded quite differently to it. Young men and women who stayed in the South for their education apparently seldom felt the need to defend our region. If they read *I'll Take My Stand* at all, they were likely to be scornful of it. Edwin Yoder, for instance, has written of his youthful response ("antiquarian and nostalgic in tone, neo-feudal in its economic and social views, a bit above-it-all"). Another Chapel Hill alumnus tells me that his copy is full of his outraged undergraduate marginalia, most often simply "Bullshit!" Both of these men have come around to a more balanced appreciation for the book in their later years, and so have I, as a matter of fact, from the other direction.

My initial response, however, was anything but "balanced," and by the time I began to have serious second thoughts, the damage was done, the die cast. That book reinforced my determination to return to the South, and by its very ambiguity encouraged me to explore—at first idly, then later for a living—just what Southernness *is*. More than thirty years and a number of books of my own later, I am still at it.

Portrait of Atlanta

We have all run into Atlantans for whom "the one thing they can't stand"—as one of Tom Wolfe's characters in *A Man in Full* puts it—is "the idea that somebody in New York might be calling them Southern hicks." This bad case of what the Australians call "cultural cringe" makes poking fun almost irresistible, and it's not just Yankees who can't resist: recently a Dallas sportswriter wrote that a sold-out Georgia Dome reflected not the Falcons' surprisingly strong season but the presence in town of "the semi-annual Stuckey's regional cashiers convention." Of course, it doesn't help that Atlantans' insecurity often leads to undeniably hicky behavior—like putting a sign in the airport that says "Welcome to Atlanta: A World-Class, Major-League City." And don't get me started deconstructing the opening ceremonies of the 1996 Olympics.

Anything short of fulsome praise for their city just feeds Atlantans' deep-seated rubophobia, and Wolfe's book is not exactly a puff piece. That whatever it has to say about Atlanta is being heard by a lot of people only makes matters worse. Its first printing was 1.2 million copies, it immediately jumped to number one on every bestseller list that matters, and buyers even seem to be *reading* this 742-page doorstop of a book. How else to explain the fact that within three weeks *The Art of Living* by Epictetus (who figures in the book) was at 3447 in Amazon.com's sales rankings, while the *Meditations* of Marcus Aurelius (a stoic with only Hannibal Lector's citation in *Silence of the Lambs* going for him) was at number 14,598, and poor, unblurbed Seneca's *Dialogues and Letters* was mired at 104,143? (Number one, of course, was *A Man in Full*.)

But Atlanta's image police may be getting smarter. True, something called the Buckhead Coalition withdrew Wolfe's luncheon invitation when they heard what was supposedly in the book, but the *Journal-Constitution* played it pretty cool, offsetting its mostly bad review ("Save your $28.95") with excerpts from other papers' more favorable notices, a couple of straight news stories, and an appreciative column by the estimable Michael Skube. This despite knowing, surely, that all this coverage could only remind readers how long it has been since the last bestseller about this pushy, acquisitive New South city—which raises the question of why Atlanta produces or even attracts so few good writers, which raises the question of what "world-class" really means. . . .

Anyway, the *Journal-Constitution*'s handling of Wolfe's book was, if not world-class, at least not hysterical, and most of the city's spin doctors managed to stay on-message when the outside press came knocking. "It's a fictional book," the president of the Chamber of Commerce told the *Washington Post*. "It's fiction!" said the head flack for Georgia Tech. *Atlanta* magazine's editor-in-chief agreed: "It's just a book." But the *Post* wasn't ready to let Atlantans get away with affecting New Yorkerly indifference. It quoted Mayor Bill Campbell—"Atlanta is very secure in who we are, and what we are"—with a clear implication of "Yeah, right," and sneered that "They are acting very sophisticated about it. . . . Very cosmopolitan." I know Atlantans have it coming, but you could almost feel sorry for them.

So what is all the fuss about? Is the *Post*'s Jonathan Yardley right when he claims that Wolfe is worse than General Sherman—leveling Atlanta without even evacuating it first? It is true that his fictional city is populated by at least the normal complement of arrivistes, weasels, thugs, and self-deceiving losers. And, like Margaret Mitchell's, it's a crass, money-grubbing kind of place, where "your 'honor' is the things you possess." But I think Yardley is off the mark when he says that "the scorn [Wolfe] heaps on the entire citizenry of Atlanta" makes his contempt for Manhattanites in *Bonfire of the Vanities* look "mild." Other reviewers have discerned in this book a kinder, gentler Tom Wolfe (I do not believe the word "compassion" appeared in any reviews of *Bonfire*), and a few have even claimed that Wolfe is *too* nice to some of his characters, notably his central one, "Cap'm Charlie" Croker, a south Georgia country boy made good as a big-time developer.

Inevitably, Wolfe has been compared to Margaret Mitchell (and one of his first Atlanta appearances after the book was published was at a six-hundred-dollar-a-plate benefit for Miss Mitchell's house). Others have invoked an earlier Southern expatriate, Mark Twain—more often mentioning Wolfe's white suits than his dark outlook, although both are apt. Wolfe himself has invited comparison to Dickens and Zola and Balzac, and Jonathan Yardley suggests John O'Hara. For a really productive parallel, though, check out the movie *Nashville* (1975). Writer Joan Tewkesbury and director Robert Altman also give us a huge and diverse cast, a wealth of subplots, a great deal of cutting back and forth, and a drawing-together of themes explored in earlier works. Like Wolfe's novel, *Nashville* was seen as critical of the city it portrayed, but Music City's offended loyalists failed to notice something that struck me immediately: sure, many of the odious characters were locals, but *all* of the admirable ones were. *A Man in Full* is not quite that loaded in favor of the natives (the most sympathetic character of all is a young Californian, the child of hippies, just trying to lead a decent bourgeois life, who winds up as a sort of latter-day Jean Valjean, then introduces Charlie Croker to Epictetus), but Wolfe, too, shows us more than enough virtuous men to save this iniquitous city from destruction.

At least comparatively speaking, in other words, this is not all bad news for Atlanta partisans. And one thing that should really please the Chamber of Commerce is Wolfe's offhand reference to Atlanta as one of the four or five most important cities in the United States. Maybe he was just being polite—I would put Atlanta somewhere in the top ten and it certainly is the Southeast's commercial capital and communications hub, but Nashville is at least as important culturally, and Houston is still, for now, the South's major international metropolis—but Wolfe's flattery plays into the kind of self-fulfilling prophecy that has always been Atlanta's specialty: time and again the city has made some ludicrous claim and then hustled to make it true. That sort of spirit is partly what this book is about, and Wolfe gets it just about right.

Another Atlanta achievement he gets about right is the famous "Atlanta Way." This genial, if cynical, accommodation is one in which racial set-asides and featherbedding are simply part of the cost of doing business, and if what you are interested in is social concord and making money it seems to work pretty well. Even the *Journal-Constitution's* reviewer, John Huey, acknowledges that Wolfe's understanding of Atlanta's "basic social compact" is accurate.

Huey denies, though, a basic premise of Wolfe's plot. He claims that even if a black football hero were accused of raping the daughter of a powerful white businessman it would not seriously divide the City Too Busy to Hate, or threaten racial violence. But Wolfe is not saying that the Klan would ride. Nobody in the book except the girl's father seems bent on vengeance: most white characters seem to want this hushed up as bad for Georgia Tech's bowl prospects. The problem, as Wolfe writes it, is that many blacks reflexively think the white girl is lying and the player is being railroaded. Now, if that wouldn't happen—if Atlanta is that different from O.J.'s hometown—well, it really is quite a place.

Most of our literati have been dismissive of Wolfe since he dissed them in his 1972 essay "Why Aren't They Writing the Great American Novel Anymore?" John Updike sniffed in the *New Yorker* that *A Man in Full* is not literature but "entertainment." (He is right about the last part: Robert Altman could make a great movie from this book, although I'll bet Hollywood makes the same hash of it that it did of *Bonfire of the Vanities.*) But Wolfe plainly doesn't give a damn what the *New Yorker*—or much of anybody else, I'd guess—thinks of him. Someone who really wants to be celebrated by the Updikes of the world does not write about law firms named Tripp, Snayer & Billings. (My favorite of Wolfe's little jokes is a former Georgia senator named Ulrich B. "Eubie" Honeyshuck—an allusion to a distinguished historian of the Old South, and if you didn't catch it don't worry; Lord knows what *I* missed.) Wolfe is having fun, making a lot of money, trashing people who need trashing, and, like a good Southern Protestant, witnessing to the unsaved by example and exhortation. And his message has been consistent for years now: Even in our crummy modern world, it is possible to be a man.

He could not be more explicit about this (I mean, just read his title). Consequently, some of the hostile criticism of this book is rather beside the point. It is true that most of Wolfe's female characters are two-dimensional, and some racists and homophobes are treated sympathetically. (It is conventional these days to do it the other way around.) But as the English historian S. J. D. Green has suggested, manliness can imply a contrast, not with the feminine, but with the childish. Sometimes it's not about being masculine, it's about being grown up. Women have their own version of this problem, and Wolfe makes a gesture toward exploring it in the story of Martha Croker, Charlie's cast-off first wife, but this is not really a book about women. It is about the world—or rather worlds—of men, and being a man has a lot to do with honor, a pre-Christian concept and maybe one the stoics can help us with. In short, although it may be hard for Atlantans to believe, this book is about more than Atlanta.

But Atlanta really is its star, and if Atlantans breathe deeply and think about it they can't be unhappy with the way that Wolfe's bravura depiction of their city gives it almost mythic power. We see it both from the air (aboard Charlie's private Gulfstream-5) and from the ground (people spend a lot of time in this book driving). Both familiar and largely unknown parts of the city are vividly realized. Anyone who knows the place—and even Stuckey's cashiers go to conventions there—will see it with new eyes after reading Wolfe's descriptions of the palazzos, fitness centers, and trendy restaurants of Buckhead, the gleaming office towers of Midtown, the Southern-style slums of South Atlanta, the Asian quarter of Chamblee ("Chambodia"), even the seedy apartment complex of "Normandy Lea." The city's *social* landscape is also revealed in marvelous set-pieces: the black collegiate celebration of "Freaknic," a political rally at the Church of the Sheltering Arms, a reception at the Piedmont Driving Club, an Atlanta Symphony concert, the opening of a show of homoerotic art at the High Museum (the curator baffles Charlie by going on about "Michelle Fookoe"). . . . The list continues, and the temptation to quote at length is almost overpowering. Description like this just has to be good for any city—good for its soul, and maybe even for its pocketbook. As one perceptive booster told the *Journal-Constitution*, "If you look at what happened with Savannah and *Midnight in the Garden of Good and Evil*, the way it promoted tourism . . . I think the same thing could happen here."

Now that's the old Atlanta spirit!

Nebbish from Mississippi

Shortly after this review appeared, Independence Day *won the Pulitzer Prize for fiction.*

In several promising novels and a book of short stories Richard Ford covered some ground, literally: Mississippi to Mexico to Montana. He really established his reputation as an up-and-coming heavy hitter in 1986, however, with *The Sportswriter*, which introduced us to some characters and a setting that most book reviewers could more easily get with: writer Frank Bascombe, Frank's soon-to-be-ex-wife Ann, and the town of Haddam, New Jersey. Now Bascombe is back, in *Independence Day*, a book that *Publishers Weekly* has hyped as what the Great American Novel would look like, if such a thing were any longer possible. Could this be?

It is 1988, Ann has remarried and left Haddam with the children, but Frank is still there, and he is selling real estate, or trying to. After a hundred pages about all that has happened is that Frank has showed a house to a couple and they haven't decided whether to buy it or not. Along about here you may begin to suspect that this is going to be a book in which nothing much *does* happen, a suspicion the rest of it largely confirms. Sure, a few things happen *nearby*, but even a murder in the same motel has no consequences for the story. Promising characters float past—a trucker, a waitress, some trashy tenants, what passes these days for a good buddy, Frank's fellow realtors, his ex-wife's new husband—but they just make brief appearances and never return. Most seem to be more interesting than Frank himself, but his current lady friend is an exception. She says things like, "Something's crying out to be noticed. I just don't know what it is. But it must have to do with you and I. Don't you agree?" (Frank has no idea what she is talking about, and he's not the only one.)

Anyway, Frank visits this woman, he visits his ex-wife, he takes his unhappy son to the Baseball Hall of Fame at Cooperstown, the kid gets beaned by a pitching machine, and that's about it for plot. Lord knows the man has problems, but aside from putting his difficult clients in a rental property, he doesn't resolve much of anything. If Ford is saving all that for his next book it strikes me as a mistake, because it means that, basically, this one is just you and Frank Bascombe for 448 pages, and the question becomes, is this the kind of guy you want to hang out with?

My guess is that for most female readers the answer will be no: they will be reminded of irritating old boyfriends, or first husbands. Some middle-aged men may identify with Frank now and again, but I'm here to tell you that's not always a treat either.

Frank is actually at his best when he is talking about his job; in fact, the romance of real estate has never had a more articulate spokesman. He really believes that "you don't sell a house to someone, you sell a life," and he sees his career as a mature compromise between youthful idealism and the need to make a living. He gave up writing to become a realtor, he says, because "in this way I could still pursue my original plan to do for others while looking after Number One, which seemed a good aspiration as I entered a part of life when I'd decided to expect less, hope for modest improvements and be willing to split the difference." He likes selling real estate, he is good at it, and he has some idea why. "My greatest human flaw and strength, not surprisingly, is that I can always imagine anything—a marriage, a conversation, a government—as being different from how it is, a trait that might make one a top-notch trial lawyer or novelist or realtor, but that also seems to produce a somewhat less than reliable and morally feasible human being."

Trouble is, it also seems to produce someone who is less than stimulating company. Frank is almost a caricature of a self-absorbed leading-edge baby boomer; he has aged, but he hasn't grown up. He gives us a lot of tedious reflection along these lines: "A successful practice of my middle life, a time I think of as the Existence Period, has been to ignore much of what I don't like or that seems worrisome and embroiling, and then usually see it go away." Most of his forty-something wisdom is bogus, stuff like "ole Davy Crockett's motto, amended for use by adults: Be sure you're not completely wrong, then go ahead," or "It's not true that you can get used to anything, but you can get used to much more than you think and even learn to like it."

Unfortunately he is right when he says, "I'm no hero, as my wife suggested years ago." And despite having hurt a good many people he is not a real villain, because, damn it, he *means* well. You can tell because he is for Michael Dukakis in the election that's going on just outside the novel's field of vision. This detail adds to the general impression of ineffectuality, but Frank is not exactly a fool either (at least he's not very funny). Nor is he a victim of anything except his own fecklessness. What he is, as he puts it himself at one point, is "a doofus." (I would have said a nebbish, but that's close enough.)

Now, this may seem an odd thing for a Mississippian to be, even one who lives in New Jersey. But it is not unprecedented. We have seen similar well-meaning, dissociated, displaced Southerners before. "Of course," Frank says, "having come first to life in a true *place*, and one as monotonously, lankly *itself* as the Mississippi Gulf Coast, I couldn't be truly surprised that a simple *setting* such as Haddam—willing to be so little itself—would seem, on second look, a great relief and damned easy to cozy up to." Recognize the tone?

This is Walker Percy country, of course. *The Moviegoer* and *The Last Gentleman* have been over much of this ground, and if you like early Percy, you could like this book. But not as much.

Hollywood Chain Gangs

A third of a century after *Cool Hand Luke* was released it still resonates in American popular culture. In *Reality Bites*, when Ethan Hawke says "I can eat fifty eggs," he is quoting Paul Newman as Luke Jackson. In *Life*, when Eddie Murphy fights the biggest man in prison, he is imitating Newman, too. And anyone who says "What we've got here is failure to communicate" is echoing Strother Martin as Luke's prison warden, "Captain."

A large part of the movie's enduring appeal is its all-star cast, starting with Newman, a natural for the role of Luke (which makes it shocking to learn that Telly Savalas was originally signed for the part). There is also an Oscar-winning performance by George Kennedy as "Dragline," the alpha convict before Luke arrives, later his principal disciple. Jo Van Fleet is good as Luke's dying mother, Arletta, although you have to wonder what Bette Davis would have done with the role (she declined it).

Martin's "Captain" is a star turn ("Now I can be a good guy or I can be one real mean son-of-a-bitch. It's up to you."), and he is backed up by as chilling an assortment of bad guys as anyone could wish for. (The movie was based on a novel by Donn Pearce, who did in fact do time on a chain gang, for safecracking, and who may have been settling some scores.) A few of the guards, or "bosses," seem to take pleasure in abusing and breaking prisoners, but most display a casual, almost impersonal brutality. Three whose names we learn are Boss Carr, who tells the new inmates the rules ("Any man loses his spoon spends a night in the box."), Boss Paul, who breaks Luke after his escape and recapture ("You got your mind right, Luke?"), and—perhaps most intimidating—Boss Godfrey, the silent "man with no eyes" behind his mirrored sunglasses, who pulls the final trigger. Only one guard shows any decency: putting Luke in the punishment box he says, "Sorry, Luke. Just doin' my job. You gotta appreciate that," to which Luke replies, "Aw, callin' it your job don't make it right, boss."

There is something timeless about this film. The story of a free spirit who defies oppressive institutions and is ultimately destroyed by them is at least as old as the Gospels (and don't get me started on the heavy-handed Christ-symbols in this movie). But *Cool Hand Luke* is also obviously a movie set somewhere in the humid depths of Dixie. Although it was actually filmed outside of Stockton, California, Spanish moss was imported from Louisiana to hang on the local trees. And, although the story takes place in 1948, this is also obviously a movie shot in the 1960s: the view of the South it presents was more popular with filmmakers and audiences then than ever before or since.

Southern prison films have a history. The genre was established in 1932 by Paul Muni in *I Am a Fugitive from a Chain Gang*, and there have been dozens since, ranging from the grim to the camp to the ridiculous. A broad definition would include Roger Corman's 1955 B-movie classic *Swamp Women*, as well as such recent offerings as *Ernest Goes to Jail* and *Happy, Texas*, but almost a constant in these very different films is that the South does not come off well. To put it mildly. (One of the few movies that shows Southern justice as administered by anyone other than brutes, sadists, or buffoons is *My Cousin Vinnie*, one of my own favorite movies about the South.)

But there are fashions in these things. The South has often served America as a whipping boy and bad example, a moral cesspool and a national disgrace, but it has not always been seen that way. At the turn of the last century, for example, the need to reconcile the victorious North and vanquished South revitalized an old image of the South as the land of moonlight and magnolias, enshrined in literally hundreds of popular songs and scores of plantation novels. Gracious Southern ladies and gentlemen were served by loyal and often amusing black folk, with a few white rustics up the holler or out in the swamp to provide a little local color. The best known movie about the South from this period is D. W. Griffith's *Birth of a Nation* (1916), which essentially presented the white South's view of itself (and celebrated the Ku Klux Klan). It was shown in the White House, where President Woodrow Wilson is said to have exclaimed that it was "like writing history with lightning" and "all so terribly true."

But when the need for national unity waned, after World War I, the dominant view of the South changed abruptly. Crusading journalists and documentary photographers gave new life to images of the region's continuing deficiencies. Hookworm, pellagra, sharecropping, lynching—all had been around for some time, but they received new attention and exposure. The Scopes "monkey trial" in 1925 was one of the defining events of what historian George Tindall has called "the benighted South." It was against this background that Muni gave his memorable performance in *Fugitive*.

But this era, too, passed. With the phenomenal success of *Gone with the Wind* in 1939, it was back to romantic images of the Old South. The need to pull together, first against the Nazis and the Japanese Empire, then against the Soviets and Red Chinese, kept sectional conflict muted until the civil rights movement got underway in the late 1950s. That development brought back the benighted South with a vengeance. Once again the South was seen as a land of bigotry, oppression, and violence. (All of which, incidentally, could be seen nightly on the television news: These things are not made up out of whole cloth.) Not even in the 1920s had the South's image been worse, and Hollywood got on board with a number of major motion pictures. *Cool Hand Luke* was released in 1967. The other big movie of that year was *In the Heat of the Night*. Two years later came *Easy Rider*, which saw Captain America gunned down by vicious rednecks.

My point is that *Cool Hand Luke* is a product of its time, the late 1960s, just as *Birth of a Nation*, *I Was a Fugitive from a Chain Gang*, and *Gone with the Wind* are products of theirs. Each reflects a particular phase of relations between the South and the rest of the United States. None could have been made in any other decade.

Shortly after *Cool Hand Luke* appeared there came yet another swing of the pendulum. In the 1970s America entered another era of sectional good feeling. The civil rights movement was over. *De jure* segregation had collapsed. North Carolina Senator Sam Erwin was being celebrated as a hero of the Watergate investigation and a champion of down-home probity and wisdom. Movies about the South tended to feature fun-loving, good-timing good ol' boys, most of them played by Burt Reynolds. And the nation was preparing to elect Jimmy Carter to be president.

In 1975 Hollywood gave us a film that was something of a remake of *Cool Hand Luke*, but the differences are instructive. In an era of changing sex roles the principal villain was a sadistic nurse. Jack Nicholson played the Newman role. And *One Flew over the Cuckoo's Nest* was set in Oregon.

VIII

Reflections

The Banner That Won't
Stay Furled

This essay began its life as an Olin Lecture at the University of London's Institute of United States Studies in 2001, when the Mississippi state flag controversy was in the news. I guessed that the British would be as baffled as most non-Southern Americans, so I tried to explain it.

> Furl that Banner, for 'tis weary;
> Round its staff 'tis drooping dreary;
> Furl it, fold it, it is best;
> For there's not a man to wave it,
> And there's not a sword to save it,
> And there's not one left to lave it
> In the blood which heroes gave it;
> And its foes now scorn and brave it;
> Furl it, hide it—let it rest.
> — Father Abram Joseph Ryan, "The Conquered Banner"

In April 2001, 750,000 Mississippians went to the polls to decide whether to change their state flag. The old flag, adopted in 1894, prominently incorporates the Confederate battle flag, and a committee set up by the governor had proposed to replace it with a pattern of twenty stars on a blue field. The stars were apparently to represent the thirteen original colonies, the six nations and Indian tribes associated with the state, and the state of Mississippi itself, although it was also said that they represent Mississippi's status as the twentieth state. The important point was that they were not the Confederate flag.

The summer before in South Carolina, where the battle flag had flown for nearly a half-century over the statehouse, legislators from both parties, black and white, faced with an economic boycott of the state by the National Association for the Advancement of Colored People, agreed to move the flag to a new location next to a Confederate memorial on the statehouse grounds. Nobody was really happy with that arrangement, but most parties to the dispute seemed to take some satisfaction from the fact that their opponents were unhappy, too.

And in January 2001, after a running battle that had begun well before the 1996 Atlanta Olympic Games, the Georgia legislature voted to remove the Confederate emblem from its prominent place on the Georgia state flag, adopting a new, compromise flag that includes the former flag in a sort of catalog of historic flags. It looks like—well, it looks like a flag designed by a committee, and cartoonists have had fun with it. But it, too, seems to have done the job of imposing a sort of grumpy stalemate.

These three events were only the latest in a string of conflicts over Confederate symbols. Beginning seriously in the early 1990s, we have seen controversy over high school and university emblems, names, and mascots; police and National Guard and Boy Scout and Little League baseball insignia; flags flown by parks, cemeteries, historical sites, businesses, hotels, and college fraternities; seals of towns and organizations; customized automobile license plates; Confederate holidays and monuments; junior-high-school dress codes, workers' lunch-boxes, and no doubt other things I have missed. Up to a point, the Mississippi conflict was virtually a replay of the South Carolina and Georgia disputes, and—except for its statewide scale and the national attention it received—a replay of most of the others as well. The players, the line-up, the arguments pro and con tend to be pretty much the same, again and again.

The new flag was endorsed by nearly every Mississippian that anyone ever heard of: the present governor and five other officials elected statewide; the former governor who headed the panel that proposed the new flag; the state conference of the NAACP; the bishops of the Roman Catholic, Episcopal, and Methodist churches, leaders of the Presbyterian church, and the Reverend Donald Wildmon, a nationally influential leader of the Christian Right; the Jackson *Clarion-Ledger* (Mississippi's major newspaper), all the other daily papers in the state that I was able to track down, the student newspaper at the University of Mississippi, and the *Mississippi Business Journal*; the Mississippi Tourism Association, the Mississippi Economic Council, and the Chambers of Commerce in most of the state's major towns; the Mississippi Manufacturers Association and other trade and professional associations; the management of the Grand Casino in Gulfport; the city council of Jackson (the capital); the presidents of the eight state universities, the faculty senate at Mississippi State, eighty-seven historians from colleges in the state, thirteen head coaches in football, basketball, and baseball at the four largest universities; Myrlie Evers-Williams, widow of civil rights martyr Medgar Evers and former national chairman of the NAACP; actors Morgan Freeman and Gerald McRaney; authors Ellen Douglas, Barry Hannah, and John Grisham; Jim Barksdale, former CEO of Netscape; football hero Archie Manning; and Mary Ann Mobley, Miss America 1959. (Anyone who knows Mississippi will recognize the significance of those last two names.)

This was a truly remarkable coalition of historic adversaries: civil rights activists and country-club Republicans, student newspapers and university presidents, casino managers and fundamentalist ministers, trial lawyers and industrialists, college professors and football coaches. According to a highly decorated Vietnam War veteran who wrote the *Clarion-Ledger*, even Robert E. Lee and Stonewall Jackson would have supported changing the flag, and at a conference on Christian unity one minister asked the question "What Would Jesus Do?" about it.

On the other side a ragtag assortment of old-flag loyalists also made up an uneasy, if not so unlikely, alliance. The most vocal were "heritage" organizations like the Sons of Confederate Veterans (SCV), an ostensibly nonpolitical group who nevertheless ran spot television ads in several markets around the state, defending the flag—and, by implication, the honor—of their ancestors. Sharing their views was the only supporter of the old flag widely known outside Mississippi, the novelist and historian Shelby Foote.

Although Foote and many other defenders of the Confederate heritage took pains to distance themselves from white supremacists, they found themselves allied, willy-nilly, with folks like a white "Nationalist" named Richard Barrett, who argued that "Negroes, communists and Japanese" are trying to take over Mississippi and "the Confederate flag is there to signify defiance of oppression." (Barrett also claimed that the new flag was modeled after that of Communist China, although the Southern Christian Leadership Conference, an old-time civil rights organization, protested, more plausibly, that the new flag resembled the first national flag of the Confederacy.)

The proponents of the new flag plainly won the endorsement battle. They also spent more money—$700,000, nearly a dollar per voter—much of it on a sophisticated phone bank and direct-mail campaign. Their opponents reported expenditures of less than $20,000, or about

2.5 cents per voter, some of which apparently went to buy old-flag Mardi Gras beads for the Catholic Gulf Coast.

As I said, pretty much the same story could be written about the earlier controversies in South Carolina and Georgia, which also saw a broad coalition in favor of change, collectively well-heeled, well-connected, and seemingly unstoppable. And in South Carolina and Georgia, they were unstoppable. They didn't get everything they wanted, but they got the flag off the South Carolina statehouse dome, and they got it relegated to obscurity on the new Georgia flag.

But in Mississippi the outcome was different. The pro-change forces' campaign seems to have turned out a substantially higher percentage of those who agreed with them. But the polls suggest that there simply weren't many such people in the first place, and the campaign did not change many minds. By a margin of 65 percent to 35 percent Mississippians voted against the change. Mississippi will remain for now the only state with the Confederate battle standard as a legible component of its flag.

This raises a couple of interesting questions. First of all, what is it with Mississippi? Why was the outcome there different from those in Georgia and South Carolina?

That one is easy. The outcome was different because the question was put to a popular vote. In Mississippi the forces for change were strong enough to get the question of the flag on the table (as they could not have done even a decade ago), but they were not strong enough just to tell legislators to fix it. In the other states, more urban and economically developed, legislators were persuaded to work out compromises that surveys showed would almost certainly not have won a majority in a referendum. Maybe legislators are more far-sighted than ordinary citizens; certainly they are more responsive to organized interest-group pressure. You can argue either that Georgia and South Carolina legislators betrayed their constituents or that they showed the sort of leadership that is all too rare in democratic polities—or quite possibly both.

Another, harder, question is why so many Southerners are attached to the Confederate flag. Again, let's take Mississippi as an example and look at why the numbers worked out the way they did.

Since whites outnumber blacks by about the same ratio as anti-change voters outnumbered pro-change ones—that is, by about two to one—it is tempting just to conclude that whites want to keep the old flag and blacks do not, and certainly that's a large part of the story. A *Clarion-Ledger* showed that something like 80 percent of whites who had an opinion were in favor of the old flag and almost as high a percentage of blacks were against it. But that just raises another question. Why did an overwhelming majority of white Mississippians and a significant minority of black ones want to keep the Confederate emblem on their state flag? What does that flag mean to Southerners?

It is hard to talk about this without sounding like some sort of postmodernist twit, but we need to recognize that there is no intrinsic meaning to colors on a cloth. A flag is a "text" to which different "interpretive communities" bring their own meanings. Some of these communities insist on the unique validity of their own understandings and seem incapable of recognizing other points of view. Some folks, in other words, are simply talking past each other. Others, however, understand each other all too well. Let's try to sort this out.

*   *   *

The proponents of change were often eloquent about what the old flag meant to them. Most African Americans and some white liberals agreed with the black minister from Raymond, Mississippi, who told an AP reporter that the Confederate flag evokes "bad memories" of its use by opponents of the civil rights movement. (It is significant—I will come back to this—that most objections at the popular level were to how the flag was deployed in the 1960s rather than the 1860s.) A Jackson grocery store owner told the *New York Times*, "I was a freedom rider. The other side would hold the rebel flag. It was always a sign of segregation and hatred." The mayor of Mayersville, Mississippi, agreed: "When I think about the flag I think about the Ku Klux Klan and when they came along here burning crosses in my yard—they had that flag."

Look at the old films of George Wallace rallies. There is the governor of Alabama standing tall (as tall as he could) for segregation, and those who stood with him waved the flag as they did it. Wallace's pledges to "Keep Alabama Southern" and then to "Southernize America" had an unabashed racial component: He and his supporters identified the "Southern way of life" with white supremacy and were not the least bit hesitant to say so. The days when overwhelming majorities of white Southerners felt that way are gone, but it is simply ahistorical to deny that the flag's principal use in the 1960s was as a segregationist symbol—and black Southerners have not forgotten that.

No wonder that, as black columnist Donna Britt put it, "For many African Americans just seeing the battle flag—on a T-shirt or a coffee mug—is a stab to the heart." Kweisi Mfume, president of the national NAACP, said the old Mississippi flag "celebrate[s] the twisted philosophy of bigotry and hatred in this country." And the NAACP's state president interpreted the vote to retain it as a sign that "Mississippi wants to remain in the eyes of the world a racist state."

Even many black Mississippians who took a more sympathetic view of their white neighbors' attitudes felt, understandably, that the battle flag is a symbol of the white South, a symbol that excludes them and denies them respect. As Harrison County Supervisor William Martin told the AP, "I want to be counted. I'm a citizen in this state. I want a flag that represents me, too."

Some white Mississippians agreed that the state flag should not be divisive and recognized that the existing one inevitably is. This was the line taken by the religious leaders and most of the academics who spoke out on the matter. One letter-writer in the *Clarion-Ledger* asked his fellow white Mississippians to "consider the fact that our present flag is offensive to a large percent of our population" and implored them, "in a spirit of good will, [to] take a positive step, make the change and show the people it offends we care and are willing to do something about it." Others put it as just a matter of good manners. One white man argued at a public meeting in Jackson that "a state flag should not cause pain to its own people," and the author John Grisham made the same case, arguing that the flag should be changed to "something not offensive to 35 percent of our population."

Many white Mississippians who made this argument made it clear that they didn't see the flag as racist, and regretted that others did. Author Barry Hannah, for example, said that he never saw the battle flag "as the flag of hostility and hate" and that he "still feel[s] reverence to the troops who fought the war." He said it is "a damn crying shame we can't celebrate them because of the Klan and idiots that began grabbing the flag," but "if [the new flag]'s what times call for, so be it." And Mary Ann Mobley, the former Miss America, said simply, "I've never thought of that flag as racist, but I'm also not African American."

The most common argument against the old flag, however, at least in the published record, was that it was bad for Mississippi's public relations and ultimately for tourism and industrial recruitment. (The fact that the campaign for change was largely funded by business interests may have something to do with that.) A spokesman for the Mississippi Economic Council (the state Chamber of Commerce) said that organization's support for changing the flag was "a strategic business decision," adding that "it can help create a more positive business climate for our state." The president of the Mississippi Tourism Association concurred: Changing the flag "will enhance our state's economic development efforts," he said. And the *Mississippi Business Journal* ran an editorial headlined simply: BAD FOR BUSINESS.

The largest donor to the campaign for change was Jim Barksdale, a Jackson native and internet millionaire who made it clear that he is kin to Mississippi's best-known Confederate general. Barksdale gave $185,000 to the Mississippi Legacy Fund, the major pro-change PAC, remarking that the old flag "doesn't send a positive signal outside the state." (It did not escape notice that he made this observation from his home in California.) Barksdale argued that the flag "prompts some businesses to steer clear of Mississippi," and his money went to pay for fliers stating that "The current flag is . . . discouraging companies from bringing good paying jobs to our people" and radio spots in which a man's voice said "Changing Mississippi's flag tells companies that we're ready to work."

In retrospect, it might have been better to emphasize the argument from good manners, or from Christian charity, rather than the pocketbook case for change, which put a new spin on Jefferson's remark that "merchants have no country" (or, as Pat Buchanan put it, "Money has no flag"). Shelby Foote dismissed the economic argument with aristocratic contempt. "I think the people who want a new flag are worried about tourists," he said. "I never cared much for tourists myself." A few defenders of the old flag pointed out the absence of any actual evidence for the proposition that it discouraged outside investment in the state. "Industry's going to come here because of the deal they get, not because of the flag," one said. Another even wrote the *Clarion-Ledger* to point out—and regret—that the flag had not kept the national Gannett newspaper chain from buying the *Clarion-Ledger*. And a Vicksburg woman told pollsters, "I don't see that many companies looking to come to Mississippi anyway."

My guess is that most non-Southerners at least understand the arguments for changing the flag, but what could the other two-thirds of Mississippi voters have been thinking? Why did they turn out in such numbers to crush the proposal for change? And I don't want to pick on Mississippi: Why would so many Georgians and South Carolinians and other Southerners have done the same, given the chance?

Some—a dwindling, if not insignificant number—like the flag for the same reason the NAACP despises it: because they see it as a symbol of white supremacy. There is a strange sort of agreement here. In fact, a couple of years ago, a black man suing to change the Georgia state flag called the leader of the Southern White Knights of the Ku Klux Klan as a friendly witness to testify that the battle flag does indeed stand for "segregation, white supremacy and states' rights."

I don't want to belabor this point, but when skinheads turned out to decorate Confederate graves with battle flags (as they did not long ago in Alabama), when Byron de la Beckwith wore a flag pin in his label at his trial for the murder of Medgar Evers, when a householder in my town flies the flag on Martin Luther King's birthday—well, there is no question that they mean by the flag the same thing that the opponents of the civil rights movement meant by it forty years ago, and that message is understood by their adversaries, as it is meant to be.

Such outspoken white racists were, in fact, rarely heard from in the referendum debate, but even if such folks are now relegated to the lunatic fringe, they are still there, and they have websites, where they made their views known. And you can make what you will of the fact that some of the old flag's supporters had ties to the Council of Conservative Citizens, the successor group to the old, segregationist White Citizens Council. The upshot is that when defenders of the old flag argued that the Confederate flag is not a racist symbol, their argument was less effectively refuted by their adversaries than by some of their allies, like the woman who told a meeting at Millsaps College that blacks should be grateful for slavery because they are better off in America than in Africa.

My guess is that overtly racist support cost the old flag votes, on balance. It is clearly no longer quite respectable to express such views in public: When the *Clarion-Ledger* poll asked people why they supported the old flag, the only response that even suggested racial animus was "[We] have given too many concessions already." (As one woman said, "If we change this, they won't be happy. They'll want to change the state flower next because they don't like the smell." Although she didn't say who "they" were, she might have had the NAACP in mind.) But that kind of response was given by only 2 percent of the flag's supporters. Clearly something else was at work here.

By far the bulk of the verbiage in defense of the old flag came from Mississippians like those who told the *Clarion-Ledger* that their reasons had to do with "history" and "heritage." To change the Mississippi flag, one opponent of the change said, would be "a slap in the face to the brave men who fought and died for the Confederacy." (That seems to have been a popular metaphor. Another white Mississippian observed at a public meeting that keeping the old flag would be "a deliberate slap in the face to the black people of Mississippi." Obviously, whatever the outcome, there was going to be some face-slapping going on in Mississippi.)

In any case, for the Sons of Confederate Veterans, for many other historically minded white folks and even a few black ones, the battle flag remains what it was originally: a symbol of the Southern Confederacy, and (some) aspects of that nation, its cause and experience. In particular, it serves as an emblem of the courage, honor, and devotion to duty of those who suffered and died for that cause. That rhetoric figures in all of the many flag disputes. Just a few examples, chosen more or less at random from literally hundreds:

- From the *Southern Partisan* magazine: "The Confederate flag is a symbol, recognized around the world, of heroism, dedication, sacrifice, and high political ideals. It serves as a symbol not only for Southerners but for all Americans."
- From Glenn McConnell, South Carolina state senator: "The flag is the emblem of our ancestors. It's the flag they saw across the battlefield and is an emblem of unity and now it flies as a war memorial for those folks who went off to battle."
- From the commander of the North Carolina Division of the SCV: "[The flag represents] the honor of all who willingly made a sacrifice for their state and nation that few today could even imagine, much less emulate. . . . The blood-stained banner helps us remember [those] who made the ultimate sacrifice, many still buried in long-forgotten, unmarked graves."
- And, in Mississippi, from the ever-quotable Shelby Foote: "I'm for the Confederate flag always and forever. Many among the finest people this country has ever produced died in that war. To take it and call it a symbol of evil is a misrepresentation."

This has been a consistent interpretation of the flag since at least 1889, when the United Confederate Veterans adopted it as their emblem. I for one find it worthy of respect and, in fact, largely share that view, if not the desire to impose it on others. Only recently has this attitude has become at all controversial. The online magazine *Slate* got it exactly backward in January 2001 when, in an article called "Tricky Dixie," it argued that "Confederate ideology" was being "mainstreamed." Observing that two of President Bush's cabinet nominees, Attorney General–designate John Ashcroft and Secretary of the Interior nominee Gale Norton, had both "expressed a measure of sympathy for the ideals of the Old South," *Slate* remarked that "defending Dixie [has] become suddenly fashionable," and asked, "Is this the onset of reactionary chic?" But Norton and Ashcroft were not on the cutting edge of fashion at all: The views they expressed were decidedly old-fashioned, reflecting what was virtually a national consensus for over a hundred years about how the Confederacy should be viewed. The conflict over how Confederate symbols should be deployed reflects the breakdown of that consensus.

This understanding, which reached full flower in the 1890s and the early years of the last century, required that ex-Confederates and their families acknowledge that the preservation of the Union and the abolition of slavery were good things, even providential. Most did. Joel Chandler Harris, Uncle Remus's amanuensis, put it this way: "I am keenly alive to the happier results of the war, and I hope I appreciate at their full value the emancipation of both whites and blacks from the deadly effects of negro slavery, and the wonderful development of our material resources that the war has rendered possible." (As an Atlanta booster he would of course mention economic development.)

In return for these concessions, former Confederates were allowed to fly their flags, sing their songs, honor their heroes, and celebrate their holidays. And not just as a private devotion: Confederate Memorial Day and the birthdays of Confederate leaders became state holidays in the South, and it was at this time that state flags began to incorporate or otherwise refer to the Confederate flag. (The Alabama, Arkansas, and Florida flags contain more subtle references to the Confederacy; we may hear about them next.) But there was more to this than simple toleration. An important step on what has been called the "road to reunion" was that "everyone" (that is in quotation marks for later reference) agreed that Unionists and Confederates alike were answering the call of duty, that both sides were courageous and acted in good faith. Innumerable works of popular fiction were written, as one scholar has put it, "to show both North and South that the adversaries were people who were kind and honorable and had fought for what they thought was right."

The former adversaries even agreed, in principle, to honor one another. When the composer Dan Emmett died in 1904, he was buried near his home in Mount Vernon, Ohio, under a tombstone that says his song "'Dixie Land' inspired the courage and devotion of the Southern people and now thrills the hearts of a united nation." And a significant milestone was the 1913 joint reunion of the Union and Confederate veterans' organizations, funded in part by the federal government, which brought over fifty thousand old soldiers from both sides to Gettysburg for four days of reminiscence and reenactment.

Another part of the deal was that the role of slavery in precipitating the conflict was downplayed. Let me be clear here: To say that the Confederate states seceded to protect their peculiar institution says nothing about the motives of individual Confederate soldiers. But on the road to reunion ex-Confederates not only agreed that they were better off without slavery, they almost denied that it had anything to do with the war. As Basil Lanneau Gildersleeve, distinguished classical philologist and veteran of the Confederate cavalry, wrote forty years after the war: "That the cause we fought for and our brothers died for was the cause of civil liberty and not the cause of human slavery, is a thesis which we feel ourselves bound to maintain whenever our motives are challenged or misunderstood, if only for our children's sake."

And to repudiate slavery was not to reject white supremacy. Quite the contrary. The ideology of the Lost Cause included a rose-colored view of life in the Old South, a frightening account of the horrors of black rule after the war, and a forthright racism that not only justified but virtually required white domination. White Southerners successfully exported most of this to the rest of white America, which was more than ready to hear it. In 1915 the movie *Birth of a Nation* presented a heroic view of the Confederacy and a distinctly unreconstructed view of Reconstruction, celebrated the Ku Klux Klan as saviors of white civilization, and attracted record-breaking and appreciative audiences nationwide. President Wilson watched it in the White House and said it was "like writing history with lightning" and "all so terribly true."

This rapprochement held for decades; several generations of Americans, including mine, grew up under it. The federal government commemorated Lee and Jackson on a postage stamp in the 1930s, and in the 1950s honored the United Confederate Veterans with a stamp on the occasion of their last encampment. A few years later President Eisenhower's proclamation marking the centennial of the war praised the "heroism and sacrifice by men and women of both sides, who valued principles above life itself and whose devotion to duty is a proud part of our national inheritance." Soldiers of both sides, he said, were "as good as any who ever fought under any flag," and the war was a "great chapter in our Nation's history."

But even as the Civil War centennial was being celebrated, with compliments all around, what I have taken to calling the "old settlement" was beginning to unravel. When I said that "everyone" had signed off on it, I meant everyone whose opinion mattered. Black Americans, in particular, were not consulted. Had they been, of course, it would have been a different story. Most African Americans' views of the Old South and of Reconstruction differed radically from the Authorized Version.

They tried to dissent—in 1915 the fledgling NAACP organized protests in several (Northern) cities against *Birth of a Nation*—but no one was listening. No one had to listen. Especially in the South, where blacks were effectively disfranchised, no one in authority had to pay any attention to their opinions on any subject. But a hundred years after Appomattox, the Voting Rights Act of 1965 profoundly changed the public opinion calculus in the South, and nowhere more than in Mississippi. These days there are roughly eight thousand black elected officials in the United States, five thousand of them are in the South, and fifteen hundred are in Mississippi. In contemporary Southern politics, the interests of black Southerners may not prevail, but their opinions cannot simply be ignored. And, as we have seen, they do have opinions about the Confederate battle flag.

Thirty years ago, in a small-town Southern hamburger joint, I saw a group of high-school girls in battle-flag T-shirts with the legend "Proud to Be a Rebel." They were cheerleaders, and the Rebels were their team. One of the girls was black, and at the time I took great satisfaction in that. I saw it as a universalizing of these Southern symbols (the most obvious ones available), an expansion of the Southern community to include the South's largest and most mistreated minority. But of course I hadn't really thought it through. Including folks in your community means they get to have a voice in it, including a voice about what the symbols of that community are to be. And when it comes to the Confederate flag, by far the most common view among black Southerners seems to be the one we have already examined: that it has been irremediably tainted by its use as a symbol of opposition to the civil rights movement.

In response, both the national Sons of Confederate Veterans and innumerable local "camps" have passed resolutions denouncing, as one put it, anyone "whose actions tarnish or bring dishonor upon the Confederate soldier or his reason for fighting," especially those "using our cherished flag as a symbol of hatred." Another says plainly that "Philosophies, attitudes and activities advanced by white supremacist organizations and other groups designed to subordinate the lives, intrinsic value and contributions of people because of their race are both morally repugnant and inconsistent with the purpose of the Sons of Confederate Veterans." But these resolutions are apparently too little, too late. Most African American voters in Mississippi were having none of it. They know what they know, and they don't like being told they are mistaken any more than Sons of Confederate Veterans do.

Now, for the record, it should be said that a handful of black Mississippians expressed essentially the same views as the Sons of Confederate Veterans. Some in fact may have *been* Sons of Confederate Veterans: an estimated two dozen members of that organization, nationwide, are African American. Anthony Hervey, a young Mississippian (with a master's degree from the University of London, by the way) who has started something called the Black Confederate Soldier Foundation, said the battle flag "stands for freedom and states' rights." The Reverend Walter Bowie of Jackson's Koinonia Baptist Church more or less agreed: "The so-called Rebel flag is the flag of the South," he said, "the symbol of many good things about our culture and history that are dear to the hearts of southerners, white, black and red. It becomes racist only in the hands of a racist." But this was decidedly a minority view among black Mississippians; in fact, these are the only two examples I found, and their opinions were, to say the least, unpopular. The mildest epithet directed at blacks who felt that way came from the president of the Columbia County branch of the NAACP who called them "house Negroes." Anthony Hervey even claims that somebody took a shot at him.

Both the poll data and the written record suggest that far more common among black Mississippians was the sort of workaday pluralism expressed by the actor Morgan Freeman, who said, "Personally, I have every appreciation for those Mississippians who say the flag represents their heritage. But it's not everybody's heritage." Or the black cab driver in Jackson, who told a *Washington Post* reporter, "You don't need to have this flag flying over all the state office buildings and everything. . . . Just put one in your yard or your house or your bedroom, and you'll have all your heritage right there in your house." In other words: Go ahead and celebrate your heritage. Just don't make everybody do it.

But to this the SCV and other "heritage" groups respond that the Confederate heritage is the heritage of all Mississippians, black as well as white. In the last few years, some members of these groups have taken the argument that the Lost Cause was not about slavery a giant step farther. Read their literature, go to their websites, and you will find them arguing that scores of thousands of black men actually took up arms for the Confederacy. We are not talking just about enslaved teamsters and cooks and laborers, not just about the odd body servant who took a few potshots at the Yankees, or the handful of blacks who were enlisted in the last desperate days of the war, but regular combat troops, fighting for their homeland. Black and white together, they were overcome.

As history—well, let's just say that the legend of black Confederates is not quite in the same genus as tales of alien abduction and satanic ritual abuse, but the numbers have been greatly exaggerated. Mississippi historian Robert McElvaine pointed out in the *New York Times* that this kind of "feel-good history" has a lot in common with Afrocentrism, but he argues that it is a sign of progress that slavery and racism are no longer "honored as part of the Southern heritage," even if it means that "it has left a sizable number of people clinging to a pseudo-historical mythology." I agree that it is progress, but I doubt that many black Southerners are going to be persuaded that their ancestors were on the Confederacy's side, or vice versa. Even if it were true, it would be a hard sell. No, for the foreseeable future, as Rip Daniels, a black businessman from Gulfport, said during the Mississippi debate, "You leave me no choice but to be your enemy as long as you wave a battle flag. If it is your heritage, then it is my heritage to resist it with every fiber of my being."

Notice that, on both sides, the argument has turned increasingly historical. Some of the flag's defenders are now saying not just that it should be a symbol of trans-racial Southern unity and that its deployment by racists in the 1950s and '60s was a regrettable aberration, but that it has always been a symbol of unity. On the other side, although the most common objection is still to the flag's use by twentieth-century segregationists, lately we have heard more and more about its use by the Confederate States of America. At last, and predictably, the entire post-Civil War settlement is being challenged, primarily by African Americans whose forebears were not parties to it.

To be sure, the old settlement, the old deal, still prevails in some circles. Last year the Sons of Union Veterans passed a resolution noting that their ancestors "met in joint reunions with the confederate veterans under both flags in . . . bonds of Fraternal Friendship," and expressing their "support and admiration for those gallant soldiers and of their respective flags." But compare that, or President Eisenhower's words about the Civil War as "a great chapter in our Nation's history," to Congressman John Lewis's recent remark that "It is unfortunate and somewhat tragic that after all these many years, people are still looking to this part of our history as some glorious time. It's not something we can be very proud of." Or consider the legislation recently introduced by Mississippi congressman Bennie Thompson condemning the use of the Confederate flag for "any reason other than as a historic reminder of the secession of the Confederate States, which prompted the violent, bloody, and divisive Civil War, and of the Confederacy's flagrant disregard for the equality of all Americans in accordance with the United States Constitution and in the eyes of God." Thompson (the only member of Congress who doesn't have a state flag outside his office) says his bill "is intended to set the record straight. The leaders of the Confederate States of America were traitors."

And it is not only African Americans who are challenging the old settlement. I had a letter recently from a former student, in Chatham County, North Carolina, who wrote that a Yankee couple who attended an SCV meeting to hear a historical lecture had written to complain about the SCV's practice of saluting the state and Confederate flags, after the Pledge of Allegiance to the Stars and Stripes. "I can see myself one day," my friend wrote, "belly down on the west bank of Jordan Lake, picking off Yankee cars as they cross over the Highway 64 bridge. Even better on the northern front, where we have the high ground overlooking the two-lane Haw River bridge." "John, I was at that meeting," he continued, "and nobody was mean or ugly. Everybody, in fact, was nice and friendly."

The former commander of the Mississippi SCV echoed this frustration when he told the *Washington Post* that people "label us and malign us and abuse us just because we want to protect our Confederate emblems," which are, after all, symbols of "courage, devotion to duty, devotion to family, honor, valor, and a lot of other qualities that we should aspire to in life." If Sons of Confederate Veterans sound a little aggrieved these days, it is because they feel betrayed. They have kept their side of the bargain: Their meetings begin with the Pledge of Allegiance. Many honestly don't understand why the old settlement doesn't work anymore. I think others do understand—but, after all, lost causes are what they are all about.

*　　*　　*

We are going to hear a lot more about heritage and hate—pride and prejudice—in Mississippi and elsewhere for years to come. But there was another factor—perhaps the determining factor—in the

Mississippi vote that we heard much less about. Consider: a half-million Mississippians, including what had to be tens of thousands of black Mississippians, voted to keep the old flag. This is vastly greater than the membership of all the "heritage" groups put together. (The largest, the SCV, has only 1,639 members in the state.) Many of these voters were expressing rebel pride, certainly, but of a less historical sort.

Sometime around the middle of the last century, the Confederate battle flag took on yet another meaning. Especially in the South, but not only there, it began to send a message of generalized defiance, directed at authority and to some extent at respectability. People who use the flag this way may not care if it offends black folks or Yankees, but those groups are somewhere behind high-school principals on the list of targets.

You can see this use of the flag in the world of popular music, where it came to stand for a hell-raising, good-timing, boogie-till-you-puke spirit associated with Southern rock and country musicians like Alabama, Hank Williams Jr., Charlie Daniels, and Lynyrd Skynyrd. Similarly, on the television program *The Dukes of Hazzard*, in the early 1980s, Bo and Luke Duke had a car called the General Lee: Its horn played "Dixie" and it had a battle flag painted on the roof, but there was never any indication that Bo and Luke were acquainted with their heritage—although they probably would be ready to fight about it.

In short, for many Southerners the flag represents a sort of don't-tread-on-me attitude that I suspect had a lot to do with the Mississippi vote, an attitude displayed by the woman who was cheered at a public meeting when she said, "If you don't like the state flag, there are forty-nine other states you can move to!" American Southerners don't have that pungent British phrase "bloody-minded," but we certainly have the behavior it describes. In fact, a reporter for the *Irish Times* found the whole Mississippi controversy eerily reminiscent of Ulster, where they also "do battle over the right to flaunt symbols of division in the name of irreconcilable versions of history." Certainly many in Northern Ireland share the ornery streak that Donald Wildmon, the Christian Right leader, said he feared would lead Mississippians to vote for the old flag "not because they are opposed to a new flag, but because they feel that someone is trying to force them to do something."

And who might this "someone" be? Well, recall that list of endorsements. It included the NAACP, to be sure, but it also included nearly all of the Great and the Good in Mississippi. My bet is that many

Mississippians who are neither great nor good (in the sense of that phrase) suspect that there is an element of social-class prejudice at work—and they are not wholly wrong about that. When I interviewed upper-middle-class college students about the flag a few years ago, many of them saw as a "redneck" symbol. Not without reason, they associated it with trailer parks, tattoo parlors, and outlaw bikers. (As one girl said, "When I see the Confederate flag I think of a pickup truck with a gun rack and a bumper sticker that says 'I DON'T BRAKE FOR SMALL ANIMALS.'") In other words, to at least some cosmopolitan Southerners the flag symbolizes not race but social class—not to put too fine a point on it, they are snobs—and nobody likes being told what to do by people they suspect of looking down on them. Of course, even worse, Mississippians were being told what to do by the *national* elite, whose opinion that all Mississippians are ignorant yahoos could have gone without saying—but didn't. One columnist said, for instance, that he found the flag debate "encouraging" because "it's always nice to see states worry about entering the 20th century."

As Kirk Fordice, Mississippi's Republican former governor, explained, "people have to understand . . . that Mississippians resent the heck" out of that sort of thing. Is it surprising that a great many of them seized the chance to cock a snoot at the agents of enlightened opinion and tell them to go to hell? Keeping their old flag may cost Mississippians in the end, both financially and otherwise. But Southerners like to joke that the most common last words in our region are "Hey, y'all—Watch this!"

The Most Southern State?

I confess that, now and then, I have taken some cheap shots at Florida's expense. In a talk I often give to civic clubs and other groups, for example, I try to draw some sensible geographic boundaries for the South. Starting with the common understanding that there is such a thing and the general agreement that Mississippi and Alabama are in it, and working out from there, I talk about Texas and Kentucky and other, more marginal Southern states. I can always get a laugh by asking, "And what do we do about Florida?"

Florida is a problem. Just as the South has been largely defined by how it differs from the rest of the United States, so Florida can serve as a sort of Southern counterpoint: Almost anything you can say about the South—about speech, religion, music, demography, whatever—isn't true of Florida. In most respects, these days, the most southerly state in the South is the least "Southern."

To be sure, as Floridians understand (and, I hasten to add, I do, too), Saint Augustine and Deland and Pensacola and Fernandina and Vernon are Southern if anywhere is. The Mississippi Delta south of Memphis is usually described as "the most Southern place on earth," but I have been to the Florabama Lounge on Perdida Key and it is a contender. But that's not what most Americans think of when they hear "Florida." Not these days.

No, the problem is mostly *South* Florida. In a book called *1001 Things Everyone Should Know about the South,* my wife Dale and I included this entry:

> *South Florida* begins somewhere south of Daytona Beach, and it is very different—ecologically, economically, ethnically, however you want to look at it—from other parts of the South, including north Florida. It is an urban place, increasingly so, with an economy based on tourism, retirement, and drugs. Well over half of its residents were not born in the South, much less in Florida, and

many were born outside the United States. It would be tempting to exclude it from the South altogether, if there were anywhere else to put it.

Of course, once upon a time, back when hardly anyone lived south of Daytona, Florida was very Southern indeed. Antebellum Florida was an integral part of the Cotton Kingdom: By the 1830s slaves and free blacks made up 52 percent of the population of Duval, Nassau, and St. Johns counties, and when the cotton states seceded after the election of Abraham Lincoln, to protect slavery and the interests of plantation agriculture, Florida was in the vanguard. It left the Union just after South Carolina and Mississippi, ahead of the other Deep South states, and well before the states of the upper South, which only joined the Rebs after Lincoln's call for volunteers turned the conflict into a states' rights struggle.

After four years of civil war, Florida shared fully in the "Southern" experiences of defeat and military occupation. In the Jim Crow era that followed the restoration of white Democratic rule, Florida, like the rest of the Southern states, wrote racial segregation into state law—and worse. According to the grisly statistics compiled by the Tuskegee Institute, in the decades after 1882 Floridians lynched 282 victims (257 of them black), by far the highest ratio of lynchings to population in the country: 40 percent higher than Mississippi's, nearly twice Georgia's, and ten times Virginia's and North Carolina's. This pattern of white supremacist violence culminated in the Rosewood massacre of January 1923, only recently retrieved from the memory hole to which it had been consigned.

It is ironic that many—possibly most—of the Floridians who came out of this unpromising matrix to achieve lasting reputations were black. One was A. Philip Randolph, born in 1889 in Crescent City, who used his platform as head of the Brotherhood of Sleeping Car Porters to become the leading civil rights advocate of the 1940s and organizer of the 1963 March on Washington, and who learned in his boyhood the lesson that "At the banquet table of nature there are no reserved seats. You get what you can take, and you keep what you can hold." Another was novelist and folklorist Zora Neale Hurston of Eatonville, a leading figure of the Harlem Renaissance in the 1920s; rediscovered after her death in the 1960s, she was rightly hailed on the tombstone erected by novelist Alice Walker as "A Genius of the South." Yet a third was Mary McLeod Bethune, a South Carolinian by birth, who founded the Daytona Educational and Industrial School for Negro Girls (now part of Bethune-Cookman College) in 1904; the first president of the National Council of Negro Women, she served as advisor to every president from Coolidge to Truman.

During this era, Florida was a reliable component of the political Solid South. After the state's disputed electoral votes were awarded to Republican Rutherford B. Hayes in the so-called Compromise of 1876, effectively ending Reconstruction, Florida and the other Southern states moved in various ways to disfranchise black voters, and for decades thereafter Southern white voters were "solid" for the Democrats, the party of white supremacy and states' rights. In seventeen of the next eighteen presidential elections Florida gave its electoral votes to the Democratic candidate, usually by lopsided majorities. Like several other Southern states, Florida balked at the Roman Catholic "wet," Al Smith, in 1928, and went for Herbert Hoover, but in 1932 it returned to the Democratic column with a 74 percent vote for Franklin Roosevelt. Not until the Eisenhower-Stevenson campaigns of the 1950s were presidential elections in Florida truly competitive.

As political scientists Merle and Earl Black have shown, the South's most consistent "yellow dog Democrats" (who would vote for a yellow dog before a Republican) were whites from rural areas with large black populations (30 percent or more). In 1920 nearly all of Florida north of Orlando and east of Panama City fit that description, containing 35 percent of the state's voters. That percentage was the same as Louisiana's and higher than that for Alabama; only South Carolina, Georgia, and Mississippi were more "Southern" than Florida, in this sense.

But twentieth-century urbanization and migration patterns changed all that, and nowhere more than in Florida. In every Southern state there are now fewer rural counties with large black populations, and a smaller percentage of voters live in even the counties that *used* to be such counties. As the Blacks' statistics show, however, this is especially true—startlingly true—of Florida. By 1980 there were only four such counties in the state, all on the Georgia border, and they contained only a negligible 1 percent of Florida voters. (The only other Southern state with as low a percentage was Texas.) When a presidential candidate these days decides to simply to write off white Southern conservative voters, as Al Gore did in 2000, he will lose most of the South—but not necessarily Florida.

Of course, a major factor in making Florida less Southern—politically and otherwise—has been the influx of non-Southern migrants that began in earnest with the land boom of the 1920s. As early as 1930, 30 percent of Florida's residents had been born outside the South (among other Southern states only Virginia, at 11 percent, was in double digits) and by 1980, a majority (51 percent) had been. These migrants brought non-Southern ways with them, and settled in concentrations large enough that they were able to sustain them and pass them on to succeeding generations.

And the "non-Southern ways" they brought came in many different flavors. Even before the 1920s Florida was the most ethnically diverse of the Southern states (with the possible exception of Texas, which had, of course, a lot more room in which to be diverse). The Seminoles, although few in number, were nevertheless one of the largest Native American groups east of the Mississippi. Greek sponge fishermen had settled in Tarpon Springs (where their descendants now make up over one-sixth of the population). The cigar industry had brought Cubans, Spaniards, Italians, and Germans to Ybor City. But, after 1920, migration to the Sunshine State also gave the state's Gold Coast the third largest concentration of Jews in the United States, after New York and Los Angeles. More recently, Greater Miami has become home to a majority of the nation's Cuban Americans; South Florida's Latin American and Caribbean connections have also given the state most of the South's Central and South Americans, Puerto Ricans, Jamaicans, Barbadians, and Haitians; and the labor needs of agriculture have given southwest Florida a concentration of Mexican American agricultural workers rivaled in the South only in Texas.

So, *would* we put Florida in the South these days, if there were anywhere else to put it? If we define the South as where Southerners live, maybe not. Only a bare majority of Floridians—51 percent—tell the Southern Focus Poll that they are Southerners, the lowest percentage (by far) of any Southern state. And in South Florida, Southerners are a decided minority. Writer Joel Garreau had a suggestion: In his boundary-drawing book *The Nine Nations of North America* he splits the state, putting northern Florida with the rest of the South, in the "nation" he calls *Dixie*, while South Florida goes in *The Islands*, with the Caribbean—and Miami is that nation's capital.

But let's not be hasty. Yes, Florida is now the least Southern state in the South, but much of the South now seems to be following Florida's lead. Could it be that Florida is not out of step at all, but rather setting the pace?

Consider: What *is* typical of the South these days? Not the Black Belt, or Appalachia, or South Texas; the old patterns of rural poverty persist in those parts, but most Southerners don't live there. As Peter Applebome observed in his recent book *Dixie Rising*, the tone for the whole region is increasingly set by the metropolitan South, by places like Atlanta and Charlotte and Nashville. We heard a good deal about this South in 1976, when Jimmy Carter's election provoked a lot of blather about an emerging "Sunbelt." That was an exaggeration, a caricature, maybe a bad idea, certainly premature, but it contained a grain of truth, if not an entire peck.

When I look around me in North Carolina these days, what I see is new jobs, new subdivisions, new shopping centers, new people. (And new problems, too—especially ecological ones.) In the 1990s North Carolina's population grew by 21 percent, an increase almost as great as Florida's 24 percent. Yankees are retiring to our mountains, to our coast, to golfing communities in between. (Many have come by way of Florida and are known as "halfbacks" because they have moved halfway back to where they came from). Our "Hispanic" population quadrupled between 1990 and 2000, to some 5 percent of the total— and these are the ones we know about. Throughout the South we are having to adjust to unprecedented religious diversity—not just more Catholics and Jews but more Muslims and Hindus and Buddhists. (One reporter for the Atlanta *Journal-Constitution* offered a characteristically Southern response: she wrote an etiquette book on how to deal with non-Christian friends.)

Walker Percy saw this coming as long ago as the 1960s. In *The Last Gentleman* (1966), Percy's character Will Barrett observed that "everything was being torn down and built anew. The earth itself was transformed overnight, gouged and filled, flattened and hilled, like a big sandpile. The whole South throbbed like a diesel." Does this sound familiar? If present trends continue, what it means to be "Southern" is certainly going to change. And that could mean, ironically, that Florida will again be one of the most Southern of the Southern states.

Brits and Grits

This essay and the next were among the half-dozen columns I wrote for a magazine called Brightleaf. *A sort of* North Carolina Review of Books, *it lived fast and died young, but left beautiful memories.*

During the Civil War, Henry Adams, serving as private secretary to his father, Lincoln's minister to London, reported with dismay that England "is unanimously against us and becomes more firmly set every day." The young Adams was exaggerating, but sometimes it did seem that everyone—at least everyone whose opinion mattered—sympathized with the Richmond government, not the one in Washington. The *Times* of London and the *Manchester Guardian*, the Liberal Gladstone and the Conservative Disraeli, the Evangelical Lord Shaftesbury and the Anglo-Catholic Bishop Wilberforce—all were pro-Confederate. As the London *Spectator* remarked, "the educated million in England, with here and there an exception, have become unmistakably Southern."

There were several reasons for that, as Sheldon Vanauken points out in his study, *The Glittering Illusion: English Sympathy for the Southern Confederacy*. Liberals' support for free trade and their sympathy for a small nation fighting for its liberty combined with longstanding Tory disdain for American democracy to guarantee that few among "the educated million" had a good word for the North. So successfully had the Lincoln administration argued that the war was not to free the slaves but to preserve the Union that even many abolitionists favored the Confederate cause.

And one reason for English sympathy crossed party lines: Whigs and Tories alike admired Southerners' *style*. In 1864, the Marquess of Lothian spoke for many others when he compared the North's "deep and widely-extended corruption," its "brutal inhumanity in the conduct of the war itself," and its exercise of "arbitrary power" at the expense of "the liberty of the citizen" to Confederate "ardour and devotedness of patriotism," "stainless good faith," "heroism in the field," and "scrupulous regard for the rights of hostile property"—all adding up to what his lordship saw as the "most splendid instance of a nation's defense of its liberties that the world has seen."

Of course, this being England, the explanation was found in social class. A. J. B. Beresford Hope, founder of the *Saturday Review*, husband of Lady Mildred Cecil, and author of three pro-Confederate books, argued that in the South, "owing to the large landed proprietors and the conditions of the country, the mob has not the same power [as in the North]. A certain number of the gentry have leisure to study politics as they ought to be studied." As for valor and chivalry—well, Richard Monckton Milnes, Lord Houghton, said, "It is just as if the younger sons of the Irish and Scottish nobility were turned loose against the bourgeoisie of Leeds."

To be sure, most English ladies and gentlemen in the 1860s were better acquainted with the literate and cosmopolitan gentry of Virginia and the Carolinas than with the less polished, Jacksonian denizens of Alabama and Tennessee, not to mention those of Arkansas and Texas. They saw the Confederates as dashing gallants in plumed hats, not ragged farm boys singing about goober peas and "Yellow Rose" and electing their own officers. They knew the Lees and Stuarts and Wade Hamptons; they didn't know—and probably could not have imagined— Bedford Forrest. But, as Vanauken shows, this selective ignorance allowed them to see the war as a conflict between Southern gentlemen and Northern cads. And, with friends like those, it is not surprising that the Confederacy found its most vocal English opponents primarily among those with little use for gentlemen—in particular, among the articulate elements of the English working class, whose sympathies, according to the historian Max Beloff, were less pro-Northern (and much less pro-Negro) than anti-aristocratic.

Well, I recently spent the better part of a year trying to teach the cream of present-day British youth something about the American South, and I am here to tell you that things have changed. The English Establishment has a much less flattering image of Dixie these days, but the working class is coming around.

Now, it is true that cultivated Brits are often inclined to feel superior to *all* Americans. This is nothing new, it's pretty harmless (no more sinister than the American tendency to regard England as a cute little country), and Southerners may actually get off easier than Californians. Still, English newspapers and magazines are full of stuff about Southerners that, if applied to a designated victim group on any American college campus, would mobilize the Sensitivity Police—that is, pretty much what Northern newspapers and magazines say about us, except maybe funnier. In the space of a couple of weeks, for instance, I encountered (1) an offhand reference in the *Sunday Times* to "the more moronic reaches of Southern redneck life"; (2) a comic novel set partly in a Southern mansion called the Villa Pellagra (near the dreary town of Bibliopolis, on the steamy Ptomaine River); and (3) a review of the London opening of "a wild, camp farce," starring a character named Harlot Mascara. No, if you want admiration for the South these days, don't turn to the ladies and gentlemen of England.

But somebody packed the Cambridge Corn Exchange to hear Don and Phil Everly. Somebody goes on the last Wednesday of each month to hear the Elvis impersonator at a local pub, and buys all those CDs of pimply Anglo-Saxon lads trying to sound like Muddy Waters. Somebody eats the chip shop's "Southern Fried Chicken" and watches the weekly NFL highlights on the telly. Who might that be?

People like a cabdriver I met in Nottingham, that's who. When he heard my accent he asked where I'm from, then regaled me with an account of his thirty-year love affair with the blues and rockabilly and country music, concluding with the detailed itinerary of a nine-week pilgrimage that took him in a rented car from Florida (a cheap flight) across the Deep South to New Orleans, north to Memphis, over to Nashville, on to the Smokies, then back to Florida. "The dream of a lifetime" he called it (and it sounded pretty good to me).

In short, those of my Cambridge neighbors who have helped to make East Anglia the line-dancing capital of England, Southern Comfort the world's best-selling liqueur, and the Confederate battle flag an international symbol of nose-thumbing rebellion are not university students, much less the dons who rooted for Jeff Davis and his team, but those very working-class folk whose ancestors had no use for us in 1862 or thereabouts.

How to explain this reversal? Once again, I think, selective ignorance is at work. In the South portrayed by our increasingly international popular culture, the aristocrats have become villains or comic figures (or both), and the white plain folk are likely to be vicious or grotesque—at best, amusing. About the only admirable figures identifiable as Southerners are the working-class heroes and heroines of sports, country music, and old Burt Reynolds movies. The educated millions in England are less likely than their working-class compatriots to encounter these tough, good-humored, and free-spirited characters in the first place, and less likely to admire them if they do. But in truth they are not all that different from Johnny Reb.

Missing

Back from a year in England, I was flooded with reminders of what I had missed about the South—sometimes without realizing that I had missed it. Southern food, for example. Thanks largely to the European Community and the influx of "New Commonwealth" immigrants, you can eat very well in England these days, and a year of pub grub and college feasts added a couple of inches to my waistline. But in our first weeks back home I scurried around to check out old Southern favorites. Just here in North Carolina, there was Mama Dip's sweet-potato pie in Chapel Hill, Lexington barbecue and tangy red slaw at Honey Monk's, crackling cornbread and collard greens at The Old Place in Bonlee, and, of course, sweet ice tea by the gallon. The British do not understand these things—especially ice tea. Hell, they don't even understand ice *water*.

I realized that I had missed Southern humor, too. England was constantly amusing, but their way is not ours. I can't imagine a bumper sticker in Cambridge like the one my daughter saw in Houston that said "Keep Honking, I'm Reloading." You just don't run into people like the Mississippi bluesman who plays a one-string guitar and bills himself as "the King of the String." You don't see advertisements like the one my buddy Hardy sent from Alabama about a local guy who sells tires by the pound, and if you can find a better deal he'll give you a goat. Or signs like the one in Seagrove, North Carolina, for the "Realistic Beauty Salon." (What could their motto be? "Don't expect miracles"? "We'll do what we can"?) Or the one outside a South Carolina country store claiming to be the "Home of World Famous Pickled Pig Lips." (I especially liked the "World Famous" part. I can guaran-damn-tee you that nobody in England had ever heard—or even thought—of pickled pig lips. But they have now.)

I was even happy to see kudzu again. That feckless vegetation always makes me smile, partly because I'm glad I don't own any. But I had missed it, too. It brings back memories. I am old enough to remember *planting* the stuff, back about aught-54, to control the erosion on a gullied east Tennessee hillside. Last time I was back in Washington County the kudzu was still there. The gullies may go all the way to China by now, but by God you don't have to look at them.

I could go on about the Southern things I missed. But now that I have been back stateside for a while my thoughts naturally run more to what I miss about England.

One thing I miss is a refreshing difference that my friend Richard Blaustein summed up nicely, over a beer in a Johnson City brewpub. "Brits think a hundred miles is a long distance," he remarked. "Americans think a hundred years is a long time."

That just about sums it up. American distances really are incomprehensible to English folk who haven't actually experienced them. A woman whose husband was thinking about taking a job in the Research Triangle asked if it would be convenient for her daughter to take violin lessons in Knoxville. She had looked at a map and figured that going from North Carolina to Tennessee must be something like going from Buckinghamshire to Oxfordshire. When I started to explain by pointing out that North Carolina is slightly bigger than England, she was dumbfounded—and a little bit horrified, I think.

This attitude is catching. After a few months in Cambridge I found myself thinking things like "It's 120 miles to Southampton. I'd better plan to spend the night." One reason distances feel longer in England is that the country is just so compact. A 120-mile drive means different accents, different beers and cheeses, even different weather. (Actually, you can just sit tight for an hour and get different weather.) In that distance you'll pass through dozens of villages and towns, most with old inns, manor houses, or parish churches worth a look. I miss that.

Now don't get me wrong. America has the best of a great many things, and lots of things other places don't have at all. But we don't have *everything*. We don't have Norman cathedrals, for instance, or Tudor stately homes. It was not until the nineteenth century that we really began to have the wealth and the exuberance to do anything other than pallid, cheapjack copies of European buildings. One reason it is so important to preserve our historic architecture is that we have so little to begin with. I like a place that has a history it can take for granted, where you can run into twelfth-century buildings still in use that don't even make the guidebooks, where something called "New College" was founded in 1379.

Another thing I miss about England are people like those that I hung out with, most of them academics, journalists, and politicians with an ingrained sense of irony that largely immunized them against the orthodoxy and sentimentality that constrains and clutters so much American conversation these days. True, the mawkish national weepfest of Princess Diana's funeral suggests that I didn't meet a cross section of the population, but people who think "Seinfeld" has an ironic take on life need a few evenings at High Table.

My English friends' impatience with cant is reflected in the well-honed English art of putting each other down. Expressions like *twee* and *naff* can only be defined by example (the best translations—cute and tacky, respectively—don't begin to do the concepts justice), but even if we had these words we probably wouldn't use them often. This is not because we don't have what the words describe (Lord knows we do), but because they are rooted in social-class distinctions that we are far more squeamish about than the English. To say that cell phones are "all very well for jumped-up estate agents" (as one of my friends put it) speaks volumes about the Thatcherites' failure to make enterprise an English trait.

I also ran into a sort of temperamental conservatism that might drive me nuts if I were English, but that as an outsider I find very agreeable. The English I like best are nearly all attached to some combination of cricket, football, dogs, real ale, Europhobia, and the Church of England. I only share the last three enthusiasms (and them not always), but in general I admire people who like being what their kind of people have always been and intend to stay that way. When British Air announced that it was going to replace the Union Jack on its airplanes with something more modern and Euro-friendly—well, you'd have thought they had proposed to take the Southern Cross off the Georgia state flag.

This conservatism is not even usually political—Lady Thatcher, for instance, is not conservative in this sense (and, as far as I can tell, she also has no discernible sense of irony)—and it may not even be the majority attitude these days, but it is widespread enough that someone who shares it doesn't feel like an alien.

You remember that old Phil Harris song, "That's What I Like about the South"? Well, *that's* what I like about England.

He's Baaack

(with MerleBlack)

Merle Black and I wrote this for Newsweek *in 1996. About the time we finished, the editor who had requested it called back to say that one of their staff writers had written something similar and they no longer needed it. (He also promised us a "kill fee," but we never got it.).*

Picture a presidential candidate who calls for America to stand tall against an array of adversaries, foreign and domestic. A candidate with a pugnacious, combative style, who lashes his opponents with sarcasm and ridicule, while teasing the press corps, throwing out rhetorical red meat with a knowing smile. A candidate whose rallies resemble revivals, with what some feel is an aura of barely controlled violence. A candidate whose fiery speeches leave his audiences charged with emotion, thrilled that at last someone is talking their language and expressing their convictions in a political campaign.

Picture a candidate who mocks Washington bureaucrats and promises to send them home, who articulates the deep sense of alienation and frustration among his working- and lower-middle-class followers, and who raises issues of race and class that mainstream politicians of both major parties would prefer to ignore. A candidate whose position on those issues often contradicts his own party's longstanding traditions.

Imagine that this candidate starts winning primaries and running strong even when he doesn't win. Imagine the dismay of party leaders and the glee of the incumbent opposition.

Now picture him gunned down in the parking lot of a Maryland shopping center. Because it is 1972 we are talking about, not 1996. And the candidate is George Wallace, not Pat Buchanan.

Those who remember Wallace's presidential campaigns (as an independent in 1968 and seeking the Democratic nomination in 1964 and 1972) will surely be struck by how Buchanan's rhetoric, his style, his base of support, and many of his positions resemble those of the Alabama governor.

There are differences, of course. Most obviously, Wallace was a Democrat; Buchanan is a Republican. Wallace was a career politician, a popular governor of his state; Buchanan is a wordsmith who has never held elected office. And where Wallace was unabashedly a man of the Deep South, Buchanan (despite his references to his Confederate ancestors) is a Yankee, from Washington, and to do well in Dixie he must overcome some lingering prejudice against his pre-Vatican-II Catholicism.

But Wallace's message had widespread appeal outside the South even thirty years ago. Historian Dan Carter reports that after the famous "stand in the schoolhouse door," Wallace's unsuccessful attempt to prevent the desegregation of the University of Alabama, more than half of the hundred thousand letters and telegrams he received came from outside the South, and 95 percent supported him. In 1964 Wallace won a majority of the white vote in Maryland's Democratic primary, and he ran strong in Indiana and Wisconsin as well. Although few believed that Wallace could ever have won the nomination at a 1972 Democratic convention that Tip O'Neill said resembled "the cast of *Hair*," when he was shot he had received more primary votes than any other candidate in the race, and he was giving national Democrats the heebie-jeebies.

And Buchanan's no Al Smith. No, the differences between him and Wallace pale beside the similarities.

Consider: Thirty years ago Wallace was calling on voters to "Stand Up for America" against an array of domestic foes that included street thugs who "turned to rape and murder because they didn't get enough broccoli when they were little boys," "hypocrites who send your kids half-way across town while they have their chauffeur drop their children off at private schools," "briefcase-carrying bureaucrats [who] can't even park their bicycles straight," and "intellectual snobs who don't know the difference between smut and great literature." To a New York audience, he explained why Alabama had no riots: "They start a riot down here, first one of 'em to pick up a brick gets a bullet in the brain, that's all. Then you walk over to the next one and say, 'All right, pick up a brick. We just want to see you pick up one of them bricks, now!'"

Unlike Buchanan, who assails Wall Street, predatory capitalism, and the ethic of the bottom line, Wallace generally avoided criticism of big business (he was trying to recruit it to Alabama, after all). But he sometimes referred darkly to "Eastern money power," and he once said, "I'm no ultra-conservative because those ultra-conservatives are conservative about just one thing—money."

Wallace polarized the electorate. Voters either loved him or hated him; like Buchanan, he was almost no one's second choice. He spoke for the white have-nots and have-littles—for America's "producers," "the beauticians, the truck drivers, the office workers, the policemen and the small businessmen"—and that's where the bulk of his support came from. For their part, the American elite returned his contempt, viewing him with disdain—or with fear. Richard Stroud wrote in *The New Republic*, for instance, of the "menace in the blood shout of the crowd" at Madison Square Garden in 1968, and drew the parallel to Nazi rallies of the 1930s. Wallace, of course, protested such comparisons, complaining that "They called me a bigot, a liar, a racist, an agitator, a trespasser. They pictured my supporters with Ku Klux Klan hoods."

But Wallace did begin as a racist, and an unapologetic one; in 1964 he told *Newsweek*, "All those countries with niggers in 'em have stayed the same for a thousand years. Tell me anyplace where white people and niggers mix." Buchanan doesn't talk that way, but he does have a knack for affronting conventional pieties on racial matters, as in his famous remark about the relative difficulty of assimilating Englishmen and Zulus in Virginia.

Perhaps even more striking than the similarities of substance are those of style. As Earl and Merle Black have observed, "Connoisseurs generally agreed that Wallace exhibited the boldest sneer, the finest snarl, the most unforced 'heh, heh, heh' in American politics." Here, too, Buchanan is giving the governor a run for his money.

The oddest resemblance was noted recently by University of South Carolina linguist Michael Montgomery, who observes that even the rhythm and intonation of Buchanan's speech, especially his pronunciation of vowels, make his accent in some ways the most "Southern" left in the race. (Lamar Alexander's basic "Tennessee homeboy," Montgomery says, has been "significantly smoothed over.")

All of this makes it passing strange that Dan Carter's recent biography argues that Wallace was the Godfather of modern Southern Republicanism. After all, one thing Newt Gingrich, Phil Gramm, Dick Armey, and Haley Barber have in common seems to be fear and loathing for Pat Buchanan, whose success almost renders Rush Limbaugh (of Cape Girardeau, Missouri) speechless. But forget the Contract with America: *this* is what George Wallace looks like as a Republican.

Wallace campaigned on a pledge to "Southernize America." Now, a quarter-century later, some might say that this unlikely promise has been fulfilled. A Southern president sits in the White House and Southerners dominate the leadership of both houses of Congress. But of course that is not what Wallace meant. Not at all. It seems that those who share his vision may have to turn to a Yankee—and an Irish Catholic at that—to do the job.

Whatever the size of the Buchanan vote in the Southern primaries, though, there is one vote he won't get. The aging George Wallace recently endorsed Bob Dole.

If at First You Don't Secede . . .

Last summer I went to an academic conference on the beautiful campus of Washington and Lee University, where we heard a paper that repaid that institution's hospitality by traducing the Confederate general whose name it bears. The historian who wrote the paper argued that, although Lee may have behaved in an appropriately submissive way after Appomattox, his constant harping on concepts like duty and reconciliation masked the persistence of some thoroughly unacceptable attitudes. One of the quotations presented as self-evidently incorrect was this, from a private letter Lee wrote to his admirer Lord Acton in 1866:

> I yet believe . . . the maintenance of the rights and authority reserved to the states and to the people not only essential to the adjustment of the general system, but the safeguard to the continuance of a free government. I consider it as the chief source of stability to our political system, whereas the consolidation of the states into one vast republic, sure to be aggressive abroad and despotic at home, will be the certain precursor of that ruin which has overwhelmed all those who have preceded it.

In the question period I asked this annoying Yankee, as one child of the sixties to another, just which part of that analysis he disagreed with.

Certainly Lee would get no argument from the scholar-diplomat George Kennan, who in his 1993 book *Around the Cragged Hill* proposed a "pipe dream," in which the United States would be devolved into a dozen "constituent republics." In Kennan's scheme each of these regional republics would exercise "a larger part of the present federal powers than one might suspect—large enough, in fact, to make most people gasp." Kennan proposed this arrangement because, in his view, "excessive size in a country results unavoidably in a diminished sensitivity of its laws and regulations to the particular needs . . . of individual localities and communities," especially in a country, like ours, with a tendency to legalistic and formulaic regulation rather than government based on "common sense and reasonable discrimination." The resulting "loss of intimacy between rulers and ruled," he argued, leads to "the impression of remoteness and impersonality on the part of government and of insignificance and helplessness on the part of the individual, and thus impair[s] the very meaning of citizenship." Moreover, Kennan observed, big countries suffer "the hubris of inordinate size," manifest in "a certain lack of modesty in the national self-image" and "a vulnerability to dreams of power and glory to which the smaller state is less easily inclined." In short, Kennan believes that centralized government in a nation as big as ours inevitably leads to—well, to despotism at home and aggression abroad.

Suspicion of centralized power has been a recurrent theme in American political thought, well established long before Patrick Henry and the Anti-Federalists opposed the ratification of the federal constitution. We might call it the Jeffersonian side of our national character as opposed to the Hamiltonian (although John Randolph and his fellow Tertium Quids thought Jefferson had dangerous monarchical tendencies). But the relative balance of regional and national loyalties has varied, both from time to time and from one part of the country to another.

Our nation's first two hundred years saw a seemingly irreversible consolidation of power at the federal level, proceeding by fits and starts, but always proceeding. Before the 1860s—some would say before the 1930s—we didn't have much of a central government, at least by modern standards, but now the Anti-Federalists' fears have been realized to a greater extent than they could have imagined. Corresponding to this political centralization, both as cause and effect, has been a long-term increase in national sentiment. Shelby Foote points out that before the Civil War the phrase *the United States* took a plural verb; for many antebellum Americans (and not just Southerners) their "country" was effectively their state. But the struggle ostensibly to preserve the Union in fact largely created one—certainly it created an overarching national identity quite different from what had existed before. In the years after Reconstruction American nationalism flourished, and it peaked in the 1890s, when even ex-Confederates and their children donned blue uniforms and went off to pursue America's imperial destiny overseas. A popular song of 1898 chortled that

Old Virginia's heart is happy,
And the Southland's fill'd with glee—
They are goin' to march to Cuba
Under Major General Lee!

(That was Fitzhugh Lee, Robert's nephew.)

But notice the words of that song. Southerners' renewed American patriotism did not make their sectional loyalties obsolete; in fact, those lower-level attachments largely reinforced the higher, as any Burkean would say they normally do. In 1898 and again during World War I, Southern boys were fighting (as another Tin Pan Alley song put it) "For Dixie and Uncle Sam." After Fort Sumter Southerners had been forced to choose between their regional and national identities; by the turn of the century, however, erstwhile Confederates had only to acknowledge that the preservation of the Union had been providential—in exchange, Congress returned captured Confederate battle flags to the Southern states, "Dixie" began to appear in compilations of *American* patriotic songs, and Robert E. Lee (though not Jefferson Davis) was taken into the national pantheon.

For almost a century that old compromise served the purpose of national unity well. (National *white* unity, that is: it is not accidental that it has come under attack with the increase in effective political representation of black Americans.) To be sure, sectional antagonism did occasionally surface. In 1930, for example, twelve Southerners, most of them associated with Vanderbilt University, published a manifesto called *I'll Take My Stand*, which one of them, Frank Owsley, later characterized as a protest against the North's "brazen and contemptuous treatment" of the South "as a colony and as a conquered province." A couple of the contributors went on to propose Kennanesque constitutional revisions, granting greater autonomy to the regions, and Donald Davidson warned that something of the sort was necessary if the United States was to endure. He imagined some future historian lecturing on the 1930s, saying: "At this point regional differences passed beyond the possibility of adjustment under the Federal system, and here, therefore, began the dismemberment of the United States, long since foreshadowed in the struggles of the eighteen-sixties."

But *I'll Take My Stand* was an aberration, of interest today mostly because several of the young contributors went on to become distinguished men of letters. The separatist impulse was never widespread, and in the event it was simply overwhelmed by the apparent need for national mobilization to address the economic distress of the Great Depression, then by mobilization for another World War, finally by the semipermanent mobilization of the Cold War. The need for Americans to pull together kept sectionalism in line; regional identities were seen as, at most, only colorful variations on a basic Americanism. And the rhetoric of "the American century" did have an appealing ring even to Southerners. Maybe especially to Southerners.

By now, the reader will have noticed that I have been speaking almost entirely of the South. As one of America's oldest regions, historically its most distinctive, and undeniably its most obstreperous, the South has usually taken the lead in these matters. (It has also done more than any other region to bring states' rights into disrepute, by linking that doctrine to propositions that were not just morally indefensible, at least in retrospect, but politically doomed.) True, when New Englanders found themselves being dragged into wars with England or Mexico, or obliged to abide by a federal fugitive slave law, even they could sound a lot like John C. Calhoun. But after Appomattox established who was to run the American show, it was mostly Southerners who were seen, and saw themselves, as "different." Other Americans were the norm from which Southerners differed.

It seems that the tables may now be turning. The shift in the regional balance of power that Kevin Phillips applauded in *The Emerging Republican Majority* (1969) and Kirkpatrick Sale deplored in *Power Shift: The Rise of the Southern Rim and Its Challenge to the Eastern Establishment* (1975) continues apace, and in *Dixie Rising: How the South Is Shaping American Values, Politics, and Culture* (1996), journalist Peter Applebome even claims that Southern dominance is beginning to extend to the cultural sphere. Things have reached the point where James Cobb, a recent president of the Southern Historical Association, wonders, in *his* book, *Redefining Southern Culture*, whether Southern identity will survive. What happens to an identity largely based on grievance, he asks, when there is not much left to complain about?

But Cobb's question is at least premature. The 1999 debut of the secessionist Southern Party got a good deal of media coverage, but it was announced in August, always a slow news month, and polls usually show support for Southern independence only in the high single digits. But Southern identification of a less political sort is a good deal more common than that. Nearly a third of self-identified Southerners say that being Southern is "very important" to them, two-thirds say it is at least "somewhat important," and, unlike neo-Confederatism, this attachment to the region cuts across racial lines.

Those numbers may or may not be lower than they would have been fifty years ago (we don't know for sure), but certainly the South is more like the rest of the country than it used to be—economically, demographically, and politically. While the South may be (as observers have liked to say for the past century) "rejoining the Union," though, some other American regions, largely dormant or merely latent for most of this century, may be becoming more important and self-conscious. Why this should be is the subject for another article or, better, for a book. Fortunately, the book exists. In *The Nine Nations of North America* (1981), journalist Joel Garreau observes that an increasing amount of the national action is now taking place at the level of entities like "Mex-America" (the Southwest), "Ecotopia" (the Pacific Northwest), and "the Breadbasket" (the Plains states). The boundaries of these diverse (in some ways increasingly diverse) regions do not correspond well to state or even national borders, but anyone who doubts their existence must lead a very sheltered life. The persistence of American regionalism is the flip side of George Kennan's observation that the United States is too big. A continental nation like ours *is* too big not to have distinctive regions.

And, as Kennan observed, a centralized government is virtually incapable of responding flexibly and creatively to that fact. Its laws and regulations by their nature treat citizens as interchangeable monads, the same in New Mexico, Oregon, Nebraska, and West Virginia. Whether run by Democrats or Republicans, subject only to the half-hearted restraint of the federal judiciary, it tends literally to make a federal case out of everything from cable television rates to the color of school buses, and—for all that many of these laws and regulations are passed in response to public opinion—is experienced by its citizens as ever more arrogant and intrusive. The heretofore "Southern" experience of seeing the institutions of government, commerce, and culture in alien hands is increasingly widespread.

At the same time, paradoxically, economic and political globalization may be increasing the significance of regional and other subnational loyalties, if only by reducing the importance and even the legitimacy of the nation-state. Each year offshore and multinational and cyber businesses render national economies less relevant and national authorities more frantic. It is not coincidence that the rise of "Europe" has corresponded with the revitalization of Scottish, Catalan, Lombard, and a half-dozen other autonomist movements.

In the American case, the collapse of Soviet Communism has removed a powerful external adhesive, and it remains to be seen what, if anything, will replace it. The "New World Order" is a concept that only a banker could love and only a mercenary would fight for. (As I heard a West Point professor ask recently, who wants to lie in "a corner of a foreign field that is forever NATO"?) If we are not to rally around the Stars and Stripes, most normal Americans will find subnational loyalties more plausible alternatives than attachment to some transnational alphabet organization.

So far regional sentiment and regional interests have received only muted expression in American politics (the South as usual aside), but I sometimes wonder whether we are not about to see a resurgence of sectionalism. If we do, it won't be just Southern this time.

Party Down

As the preceding essay mentions, the formation of the secessionist Southern Party was briefly big news, and Van Denton of the Raleigh News and Observer *"interviewed" me (by email) about it.*

N&O: So are folks who talk about the South seceding from the Union just whistling Dixie?

JSR: Well, you can judge for yourself. They want to talk to you about it, and they have things like websites to do it with. Some of them are just teasing, of course, but others are in dead earnest.

N&O: How seriously should we take the notion of a political party organizing with the goal of getting sixteen Southern states to secede?

JSR: In the short run, I think not very seriously. They intend to run candidates, and at the local level they may even elect a few, but I don't see them electing statewide candidates or US representatives any time soon. The major parties have arranged things so it is very difficult for third parties of any sort—ask any Libertarian. If they have any effect, I suspect it will come the way most third parties have made a difference: that is, by influencing major- party candidates, by endorsing them or threatening to run a spoiler candidate. If they get off the ground, we may hear more discussion about the appropriate balance of state and federal power, the meaning of the Tenth Amendment, and so on. Long-term, who knows? It has always puzzled me why a country as big and diverse as the United States should be assumed to be immune to the kind of separatist movements that you see in so many other, smaller, and historically more unified countries. These neo-secessionist folks are well aware of their European and Canadian counterparts, too—I imagine they keep in touch. Elsewhere in the world, it seems that globalization is increasing the importance of regions, if only by decreasing the importance of the old nation-states. That could happen here, I suppose.

N&O: The Southern Focus Poll shows that most people disagree that the South would be better off as a separate country today. What would you look for in the South that would signal a change in that attitude?

JSR: We've asked that question several times over the past seven years and you're right: support for an independent South tends to be in the high single or low double digits—and it depends to a considerable extent on how the question is asked, which suggests that it is not a very firm or well thought-out opinion. If more people are going to say that the South would be better off as a separate country, either they'll have to be persuaded or conditions will have to change. And persuading them won't be easy: it looks to me as if the South is doing pretty well these days. In fact, some other Americans have started to grumble about Southerners taking over the country. On the other hand, when it comes to a matter that isn't really on the agenda poll numbers may be mis-leading. Thirty-five years ago about the same percentage of Quebecois said they favored separation from Canada. That changed very quickly after the Parti Quebecois came along and made it a real possibility. I presume the Southern Party is hoping for something similar.

N&O: In 1948, we had Dixiecrats in the South who campaigned for states' rights. Do you see any similarities between the Dixiecrats of fifty years ago and the organizers of the Southern Party?

JSR: I am more struck by the differences. The Dixiecrats' official name was the National States Rights Democratic Party—notice the "National"—and by "states rights" they really meant the rights of Southern states to maintain racial segregation. They made no secret about that. They were unapologetic white supremacists. Their inten-tion from the get-go was to throw the presidential election into the House of Representatives and win some concessions from one or the other major party. The Southern Party folks I've read pretty vigor-ously deny that they have a racial agenda. Now, given the historical record of Southern nationalism, you probably ought to be suspicious about that, but it certainly is a rhetorical change of some importance.

N&O: In the 1990s, why do we find ourselves still talking about the South as a place apart from the rest of the United States?

JSR: Why not? In some respects it is. It is certainly the most distinctive and self-conscious of the major American regions right now, not to mention its distinctive history.

N&O: What makes the South distinct from the rest of the nation as a region and a culture?

JSR: Well, there's that history, for starters. But, in addition, there are differences in racial and religious composition, in attitudes toward a whole range of social issues, in more subtle things like speech and manners and taste. These are statistical differences, of course—tendencies, that's all—but that's pretty much true of ethnic and regional differences everywhere. Whether they're seen as important or not has less to do with how big they are than with whether they take on political significance or somehow become badges of identity.

N&O: Are we as different when it comes to political and economic philosophies as we are in some of those cultural factors?

JSR: Generally speaking, Southerners are more conservative on most issues. This is certainly true for Southern whites and on many issues for Southern blacks as well. So far these differences have been accommodated within the two-party system, though.

N&O: Let's talk about symbols for a second. The Southern Party has the Dixie Dingo as its official mascot. If a Southern country formed from the states of the old Confederacy, what would some of the other symbols be?

JSR: I haven't seen the Dixie Dingo, but any Southern separatist movement is going to have a problem when it comes to symbols. The obvious choice is to use the Confederate ones, as the Southern Party does, but that ties you to that particular version of what the South is all about, and greatly restricts your scope. For starters, it virtually guarantees that you'll be an almost all-white enterprise. Something with more universal appeal—say, one of those dancing pigs you see on the signs of barbecue joints—doesn't do as good a job of mobilizing your core support: I mean, nobody has died for it. It's a tricky business. You get a similar problem when you ask what positions you're going to take (or whether you're going to take any positions at all) on issues other than regional autonomy. Some nationalist groups elsewhere in the world have strong political agendas—some left-wing, some right-wing—and attract a cadre of activists who see independence as a way to enact those agendas. Others just say "We want independence—we'll fight about what to do with it after we have it." It seems to me that the more you include in your program the more strongly it will appeal to those who agree with it, but the fewer who will agree with it in the first place.

N&O: How about you. You're a Southerner. Are you ready for North Carolina to secede?

JSR: Not yet.

Our Kind of Yankee

This was written for a special issue of The American Enterprise *magazine on New York City, in response to the terrorist attack on the World Trade Center.*

In the days after September 11, when Americans were watching a lot of television, many of us heard a Texas man-in-the-street tell a network interviewer something like, "Being a Texan or New Yorker just isn't very important right now. We're all Americans." Soon after that, we heard about some South Carolina middle-school students who raised the money to buy a truck for some Brooklyn firefighters who lost theirs (along with seven comrades) at the World Trade Center.

What is going on here? Texans and South Carolinians playing kissy-face with *New York City*? Isn't New York the heart of Yankeedom? Isn't it the city Southerners love to hate?   ·

Well, like other Americans in that great red, Republican interior on the 2000 presidential election map, many Southerners do think at least occasionally of New York City as the Great Wen, the cesspool of iniquity, home of everything alien and vile. It has been suggested, not entirely in jest, that the city's evolution vindicates the Confederacy. The bill of particulars has several components.

First of all, there is a lot for everybody to dislike about New York: violent crack-heads, the welfare culture, deranged street people, dysfunctional public schools, periodic brushes with bankruptcy, wack-job politicians—even many New Yorkers complain about this stuff (often while taking a perverse sort of pride in being able to cope with it).

But Southerners have had some special reasons to dislike New York, starting with the fact that it is simply the most urban corner of America. A good many Southerners have seen city life as bad for both morals and manners. When Thomas Jefferson celebrated ownership of land and the farming life as the only sound basis for culture and society, he was writing in what was already an old Southern tradition.

The most eloquent statement of the Southern case against big cities probably came in 1930, with a manifesto by twelve Southern men of letters called *I'll Take My Stand: The South and the Agrarian Tradition.* More recently, Hank Williams Jr. has often put the sentiment to music: In one song, for example, he complains about New Yorkers who don't smile or speak to him because they are too busy trying to make money. Another of his songs, "If Heaven Ain't a Lot Like Dixie," says that if it ain't he would as soon go to hell—or to New York City.

Many Southerners have also taken a dim view of New York for serving as the great reception center and repository for foreign immigration. Although this may be changing, it was not that long ago that our Chambers of Commerce bragged about our "native-born" labor force. And John Rocker of Macon, Georgia, and the Atlanta Braves is not the only Southern boy who thinks Americans ought to speak English.

In general, ever since New York displaced Boston as the home of the ultra-Yankee, Southerners have tended to see whatever we dislike about Northerners as concentrated there. When we describe ourselves to pollsters as friendly, polite, hospitable, leisurely, religious, patriotic, traditional, conservative—well, it goes without saying who is not that way.

And what many of us really dislike about Northerners, and thus loathe in spades about New Yorkers, is their view of Southerners as yokels—if not as *Deliverance*-style Neanderthals. Wherever Northerners got their ideas of the South (and of course a Southerner wrote *Deliverance*), some of them have indeed been inclined to view us as a lesser breed. Consider Kirkpatrick Sale's scaremongering 1975 book, *Power Shift: The Rise of the Southern Rim and Its Challenge to the Eastern Establishment*, which extrapolated from economic and demographic trends to project the sort of nightmare future in which Sale's northeastern readers would have to choose between, say, a governor of Texas and a former senator from Tennessee for president. (One of the few pleasures of the 1992 Democratic convention for this Southerner was watching the expression on Mario Cuomo's face every time he said the word "Arkansas.")

I could go on, but the point is that there has been no love lost, in either direction, between New York City and the South. And in this, the South has merely been a hundred-proof stand-in for places like Nebraska, Idaho, Ohio, and many other parts of what some New Yorkers call "flyover country." Everybody knows this, don't they?

But, of course, it has not been quite that simple. Southerners, like other American heartlanders, have always been of two minds about the city. Some have looked on New York and New Yorkers with admiration, occasionally envy. Most of us can find at least something to admire about the place and its people.

For decades, of course, New York looked pretty good to *black* Southerners. In the first half of the twentieth century, hundreds of thousands, especially from Georgia and the Carolinas, packed their worldly goods and box lunches and rode the Chickenbone Special out of the Jim Crow South, following the drinking gourd to seek a better life in Harlem and Bedford Stuyvesant.

Many whites joined this exodus, especially a certain type of young Southern intellectual for whom The City has always been where it's happening (whatever "it" may be). North Carolina's Thomas Wolfe set the pattern in the 1920s, and forty years later Mississippi's Willie Morris epitomized it. Morris's wince-making memoir *New York Days* is awash in isn't-it-wonderful-that-I'm-a-part-of-you New York, New York gush. Even as confident and self-aware an expat as Tom Wolfe the younger (the Virginian who pretty well peeled, cored, and sliced the Big Apple in *Bonfire of the Vanities*) once confessed, "I still find New York exciting, to tell the truth. It's not the easiest way to live in the world, but I still get a terrific kick out of riding down Park Avenue in a cab at 2:30 in the morning and seeing the glass buildings all around. I have a real cornball attitude toward it, I suppose, which I think only somebody born far away from there would still have."

Southern writers and artists have historically *had* to look north to New York, because that is pretty much where the literary and artistic action was. Yet arty folk are not the only ones who have feared, deep down, that nothing signifies unless it is noticed on that thin sliver of asphalt stretching between the Hudson and the East River; plenty of hardheaded businesspeople feel the same. Atlanta, in particular, is full of the kind of strivers for whom the only thing worse than being looked down on by New Yorkers is being ignored by them. (For some reason, it seems to me, Houstonians aren't as other-directed. On the rare occasions when they think of New Yorkers at all, they're likely to feel sorry for them because they're not Texans.)

One might have thought that the South's astonishing economic development, the rise of Southern cities, and the end of *de jure* segregation—all of which have made the South more like New York, for better or for worse—would make New York City less alluring to some, and less repugnant to others. Increasingly, Southerners don't have to leave home to find urban, cosmopolitan, polyglot settings. Now that we have our own street crime, pollution, and traffic problems, there should be less reason to feel superior. Now that we have our own operas and publishing houses and big-league sports, there would seem to be less reason to be envious. But we still think of New York as different, and, in some ways, special.

No matter where we grew up, few of us have entirely escaped the romance of The City. We know about the mean streets, sure, but we can't shake the image of Gene Kelly dancing in them. Thanks to *Mad* magazine and the *New Yorker*, to Irving Berlin and Hollywood, I knew about Coney Island and Harlem long before I ever set foot in New York; I recognized that socialites lived on Park Avenue, bums in the Bowery, bohemians in Greenwich Village; I understood who worked on Wall Street, and Madison Avenue, and Broadway, and Tin Pan Alley.

New York is part of the mental furniture of all Americans, and—this is important—many of us think of the good things about New York as in some sense *ours.* We have proprietary feelings about the Metropolitan Opera, the Rockettes, the Statue of Liberty, and, yes, the World Trade Center. We feel attached to them whether we have seen them or not (and we may actually be more likely than the natives to have visited them). To say that those who destroyed the Twin Towers attacked New York City is like calling an assault on Mount Rushmore an attack on South Dakota.

* * *

But there is something more going on here. The aftermath of 9/11 reminded us that the New Yorkers we most often hear from are not the only people who live there. When Southerners and other outsiders dislike (or fawn on) "New Yorkers," the people they usually have in mind are the media and show business figures, politicians, business titans, and intellectuals we encounter on television: sophisticated, worldly, cosmopolitan (if you admire them); supercilious, smug, arrogant (if you don't).

These people are still there, of course, and they sure can grate. Shortly after September 11, for example, I heard Fran Leibowitz being snide on NPR about President Bush's reference to the "folks" responsible for the attacks. She apparently had that word associated with hayrides. But since last fall some of these obnoxious figures have been uncharacteristically subdued, and the attacks have highlighted a different kind of

New Yorker, one many Southerners and other Americans find more sympathetic.

There has always been more to New York City than the big shots. Ever since the heyday of Jacksonian Democracy, an on-again off-again alliance has existed between ordinary Southerners (that is, most of us) and New York's working people. After the Civil War and Reconstruction, this coalition was famously described as one of "rum, Romanism, and rebellion." Later, it elected Franklin Roosevelt to four terms. Later still, it reassembled to elect Richard Nixon and Ronald Reagan.

Most Southerners who know New York (I lived there for five years) know that there is a kind of outer-borough New York guy (it's almost always a guy) we get along with just fine. He is working-class and usually Irish, Jewish, or Italian, but these days sometimes black or Latino. He is what historian Paul Fussell called a "high prole," largely defined by his skills and "pride and a conviction of independence." When Fussell identifies disdain for social climbing, fondness for hunting and gambling and sports, and unromantic attitudes toward women as his other traits, Southerners should recognize the Northern variety of what we used to call a "good old boy" (before the label escaped captivity and lost all precision): "A solid, reliable, unpretentious, stand-up, companionable, appropriately loose, joke-sharing feller," as Roy Blount Jr. describes him.

The bond between Southerners and this kind of Northerner often does have to do with sports. Recall that "Broadway Joe" Namath of the New York Jets, the Pennsylvanian who became an archetypal New Yorker, launched his public persona as "Joe Willie" Namath of the Alabama Crimson Tide. (Namath even played a Confederate soldier in a seriously bad movie called *The Last Rebel*.) Or consider Coach Frank McGuire, from Saint Xavier High School and Saint John's University in Queens, who steered the North Carolina Tar Heels to an undefeated season and a national championship, and later coached at South Carolina. The New York players McGuire recruited used to bemuse the locals with their habit of crossing themselves before foul shots. And then there is Coach Jimmy Valvano of North Carolina State University, another New Yorker who led a Southern team to a national championship and endeared himself even to fans of rival teams with his good-old-boy humor. After his team blew a lead to lose to the archrival Tar Heels, a fan wrote Valvano, "If you ever do that again, I'll come over and shoot your dog." Valvano said that when he wrote back that he didn't have a dog, the man replied: "I'm sending you a dog. But don't get too attached to him." (True, Valvano, like McGuire, eventually ran afoul of the NCAA's picky regulations and lost his job, but Southerners don't mind a whiff of corruption in our heroes: It humanizes them.)

This is the kind of New Yorker we saw on television after September 11: policemen, firemen, rescue workers—ordinary folks. Their accents may have sounded funny to Southern ears, but they are our kind of Yankee: unpretentious, hard working when they have to be, offhandedly courageous. Mayor Giuliani may or may not be one of them by nature, but in that context he sure looked it, and most of us found him wholly admirable.

The post-9/11 fortitude and determination of New York's plain folk have led many of us to conclude that Tom Wolfe was wrong when, in one of his most famous essays, he described the stockcar racer Junior Johnson, from Ingle Hollow, Wilkes County, North Carolina, as "the last American hero." We have been reminded that there are some guys from places like Red Hook, Brooklyn, New York, who surely qualify as well.

IX

But Let's Talk About Me

Mixing in the Mountains

This was written for a Conference on Southern Autobiography organized by my friend Bill Berry at the University of Central Arkansas.

One January day in 1996, I picked up the *Wall Street Journal* to find a story headlined "Rural County Balks at Joining Global Village." It told about Hancock County, Tennessee, which straddles the Clinch River in the ridges hard up against the Cumberland Gap, where Virginia, Kentucky, and Tennessee meet. This is a county that has lost a third of its 1950 population, which was only ten thousand to begin with. A third of those left are on welfare, and half of those with jobs have to leave the county to work. The only town is Sneedville, population thirteen hundred, which has no movie theater, no hospital, no dry cleaner, no supermarket, and no department store.

I read this story with a good deal of interest, because the nearest city of any consequence is my hometown of Kingsport, thirty-five miles from Sneedville as the crow flies, but an hour and a half on mountain roads. (If you don't accept my premise that Kingsport is a city of consequence, Knoxville is a little further from Sneedville, in the opposite direction.)

The burden of the article was that many of Hancock County's citizens are indifferent to the state of Tennessee's desire to hook them up to the information superhighway—a job that will take some doing, especially for the one household in six that doesn't have a telephone. The *Journal* quoted several Hancock Countians to the effect that they didn't see the point. The reporter observed that the county offers "safe, friendly ways, pristine rivers, unspoiled forests and mountain views," and that many residents simply "like things the way they are."

So far a typical hillbilly-stereotype story. But the sentence that really got my attention was this: "Many families here belong to 100 or so Melungeon clans of Portuguese and American Indian descent, who tend to be suspicious of change and have a history of self-reliance."

Now, I picture the typical *Wall Street Journal* reader as a harried commuter on the Long Island Railroad, and I wondered what in the world he made of that. What is this "Melungeon" business? And what are *Portuguese* doing up those remote east Tennessee hollers? You might well ask.

Ethnic diversity is not what comes immediately to mind when we think of the American South—perhaps especially not when we think of the Southern mountains. The historian George Tindall once characterized the South as "the biggest single WASP nest this side of the Atlantic," and, in fact, all of the US counties where over half the inhabitants claim only English ancestry are in the Kentucky hills (not far from Sneedville, actually). But there has been more diversity in the South than many people suppose. Intermixed with these British whites, with West African blacks and the scattered remains of the South's American Indian population, there are these odd . . . enclaves. They are mostly small, but there are a *lot* of them. Louisiana has its Creoles and Cajuns, of course, but also pockets of Hungarians and Canary Islanders. Texas has its well-known German settlements, but also counties settled by Czechs and Poles. You will find Greeks in Tarpon Springs, Florida. Mississippi has Chinese in the Delta, and Lebanese here and there. There are Italians in former truck-farming colonies in Louisiana, Arkansas, and eastern North Carolina. And there are Druse in east Tennessee (also not far from Sneedville).

Few of these exotic groups have been as little-known or poorly understood as those the sociologist Edgar Thompson called the "little races" of the South. Every Southern state except Arkansas and Oklahoma has at least one group like the Red Bones of Louisiana and Texas, the Turks and Brass Ankles of South Carolina, the Issues of Virginia, the Lumbee and Haliwa and so-called Cubans of North Carolina, or the Cajans of Alabama. The 1950 census identified over twenty of these populations in the South, numbering from a few hundred to a few thousand, often isolated in swamps or mountain coves. The Melungeons are one of the largest of these groups. Estimates of their numbers are imprecise, for reasons I will get to, but they range from about five thousand to about fifteen thousand, scattered around east Tennessee, southwest Virginia, and southeastern Kentucky, and concentrated in the area around Sneedville.

Like most of the other little races, the Melungeons have been stereotyped as inbred, violent, and degenerate. The threat that "The Melungeons will get you" was once widely used to frighten small children. In one of the earliest journalistic accounts of the group, published in 1891, Miss Will Allen Dromgoole described them as "shiftless, idle, thieving, and defiant of all law, distillers of brandy, almost to a man"; "a great nuisance," "exceedingly illiterate," "unforgiving," and "in most cases filthy." She deprecated their "habit of chewing tobacco and spitting upon the floors" and "their ignorance or defiance of the distinction between *meum* and *tuum*." She observed that "they are exceedingly immoral, yet are great shouters and advocates of religion." She called them "'born rogues,' close, suspicious, inhospitable, untruthful, cowardly, and, to use their own word 'sneaky.'"

And Miss Dromgoole's was a *sympathetic* treatment. Forty years later, a compilation of east Tennessee folklore implied even worse:

> Folks left them alone because they were so wild and devil-fired and queer and witchy. If a man was fool enough to go into Melungeon country and if he come back without being shot, he was just sure to wizzen and perish away with some ailment nobody could name. Folks said terrible things went on, blood drinking and devil worship and carryings-on that would freeze a good Christian's spine bone.

Like many stereotypes, this one had a few elements of truth in it, mixed with outright slander, grotesque exaggeration, and a good deal of self-fulfilling prophecy. It is known that the Melungeons began to move into east Tennessee in the 1790s from western Virginia and North Carolina. It appears that they came simply to be left alone, to escape the contempt and persecution of their neighbors in Virginia and Carolina. As east Tennessee began to fill up with Scotch-Irish settlers, they moved on once again, this time from the fertile bottomlands up the hollers and onto the ridges. By the 1840s they were poor farmers on poor land—"poor as gully dirt" as their neighbors put it. Remote from a civil authority that was indifferent if not hostile, they were viewed as pariahs and largely a law unto themselves. Like some of the other little races, they turned to a variety of illegal activities to support themselves: among them moonshining (as we have heard), thievery, and counterfeiting.

One widely told story has it that the Melungeons were skilled metalworkers, who used to produce fine counterfeit silver pieces—very popular because they had a higher silver content than the federal issue. That may be apocryphal, but it is a matter of record that during the Civil War the "Melungeon Marauders" raided Confederate supply trains and, it is said, the homesteads of absent Confederate soldiers. This was more a matter of fighting against the Confederacy than fighting for the Union—it is also said that they raided an occasional Union supply train—but it reinforced the suspicion and fear that already existed and left a legacy of bitterness that lasted well into this century.

Who *are* these people? The adjective that occurs again and again in connection with the Melungeons is "mysterious." When Miss Dromgoole asked their Republican state representative about them, he told her, "A Malungeon [*sic*] isn't a nigger, and he isn't an Indian, and he isn't a white man. God only knows *what* he is. *I* should call him a *Democrat*, only he always votes the Republican ticket." At one time or another it has been argued that they are descended from ancient Carthaginians, the Lost Tribes of Israel, twelfth-century Welsh explorers, the DeSoto and the Pardo expeditions, the Lost Colony of Roanoke Island, and shipwrecked mariners from several different swarthy nations. One unflattering theory (from that same folklore compilation) has it that Satan was driven from Hell by his henpecking wife and settled in east Tennessee because it reminded him of home. The Melungeons, by this account, are descended from "Old Horny" and an Indian woman. The Melungeons themselves always accepted the Indian part, but as for the rest they have consistently told outsiders what they told the *Wall Street Journal* reporter: that they are Portuguese, or (as it used to be pronounced) "Porty-gee."

And, incidentally, until recently they have resented the word "Melungeon," which was used by outsiders as a derogatory epithet—although nobody knows *its* origins or original meaning. Some say it's from the French *mélange*, or from the Greek *melan* (black), or from "malingerer," or from some corruption of the common surname Mullins, or from the Portuguese *melungo*, which means "shipmate." As Brewton Berry concluded thirty years ago, however, "The truth is nobody has the faintest idea where the name came from."

For my purposes, what the group's remote connections may have been is less important than what they have become over the years. Recent anthropometric and genealogical studies have made it clear that the Melungeons, like most of the other little races, incorporate genetic material from a combination of whites, blacks, and Indians—that they are, in other words, what anthropologists call a "tri-racial isolate."

To be sure, they are markedly "whiter" than most other tri-racial groups. In the 1960s, one research team estimated the European contribution to the Melungeon gene pool at something between 82 and 94 percent—probably nearer the latter—and they drew this conclusion from a sample of identified group members, obviously excluding any who had chosen to "pass" into the larger white community. As it turns out, some sort of Iberian contribution is not out of the question; in fact, it looks more likely now than most outsiders would have guessed thirty years ago. But that is a lengthy and still largely speculative excursion that I will pass up here.

This research also found clear genetic evidence for the Melungeons' Indian ancestry, although the genealogical thread is elusive. One student of this matter, Virginia DeMarce, concludes that the Indian strain came to east Tennessee with the original Melungeon settlers, who acquired it in the surprising fluid racial matrix of the seventeenth-century Virginia Tidewater. That may well be, but it could also have been reinforced since then through intermarriage with sociologically "white" neighbors, many of whom are proud to claim Indian blood (usually Cherokee). In 1995 I slipped a question into a national public opinion survey, asking the respondents whether they had any American Indian ancestors. I thought the numbers would be high, but they surprised even me. Half of all black Americans claim Indian ancestry, and so do 40 percent of native Southern whites (twice the rate for non-Southern whites). White Southerners these days (especially young ones) are more likely to claim an ancestor who was an Indian than one who was a Confederate soldier. Make of that what you will.

Anyway, the Melungeons' problems, historically, have not been due to their *Indian* heritage. Like the South's other tri-racial groups, they have been ostracized and discriminated against because their neighbors suspected that they were, as one told Miss Dromgoole, "Portuguese niggers." (Do not imagine that the absence of racial diversity in the mountains means the absence of racial prejudice.) Until recently most Melungeons have vociferously denied any African American connection, and simply refused to accept the attendant legal restrictions. As one mother told Brewton Berry, "I'd sooner my chilluns grow up ig'nant like monkeys than send 'em to that nigger school." But those neighbors were probably right: DeMarce has now established clear lines from several Melungeon families back to eighteenth-century free black families in Virginia and the Carolinas.

This genealogical research is recent, however, and, as the anthropometric data suggest, most Melungeons are physically indistinguishable from the general white population. Consequently, after the Tennessee constitution of 1834 disfranchised "free persons of color," many east Tennesseans who had been "FC" (free colored) in the 1830 census turned up in 1840 as white, and the vast majority of Melungeons have been white for purposes of enumeration and segregation ever since. On those rare occasions when the question wound up in court, the Melungeon view prevailed. In an 1872 decision, for example, the Tennessee Supreme Court accepted the argument that the Melungeons were descended from the Carthaginians, thus legalizing the marriage of a Melungeon woman to a white man and legitimizing their child.

If the Melungeons escaped the more rigorous forms of legal discrimination during the Jim Crow period, however, that is not to say that they haven't faced other sorts of stigma and exclusion, as my earlier quotations suggest. But most could escape even those impediments by moving to communities where their origins weren't known, and it seems that many did. Given the group's documented high birth rates and the relative stability of their population count, it must be the case that over the years a great many have simply slipped away and joined the general white population.

Moreover, apparently love conquers all. There is undeniable evidence of more or less constant intermarriage (not to mention less formal liaisons) between Melungeons and their white neighbors. Just one indicator: To the half-dozen original Melungeon names and their dozen or so variants, one recent list of "Melungeon-related surnames" adds over a hundred others, most of them English and Scotch-Irish names common in the Southern Appalachians, obviously acquired by intermarriage. It probably helps that to the extent that there is a distinctive Melungeon "look," it is a strikingly attractive one, among both men and women.

Anyway, one result of this race-mixing (to use the old-fashioned term) is that the Melungeon population must be even "whiter" than it used to be. Another is that a great many natives of present-day east Tennessee and southwest Virginia must have Melungeon cousins, if not Melungeon ancestors.

And here we come to autobiography.

When I was growing up in east Tennessee, I heard about the Melungeons, these strange folk who lived back in the hills and had olive complexions. My father, a doctor, also told me that they often have six fingers. (Now, the literature I have been reading lately does not mention that. Some tri-racial groups like the Wesort of Delaware do have a tendency to "polydactylism," but if the Melungeons do, it hasn't made the papers. Nevertheless, as a child I believed what my father told me.)

Dad also told me a story. It seems there was this Melungeon woman who sold whiskey from her cabin and was so enormously fat that

when the revenue agents came to arrest her they couldn't get her out
the door. When she died they had to knock out a wall to remove her
body.

This story has been widespread. It turns up in east Tennessee folklore, it figures in a novel by Kentucky writer Jesse Stuart, and it turns
out to be true. The woman was Mahala "Big Haley" Mullins. Born in
the 1820s, she married a son of the Melungeon patriarch "Irish Jim"
Mullins (also known as "Hare-lipped Jim"), and bore him some nineteen or twenty children. Her weight apparently never approached the
seven hundred pounds of legend, but it did suffice to confine her to her
Hancock County cabin, from which she sold high-quality moonshine
until her death in 1902. As one deputy sent to arrest her reported, she
was "catchable" but not "fetchable."

Anyway, that was pretty much it for my youthful knowledge of
Melungeons. To the extent that they impinged on my consciousness
at all, they were not figures that inspired fear or hatred. Even as a child
I hadn't thought of them as bogeymen. As far as I can recall, I had always
thought of them as pitiful specimens or colorful exotics, although as
far as I knew, I had never met one.

One fine day when I was sixteen or seventeen and newly armed with
a driver's license, my buddy Bill and I were out cruising the countryside. We often did this, stopping along the way to examine old pecker-
wood lumber mills, buying soft drinks and two-bit punches on illegal
punchboards at country stores and filling stations, one time trying to
find someone with something to trade for Bill's broken-down motor-
cycle. . . . This day, for some reason, we started sharing our ignorance
about Melungeons. Having nothing better to do, we decided to go find
some, and we set a course for Sneedville.

I wish this story had some drama to it, some fateful encounter or
embarrassing discovery, but as a writer of nonfiction, I am stuck with
the facts. What happened was that we cruised Sneedville's down-at-
the-heels main street, circumspectly eyeing the locals (we knew better
than to stare). We were checking for extra fingers, but we didn't see
any. Nor did we see any "olive" skin, which we imagined to be green.
We stopped in a general store to buy some junk food—I was partial to
Dolly Madison cream-filled cupcakes—and we made idle conversation
with the man behind the counter. We talked about this and that, but
not about Melungeons. Oddly, for a couple of bumptious teenage city
boys, we were reluctant even to say the word: it didn't seem *polite*. So
we left Sneedville no wiser than we had come.

It must have been about that same time that the sociologist Brewton Berry went to Hancock County. He was doing research for his book *Almost White*, and, of course, scientific inquiry licenses all sorts of bad manners. But Berry didn't learn much either. Unlike Bill and me, he at least knew what his prey were likely to be named and what they actually tend to look like, but when he asked various likely prospects if they were Melungeons they invariably denied it—although they usually suggested that there were some living in the next holler.

Some twenty years later, in the 1970s, my kid sister, a writer, also went to Sneedville to research the subject. But her impolite questions were no more fruitful than Berry's. People pretended not to know what she was talking about, or denied that there were any Melungeons left. Even in the late '80s, when the English-based travel writer Bill Bryson detoured to Sneedville on a tip from a London journalist, all he got was "Don't know nothin' about that. You want your oil checked?" As he drove away, discouraged, he writes, "High up the hill I began to encounter shacks set back in clearings in the woods, and peered at them in the hope of glimpsing a Melungeon or two. But the few people I saw were white."

Now, of course, they are coming out to reporters for the *Wall Street Journal*. They're back and they're proud. You can read all about it in a book by a fellow named Brent Kennedy, who heads up an organization called the Melungeon Research Committee. Kennedy's book, published in 1994, is called *The Melungeons: The Resurrection of a Proud People. An Untold Story of Ethnic Cleansing in America*. As you might gather from its title, it is a rather rum little book, a mixture of genealogy, autobiography, more or less reliable history, and special pleading—something like this essay, as a matter of fact.

As I read it, I noticed something I found very peculiar. Kennedy's history of the Melungeons' wanderings offered a striking parallel to the history of some of my own ancestors, who moved in the first decades of the nineteenth century from Ashe County in western North Carolina to mountains of east Tennessee and southwest Virginia.

Yes, I thought: very odd. Then I encountered that list of Melungeon family names I mentioned earlier. Although none of the half-dozen classic Melungeon names can be found in my family tree, nine others from Kennedy's list turn up among the southwest Virginians on my father's side. Some of those names, like Hill, White, and Burton, are too common to signify, but Phipps and Reeves and Tolliver are rarer.

Swindall and Rasnick are rarer still, and anyone named Vanover is almost certainly kin to me.

Finally, I took a close look at Kennedy's own family tree. Some of his ancestors' names looked dimly familiar. Later, my sister told me that there is a reason for that: they are ours, too—hers and mine. If Kennedy is right about their being Melungeons (and why would anyone make *that* up?), well. . . . A few years ago, I spoke on a program with the poet and novelist Ishmael Reed, who comes from Chattanooga. He talked about his mixed ancestry—African, Indian, and Scotch-Irish—and referred offhandedly to race-mixing in the east Tennessee mountains. Since we share the same last name, I got a laugh when it came my turn to speak by referring to "my cousin Ishmael." Even then I was not joking, but now, it seems, I would have even less reason to be.

In her pioneering article on the Melungeons, Miss Dromgoole reveals an interesting misconception: "A race of Mulattoes cannot exist as these Melungeons have existed," she wrote. "The Negro race goes from Mulattoes to quadroons, from quadroons to octoroons and there it stops. *The octoroon women bear no children.*"

Think about that: "Octoroon women bear no children." Like mules. Who knows how many genteel Southern white women held that comforting belief—comforting, that is, to one who accepted the "one drop" rule of racial identification that was enshrined in the laws of many states. But in one sense Miss Dromgoole was right. Not only is there *no word* for people with one black great-great-grandparent; sociologically speaking, it is almost true that there are *no such people.*

After I read Kennedy's book, I got out my old high-school yearbook, the *Maroon and Gray* of the Dobyns-Bennett High School Indians. ("Indians," huh?) With some trepidation, I opened the book. I paged through it, looking up old friends and classmates and cousins whose privacy I will protect here, but who bear the classic Melungeon family names. As often as not, the features that looked back at me resembled those in the photographs in Brent Kennedy's book. Of course they were the same kids I had always known—it didn't matter at all—but how about that yearbook title? Gray, of course, mixes black and white. And the noun "maroon," as *Webster's* tells us, can mean "a fugitive Negro slave" or the descendant of one. . . . No, just coincidence. Surely. (Give me six, bro'!)

Among the Baptists

This was written for another of Bill Berry's conferences on autobiography, this one after he had moved to the University of Tennessee at Chattanooga.

Lately we seem to have entered the Age of the Memoir. All sorts of people are now committing their recollections to paper, despite the fact that many of them apparently don't have much of interest to recall. And those who do—well, I often find myself wishing they hadn't. Old-fashioned writers of memoirs usually asked, implicitly, to be admired for what they had accomplished, but these days a lot of folks seem to be asking to be admired not for what they have done but for what has been done to them. (I think we may have Oprah Winfrey to thank for that.) You may gather that I am not happy about this development, and you are right. I have read a lot of memoirs in the last few years, out of some warped sense of obligation, and nine times out of ten I have not wanted to thank the author for sharing.

I don't want anyone to feel that way about this autobiographical account, so you won't be hearing much about my youthful suffering. I'm not even saying that I had any. I like Bill Bennett's answer when someone asked him about using drugs in college: "If I have any confessions to make I'll make them to a priest." Just so: If I have any whining to do I'll do it to a psychotherapist. No, one of my heroes is the great libertarian Albert Jay Nock, author of *Memoirs of a Superfluous Man*, one of the most reticent autobiographies of all time. Nock wrote that

> whatever a man may do or say, the most significant thing about him is what he thinks; and significant also is how he came to think it, why he continued to think it, or if he did not continue, what the influences were which caused him to change his mind.

You may find that a desiccated, intellectual view, but it's my view and I'm sticking to it.

That means I have a problem. I have spent most of my life studying the American South, so the obvious topic is how I came to be interested in that, and why I wound up studying it the way I have. But I have told that story elsewhere, at immodest length. The only other subject I have thought about seriously is the so-called Anglo-Catholic movement in the nineteenth-century Church of England. I wrote a book about that. A rare book. I didn't plan it that way, that's just the way it worked out. (I stole that line from Will Campbell.) To judge from the sales figures, not many people share my arcane interest, but there is a biographical explanation for it, and maybe that story *is* a Southern story, of a sort.

*   *   *

I grew up an Episcopalian in Kingsport, in upper east Tennessee, which has to be one of the furthest-flung corners of the Anglican Communion. Where I come from Episcopalians were and still are a tiny minority, outnumbered not just by Baptists and Methodists but by Presbyterians and Campbellites and all manner of Pentecostals. When I was in grade school my teachers sometimes killed time by asking students to go around the room and say where they went to church. Invariably I was the only Episcopalian. (I should say that all of this was in the early 1950s—well before the Supreme Court started meddling with religious expression in the public schools.)

Now, please don't think I am complaining. I know some children don't like feeling different, but I rather enjoyed it—at least in this respect. I was cocky enough to feel that being the only Episcopalian made me special. And of course there was no stigma attached to it. I don't think my churchmanship was actually an advantage (although, looking back, I can see that it was a *sign* of advantage), but it was not a drawback, or a handicap. I was not like the poor Jehovah's Witness who had to leave the room when the class had a Halloween party, or the Jewish boy who sat outside during the weekly visit of the Bible teacher, or even the few Catholic kids, who had their own grade school and lived in a sort of parallel universe as far as we were concerned.

True, Southerners do sometimes call my people "whiskey-palians," referring to our noncompliance with the Eleventh Commandment of Evangelical Protestantism, but I never heard that label in Kingsport. The one time I ran into anything other than matter-of-fact acceptance from my schoolmates, it was not a matter of hostility but of innocent curiosity. A boy who attended the Church of God, in the mill village down the hill, approached me once and said that his preacher said that we Episcopalians "worshipped the golden calf," and he wanted to know if that was true. I denied it more vigorously than I would now that I understand what the preacher meant.

To explain how I wound up with this peculiar affiliation requires an excursion into genealogy, but Southerners tend to confuse biography and genealogy anyway. Briefly: My mother made me what I am.

There were a lot of other possibilities. Like many Southern high-landers, my father's people were mostly Germans and Scotch-Irish who came down the Great Wagon Road from Pennsylvania in the eighteenth century. They settled in the hills of southwestern Virginia, near the Kentucky and Tennessee lines. These folks were teachers, preachers, and small farmers. Most were Unionists in the 1860s, but there were enough Confederates to spice things up. Their churches were ethnic ones—Lutheran and Reformed and Brethren for the Germans, Presbyterian for the Ulstermen. Despite his Scotch-Irish name, my Grandfather Reed was born into the Church of the Brethren, a German pietist sect whose practice of baptizing by triple immersion gave them the nickname "Dunkards." Somewhere along the line a Reed evidently married a "Dutch" *frau*, and the children took their mother's religion.

My grandmother's ancestors were much the same—in fact, many were the same people, since she and my grandfather were second cousins. (Yes, there is a point at which my family tree doesn't branch.)

Granddad's first job was as a schoolteacher, but Grandmom, who was also a teacher, taught in the girl's reformatory in Richmond to put him through medical school. (He worked part-time as medical officer for the Confederate veterans' home.) After medical school they went back home to Dickinson County, but when George Eastman founded the Tennessee Eastman Corporation in 1920, to make film base for his cameras, Granddad saw his chance and took it. He moved fifty miles or so, across the state line, to the new town of Kingsport, and set up the first hospital there.

At some point (I am not sure when) he marked his upward mobility by becoming a Southern Baptist—albeit one with a marked taste for whiskey and poker—and my father was raised in Kingsport's First Baptist Church. If I had been brought up in his boyhood religion, I guess I would have to find something else to write about. But, as I said, I got my religion from my mother.

She is a Yankee girl, true blue—from Rochester, New York. My father met her when he went to the University of Rochester on an Eastman scholarship. After he finished medical school and became a doctor like his father, he married her and brought her back to Kingsport. Her maiden name was Greene, anglicized from Gruen, and she got it from a line of Alsatian millers, who may well have been Jewish in Alsace, although they got off the boat in the New World as Protestants. But her Grandfather Greene married a Griswold. That's old Yankee stock—none older. The Griswolds came to Connecticut in the early seventeenth century from Warwickshire, where they had been ever since the Angles and Saxons pushed out the Celts. In storage somewhere in the San Diego museum is a bust of my Griswold great-grandmother that was made for a turn-of-the-century anthropometric exhibit to illustrate the 100-percent pure Anglo-Saxon type. (No kidding.) Her people were mostly Congregationalists, although for some reason her son, my grandfather, was Methodist.

But my mother's religion came from *her* mother. Grandma Greene came from the Anglo-Irish, that race of poets, soldiers, and rogues whose church was the established, Protestant Church of Ireland, the Anglican church of "the ascendancy," the Irish version of Episcopalianism. My father adopted my mother's genteel religion early on, with (he says) a great sense of relief. He had never forgiven the Southern Baptists for some hellfire and damnation preaching that gave him nightmares as a boy. My brothers, sisters, and I were christened as Episcopalians before we were old enough to have an opinion in the matter, and although I have drifted away from the church now and again, I have never been tempted by any other variety of religious expression.

In the Kingsport of my youth Episcopalians were rare, as I said, but there were enough of us to support the small church of Saint Paul's. Many were transplants like my mother, the families of executives at Eastman or one of the other Yankee-owned industries that gave the so-called Model City its economic base. A few were from the old low-church tradition of Virginia, Carolina, and the Cotton South—the church that buried Robert E. Lee and Booker T. Washington and William Faulkner. (How's that for a trivia question?) What we did not have at Saint Paul's were natives of east Tennessee or southwest Virginia (a few converts like my father aside). And of course there was a social-class element to this, although I could not have articulated it at the time. Our congregation was made up mostly of the families of executives and professional men: its social range didn't extend much below the upper-middle class.

The church itself was a small stone building, built to a self-consciously Olde English model. Before the big ungainly parish hall was added, it looked like something you might have found in the Cotswolds. It was on the edge of downtown, though not on Kingsport's imposing, central "church circle." That was reserved for the columned edifices of First Baptist, First Presbyterian, First Methodist, and Broad Street Methodist. (The two Methodist churches had been built before the 1939 reunion of the Northern and Southern denominations.)

Saint Paul's was served by a remarkable priest, the man who baptized my father, me, and eventually my first child. No novelist could have invented a more English name than that of the Reverend Leicester Kent, although Mr. Kent was, in fact, from Ohio. Before he came to Kingsport he had spent some years as archdeacon of the Yukon, traveling by dogsled to remote congregations of Indians and Eskimos. He had a very distinctive voice: I can only describe it by saying that it was perfect for the role of Santa Claus, which he played every evening in December on the local radio station, reading children's letters and talking about his preparations for the big night. When his young parishioners asked how come Santa Claus sounded just like him, he said that living at the cold North Pole must have affected Santa's voice the same way living in the cold Yukon had affected his.

Mr. Kent was and still is to my mind the model of an Anglican parish clergyman. After his death I learned that he had corresponded for some years with Carl Jung, and I recall that he was an early reader and admirer of C. S. Lewis. Our little parish library stocked the Chronicles of Narnia and *The Screwtape Letters*, and, believe it or not, I remember learning as a teenager the words *agape* and *eros* from a sermon that must have been based on Lewis (although Lewis's book *Four Loves* was not published until several years later).

Mr. Kent was not on the rota of local clergymen who came, one a week, to our schools' assemblies. Someone told me later that he didn't belong to the local ministerial association because black ministers were not allowed to join, and that may have been. It would have been in character. Although he didn't preach any sort of social gospel that I recall, quiet witness was certainly his style. I remember the time when our small youth group, the House of Young Churchmen, met in the parish house with a group of black teenagers from Kingsport's AME church to make palm crosses for Palm Sunday. This was the first and only racially integrated social event I experienced until I went to college in Massachusetts. I believe it would still be unusual—and not just in the South. Certainly it was remarkable for Tennessee in 1956.

In Anglican terms, Saint Paul's was characterized by low-church liturgy and broad-church theology, although I didn't know that at the time. I was far more familiar with our differences from other Protestant denominations than with our differences from other Episcopal churches. One summer, though, when I was about fourteen, I went to church camp at Monteagle. Not only was it a novel experience to be surrounded by several hundred teenage Episcopalians, I distinctly remember some young people from Chattanooga who called their minister "Father Jim" (or something like that), distinguished themselves by what were to me unpredictable crossings and bowings in chapel, spoke of incense and other mysteries, and adopted a somewhat superior and pitying attitude toward the rest of us. This was my first encounter with "high church" Episcopalianism, and I confess that I was envious.

But back home in Kingsport I spent more time worshipping with Evangelical Protestants than with my fellow Episcopalians. Besides the ministers who came to the school assembly each week, there was an itinerant lady Bible teacher who visited each grade-school class. Naturally each morning at school began with prayer on the PA system (student-led, beginning in junior high) and our music program included a healthy dose of hymns and other more or less religious music. I remember in particular "The Old Rugged Cross" and "The Little Brown Church in the Vale." (The chorus of that last one used to crack up us nasty adolescent boys. In our weekly music assemblies we would *shout* it: "Oh-oh come! come! come! come!") When I went to college up North, one of my best friends was an Arkansas lad, raised as a Christian Scientist. Among the many things we had in common, we discovered, was nostalgic attachment to the same Baptist and Methodist hymns.

I mentioned the House of Young Churchmen (most of whom were young churchwomen, actually). It was a valiant but ultimately rather sad affair: a half-dozen of us, a dozen at most. Nothing to compare to the legions of the "MYF" (Methodist Youth Fellowship), or the Baptists' Royal Ambassadors. For some reason most of my best friends were Methodists—including eventually my girlfriend, now my wife—and I often went to the MYF, just to be with them. I even went with them one summer to the Methodist church camp at Buffalo Mountain, Tennessee. (I remember distinctly that it was the summer of the Everly Brothers'

"Bye Bye Love," which makes it 1957.) MYF piety was very much what the Brits call "happy-clappy," so there was a lot of singing and sharing on the agenda at Buffalo Mountain, but it was not oppressive: better than school, actually. The last night of camp we sat in the big outdoor amphitheater, sang and prayed and concluded by signing cards pledging that we would not drink or smoke. For most of us—fifteen years old, with no driver's license in a dry county—drinking was only an aspiration, but a good many had already taken up with Lady Nicotine. I remember walking down the hill from the service, feeling solemn and committed as only a sentimental teenager can, when a semi-hoodlum friend named Ritchie pulled a Marlborough pack from the rolled-up sleeve of his T-shirt and threw it into the woods. Amazed, I asked him if he had taken the pledge. "Naw," he said. "Damn pack's empty." That shattered the solemnity, for sure.

Not too much later, I confess, I lost my youthful faith. It was a gradual process, proceeding through a sort of deism to agnosticism, helped along by books like Thomas Paine's *Age of Reason* and Bertrand Russell on *Why I Am Not a Christian*. (I was a bookish lad, and those books could be found even in Kingsport.) There was no anguish about this, no dark night of the soul. Quite the contrary: after all, being a freethinker was even more different—more special—than being an Episcopalian. I flaunted my new opinions, scandalizing some earnest young people, annoying some older ones (including my parents), and no doubt amusing some others. I think Mr. Kent knew the score: he asked once if I had any doubts that I wanted to discuss, but I was, oddly, reluctant to tell him. For once I kept my opinions to myself—somehow I felt that he would be disappointed in me. (I am certain now that I was wrong about that.)

In 1959, when I was seventeen, my involvement with Southern religion took a different turn, a commercial one. I got a summer job at a thousand-watt radio station in the little community of Church Hill, a few miles out of Kingsport. On weekdays I ran the "Noontime All-Hymn Program" for two hours, followed by three hours of top-forty rock and roll, then an hour and forty-five minutes of "Sunset Hymn Time." I dropped my voice an octave to read "the obituary column of the air," sponsored by Bruton snuff. ("Sure as shootin', you'll like Bruton. Bruton Scotch and Bruton Sweet, Bruton snuff just can't be beat.")

On Sundays I signed the station on at 7:00 AM and worked for thirteen hours straight. Aside from patching in a broadcast of the

11:00 service at Church Hill's First Baptist Church (the station owner's church), my job was to ride herd on an all-day parade of preachers and their flocks who bought time by the half-hour to worship in our studio and to spread the gospel throughout radioland. I took their money—fifteen dollars for thirty minutes, twenty-five for a full hour—and sat at a control board behind the glass to introduce them and to close them out with something like: "You've been listening to the Four-Square Gospel Hour, with the Reverend T. H. Phipps. This ministry needs your support. Please send your free-will love offering to Reverend Phipps at Box 24, Route 17, Surgoinsville, Tennessee."

Most of these folks were Baptists of one kind or another, but a few were tongue-talking Pentecostals who could be difficult to cut off when their time was up. (I never saw any serpents in the radio station, but my dad sometimes treated folks from up around Big Stone Gap whose faith had been insufficient.) All of the patrons of the station were white, but occasionally a black preacher would show up and ask to announce a revival or something. Invariably he was greeted warmly and introduced on the air as "Brother" so-and-so, and at least one was asked to lead a prayer, which he did. I have to say that these occasions were among the very few times I saw "separate but equal" actually work out that way.

I also remember in particular one preacher, a brawny countryman who drove a truck during the week and who often came into the control room after his hour was over. We talked and joked and gradually became friends. One day, out of the blue, he asked me quietly if I knew Jesus. Even a callow youth had to recognize that he was offering me, his friend, something very important to him. As with Mr. Kent, though, I didn't want to tell him the truth. I didn't want him to think less of me. So I lied.

I worked at WMCH, "your good neighbor station in Church Hill," three summers altogether. For my fifty-three-hour week, I received forty dollars, the glory of being what was not yet called a "media personality," and an acquaintance with white gospel music that is unusual, I believe, for an Episcopalian. I must say that I also came away with a lasting respect and sympathy for the more down-home varieties of Southern religious experience. Of course, as an advanced thinker myself, I held the primitive beliefs of these people in contempt, but I could not help noticing that they were good and decent folks—better Christians, by and large, than I was used to associating with. Nearly forty years later, when I saw Robert Duval's remarkable movie *The Apostle*, it brought it all back.

But much as I admired my preacher friend's commitment to his faith, I was not drawn to it myself, any more than I was to the more saccharine piety of the Methodists and downtown Baptists. Like many Southerners who don't go to church, I always knew which one I wasn't going to.

I didn't go to it for a long time. I left Kingsport for college smug in a sort of nineteenth-century scientism, and nothing I encountered in college at MIT or graduate school at Columbia did anything to undermine that. For ten years in Massachusetts and New York, I lived in an almost entirely secular world. Nearly all of my friends were irreligious or soon became so. Religion was something we rarely thought or talked about. It was an odd thing that a very few among us unaccountably did, like rock-climbing.

For sentimental and diplomatic reasons I did go to St Paul's when I was back home in Tennessee—in particular, every Christmas Eve with my girlfriend, who midway through that decade became my wife. We were married in the mammoth sanctuary of Broad Street Methodist, her church, but we were married by Mr. Kent, in a Prayer Book service, so it counts. (Dale's minister was conveniently on vacation that week.) Except for a couple of other weddings, however, I literally never went to church in Massachusetts or New York.

Finally, with a dissertation half-written and a child on the way, I took a job in Chapel Hill, and we shook the dust of New York City off our shoes. Not long after we returned to the South, I returned to the church. I was ready, but it helped that the Episcopal church in Chapel Hill had splendid music and, in Peter Lee (later the bishop of Virginia), an intelligent and amusing rector. Once again, a lot of reading was involved—some apologetics and theology, of course, but even more church history and liturgiology.

When some Episcopalians, in their cups, sing a little song to the tune of "God Bless America" that goes, in part, "Not a Methodist, Presbyterian, / Or a Baptist white with foam, / I am an Anglican, one step from Rome"—well, they are singing my song. I always knew that much of what I missed about the Episcopal Church was precisely what set it apart from Evangelical Protestantism. I missed the brocaded vestments of priest and deacon; the dark, carved wood of the pews and stalls; the glittering brass of candlesticks and crosses; the choral processions; hymns by Christina Rossetti, William Alexander Percy, and John Mason Neale; the calm, instructive sermons; and especially the stately and sonorous cadences of Thomas Cranmer's *Book of Common Prayer*.

When I returned to the church, I was baffled and irritated to find it in the process of junking the old Prayer Book, and I read everything I could find that might shed light on why anyone would want to do that. Although there were good historical, theological, or structural reasons for a few of the changes, most had been made for reasons that struck me (and still do) as fatuous. I have ever since regarded the new book as penance imposed for my time away—although why my poor ex-Methodist wife should have to suffer, too, is a mystery.

But I learned a lot from this course of reading. In particular, I slowly came to realize that much of what I loved about Anglican worship, the actual words of the Prayer Book aside, was not unbroken tradition from before the Reformation, as I had supposed, but Victorian innovation—the result of a conscious effort to turn back the clock, an effort that began with John Henry Newman and his friends in the Oxford Movement of the 1830s and culminated in the so-called Ritualism of the 1860s and 1870s. Today's Anglo-Catholics—like those high-church teenagers from Chattanooga I had met at Monteagle—were the Ritualists' direct descendants, but over the years Anglo-Catholics had moved the entire Anglican Communion in their direction. Even the ceremonial and decoration and architecture of our little low-church parish in east Tennessee looked like that of an early Oxford Movement church, not an Anglican church of, say, 1800.

Well, now. How did this happen? Smarting over the changes to the Prayer Book, I had reasons to be interested in successful reactionary movements. As a sociologist, I knew "the literature" on social movements, and knew what questions to ask—most obviously, who took up the movement, who opposed it, and why? But the more I read, the more I came to realize the truth of a remark by the ecclesiastical historian John Kent: "Somehow, the central problem remains untouched: why did a section of the nineteenth-century Anglican Church move so dogmatically and successfully back to a style of religious behaviour that had seemed so entirely abandoned in England?" There was a vast literature on and of Anglo-Catholicism, but no one had really asked that question—or rather, those who had, put it down to the operation of the Holy Spirit. That's an answer I would not dismiss out of hand, but it is not one that would satisfy the readers of the *American Journal of Sociology*.

I laid out the problem in a research proposal for the Guggenheim Foundation and was lucky enough to receive a fellowship (maybe the Holy Ghost at work again—who knows?). It let me spend a delightful year reading Victorian pamphlets and newspapers in London and Oxford, church-crawling in the towns and countryside of England, and exploring the amazing variety of Anglican worship—choral evensong at Christ Church, Oxford; morning prayer and sermon in little Norman village churches; high mass at All Saints Margaret Street; benediction and exposition in the chapel of Pusey House, Oxford. . . . but we are getting pretty far from east Tennessee here. The product of that year was a suitcase full of notes, and nearly twenty years later I finally published that book I mentioned, a volume called *Glorious Battle*, subtitled "The Cultural Politics of Victorian Anglo-Catholicism."

Irony is cheap these days—almost as devalued as memoir—but it is a central theme in that book. Let me close with a few words about that.

The law of unanticipated consequences applies to religious movements as much as to political ones, so much so in this case that I took as an epigraph a sentence from William Morris's *A Dream of John Ball*:

> I pondered all these things and how men fight and lose the battle and the thing that they fought for comes about in spite of their defeat, and when it come it turns out not to be what they meant, and other men have to fight for what they meant under a different name.

But the ironies that are relevant here have less to do with the story of Anglo-Catholicism than with the story of my writing that book. One reason it took me so long is that I couldn't tell the story I expected to tell when I started. As I read my way into the nineteenth century, my sympathies became less one-sidedly with the Anglo-Catholics. I had originally seen them as they saw themselves—as sturdy defenders of the historic faith, rolling back the obnoxious innovations of their Protestant foes. But I came to understand that from their opponents' point of view *they* were obnoxious innovators, imposing strange new practices on congregations who were content with their accustomed forms of worship—rather like the advocates of the new Prayer Book, in fact.

And there is another irony. Many prominent Anglo-Catholics were saintly men and women, and I try to do them justice in my account, but in the early days many enthusiasts for the movement were the kind of pert and insufferable young people who like to be different because it makes them special. This often makes for an amusing story, but I didn't find it entirely amusing because, in short, in some of the movement's less attractive followers I recognized myself.

Mea culpa.

Choosing the South

This was the first paper I gave at one of Bill Berry's conferences, but it seemed the best one with which to end the book.

Being asked to talk about my life, especially in the company of artists and writers, is a heady experience. Sociologists are seldom asked to do that. I would have said that there is probably a good reason for that, except that I have just been reading a recent collection of sociologists' autobiographical essays, *Authors of Their Own Lives*, and I find that some of my colleagues are more interesting people, and better writers, than you probably suppose—or than I did, for that matter. But such sociological autobiography is rare, and Bennett Berger, the editor of that collection, suggests that is because the norms of our profession discourage it: it is seen, he says, as "risky, embarrassing, and tasteless," as bad manners and bad science.

This may be changing—the publication of Berger's collection itself suggests as much—but for the benefit of any sociological brethren who wouldn't understand, or who would be envious, I thought about adopting the camouflage of a good, sociological subtitle: something like "Marginality and Regional Consciousness." That has echoes of Georg Simmel and Everett Stonequist, and is very respectable. I also considered something flashier, like "Living on the Edge: How I Became a Professional Southerner." In the end, as you can see, I sort of split the difference.

In fact, however, this essay is sociological, at least to the extent that it employs and illustrates a hoary sociological generalization, one that holds for *any* ethnic or cultural group. Applied to Southerners, it is simply this: those who are somehow marginal to the South seem to be more likely to *think about it* than those who are more comfortably and unquestionably Southern. This proposition has the paradoxical corollary that the most self-conscious Southerners are often the least typical, men and women whose backgrounds and experiences put them somehow on the edge of the regional group. That my own biography exemplifies all this simply confirms Andrew Greeley's observation in Berger's book that nearly all sociologists think of themselves as marginal and that many of us study the phenomena that put us in that situation. But let me say a bit about regional marginality in general before I turn to my own in particular.

* * *

For Southerners, one of the most common of the many paths to marginality these days is residence outside the South. Of course, some who leave the South simply stop being Southerners; for those who don't, however, leaving often turns out to be what has lately come to be called a "consciousness-raising experience." Louis Rubin has written of the importance of this experience in the biographies of Southern writers, and I have analyzed survey data to show similar effects for ordinary folks. Southerners who have lived outside the South are more likely than those who have not to say that they have thought about the South a lot, to say that they often think of themselves as Southerners, to believe that there are important differences between Southerners and other Americans, and to be ready to tell us what those differences are. This should not be surprising. Lord Acton observed once (not talking about Southerners, of course) that "exile is the nursery of nationalism, as oppression is the school of liberalism." Why think about the South if you have never known anything else?

I'll come back to this business of leaving the South. For now, let me just observe that there are other ways than physically to do it. You can, for instance, be *born* marginal. I don't have the numbers, but it is striking how many Southerners who write about the South have come from the edges of the region, from Texas or Arkansas or Tennessee or Kentucky—parts of the South remote from the region's cultural heartland, whether that be the antebellum Virginia-Carolina heartland or the Deep South that set the region's tone and defined its agenda well into this century. If you look at twentieth-century Southern intellectuals who have taken the South as their subject, I believe you will find far more from the upland South and the Southwest than random selection would predict. Those subregions have always stood in an equivocal relation to The South proper: if growing up there produces Southerners at all, it seems to produce especially thoughtful ones.

Marginality can also be familial. Growing up with parents from the wrong place, or the wrong ethnic group, can make you think. As Eudora Welty, the Mississippi daughter of a West Virginia mother and Ohio father, put it, you learn that there is usually more than one side to a story. People can be marginalized even by vicarious exposure to outsiders, through education or the mass media, for instance. And now that so many of our cities are receiving migrants from other parts, perhaps it is not surprising to find that *urban* Southerners show higher levels of regional consciousness than rural ones.

I could go on, but put all this together, and you get a recipe for intense self-consciousness. I wrote once about the Nashville Agrarians, authors in the 1930s of *I'll Take My Stand*, pointing out that all twelve were highly educated, all had become urban, all had lived outside the South, and three-quarters came originally from the outer South. These characteristics made them very unusual Southerners in the 1930s, and also (I argued) guaranteed that they would give the South a good deal of thought.

There is a danger here. There are so many ways to become marginal that we can probably find at least one of these factors in the background of any Southerner, self-conscious or not. We need some careful statistical analysis before we conclude that there is a link between marginality and consciousness. But, as a matter of fact, I have done that analysis, in a book called *Southerners: The Social Psychology of Sectionalism*, and the link exists. Regional consciousness, it appears, is heightened (1) by urban upbringing and residence, (2) by education, (3) by exposure to the national mass media, and (4) by travel and residence outside the South.

*   *   *

OK, enough about my work. Let's talk about me. How did I become regionally conscious, to the point of spending most of my professional life writing and talking about the South? The short answer is that I had little choice: I grew up in the upper South, in a town with an abnormally high concentration of Northern immigrants, one of them my own mother. I lingered in college and graduate school indecently long, and (most important, I think) I did so in Boston and New York. Looking back I can see that my raising and even my ancestry constantly put me on the boundary between the South and the . . . *non*-South, the Other (if you will) that defines the South. I can't remember a time when I didn't know that there was a South and that it was different.

Start with where I come from. The names of the elementary schools in my hometown will tell you that to within a hundred miles: George Washington (no help there), but also Robert E. Lee and Frederick Douglass—plainly we are in the South. Add Andrew Jackson (probably the upper South), Abraham Lincoln (the reconstructed South), and (the dead giveaway) Andrew Johnson: obviously upper east Tennessee, the old State of Franklin.

Now, to be sure, east Tennessee is Southern, as those school names indicate. There are other markers as well: Baptists, moonshine whiskey, country music, family feuds, stock-car racing, Moon Pies (from Chattanooga)—all of these indicators put it firmly in the South. But it is a funny *kind* of South. For starters, it is overwhelmingly white (there were hardly enough black kids to segregate) and, partly in consequence, between 1861 and 1865 attachment to the Confederate government in Richmond was a sometime thing, at best. Many mountain men spent the war years burning each others' barns and dodging the Union and Confederate drafts with fine impartiality. I mentioned Andrew Johnson, a self-taught tailor from Greenville and an east Tennessee homeboy with little use for flatland aristocrats. Tennessee's Reconstruction governor was a Methodist preacher from Knoxville, Parson Brownlow, a low-life opportunist, perhaps, but one who had a fine Southern way with words. (After one Confederate defeat, for instance, he chortled gleefully that "F.F.V." should stand for "fleet-footed Virginians.")

Moreover, my hometown of Kingsport is a funny part of east Tennessee. For all intents and purposes, it was founded just before 1920 as a company town, site of an Eastman Kodak branch plant. So when I was growing up, engineers and executives from Rochester, New York, were constantly cycling through town, with their families. The plant and the other industries that grew up around it—a paper mill, a press, textile mills, a munitions factory, a glass plant, cement works— attracted workers and executives from other parts of the country, too, in particular from the lowland South. (My high-school girlfriend, now my wife, is the daughter of Georgians, her father an Eastman engineer.)

Given all this, perhaps it is not surprising that relatively good-natured roughhousing between Yanks and Rebs was a regular feature of my junior-high lunchtimes. Like Bill Clinton, I was a jolly fat boy and usually contrived to avoid these scuffles, but I confess that my sympathies and, when necessary, my fists were with the bluebellies, because the distinction was more political than social, and as much contemporary as historical: to a great extent Yankee and Rebel meant the same thing as Republican and Democrat, and my family is Republican on both the native and the immigrant sides.

My father's people have been in east Tennessee and southwest Virginia since the eighteenth century (because, the family joke has it, some Carolinian forebears were looking for the Cumberland Gap and couldn't find it), but most of my father's ancestors were Scotch-Irish and Germans who came down the Shenandoah Valley from Pennsylvania. (Perhaps there were some "Melungeons," too, but that's another story.) Like most folks with roots in the Southern hills, we have kin who fought on both sides and neither between 1861 and 1865. Tennessee's Confederate Senator Landon Carter Haynes may have been some kind of cousin, but family lore says that another ancestor was the captain of a Unionist home guard unit in southwest Virginia, a man who fought "the Democrats" (as his daughter put it later)—until they killed him. I don't know much about this forebear and I am reluctant to look into it because I like the story the way I have it, but as I've heard it his daughter spoke of going with a slave woman to retrieve his frozen body from the wintry mountaintop battlefield. In other words, this ancestor was apparently a slaveholding Unionist (which may suggest that my folks have always had a way of missing the point). If so, however, he must have been the sort of yeoman Daniel Hundley of Alabama described dismissively in 1859, who "works side by side with his slaves in the fields and is not dismayed when they call him familiarly by his Christian name." This image of slavery—a smallholder and one or two slaves working the fields together, calling each other "Bob" and "Jimmy"—is not the image most familiar to us, and of course it was not the experience of most slaves, but it may have been the experience of most *slaveholders*, especially in the upland South.

Anyway, in the mountains confused loyalties did not end with Appomattox (for that matter, neither did the fighting, which continued in some parts in the guise of family feuds). My grandfather was supposedly kin to "Uncle Alf" and "Fiddling Bob" Taylor, sons of a Unionist father and Confederate mother, who ran against each other for governor in the famous Tennessee election of 1886 known at the time as the War of the Roses. (Robert Love Taylor, the Democrat, won that one, but Alfred was finally elected in the Republican landslide of 1920.)

All these genealogical facts may begin to explain not only my interest in the South but my politics. Some yellow-dog Democrats I know still see support for the Democracy as a badge of Southernness and reproach me for my habit of voting Republican or staying home. But

I make no apologies for supporting the Grand Old Party of Richard Petty and Roy Acuff. No Republican ever killed a relative of mine.

Twenty-five years before me, my father left Kingsport to go to college in the North, in his case with an Eastman scholarship to the University of Rochester. There he met my mother, a Rochester girl—that is, as I said, a Yankee. She was not just a courtesy Yankee, either, but the real thing, with New England names like Peabody and Griswold scattered about the family tree, intermixed with more recent immigrants (and, speaking of marginality, with some pretty odd sorts: Alsatian Germans and Anglo-Irish). After my father finished medical school, my parents moved to New York City where he did his internship and residency, and where, to my embarrassment every time I have to show my passport, I was born. (As the Duke of Wellington growled when someone referred to his Irish birth, just because someone was born in a stable, doesn't mean he's a horse.)

Shortly after World War II we moved back to Kingsport, to the house my grandparents built, and it has always been home to me. Some of my earliest memories, however, are of summer vacations in the Finger Lakes country with Northern aunts, uncles, and cousins—that, and the interminable drive up the Shenandoah Valley on US 11, retracing in reverse the Reeds' trek of two hundred years before, past Dr. Childress's Snake and Monkey Farm, Burma-Shave signs, and historical markers for Stuart and Sheridan and Mosby, through the little towns of the Valley to Winchester, where we usually stopped for the night, then on the next morning into the North: to Hagerstown, Chambersburg, and beyond.

The upshot of all this was that I finished high school with an exceptional degree of regional *consciousness* but without a strong regional *identity* (to employ a distinction elaborated in that book *Southerners* I mentioned earlier). I certainly knew that some folks were Southerners and others were not, and despite my junior-high lunchtime Unionist sympathies, I knew I was a Southerner. (I had my Northern cousins to remind me.) But I didn't feel strongly about it. It was just a fact, one of many answers to the question "Who are you?", but pretty far down the list.

When I enrolled at the Massachusetts Institute of Technology in 1960, however, it moved up in importance. My reasons for going to college in the North had little to do with getting out of the South, or anything like that. It's just that I was pretty hot stuff in east Tennessee algebra circles, thought I wanted to be a mathematician, and MIT sounded like a good place to go if that's what you wanted to be. But

I would be lying if I said I didn't know what Thomas Wolfe meant when he wrote of going north that "every young man from the South has felt this precise and formal geography of the spirit, this tension of the nerves, . . . this gritting of the teeth and hardening of the jaws, this sense of desperate anticipation"—and so forth, at length. It *was* exciting to be on my own in a big, strange Yankee city. I learned a good many things in Cambridge, and later at graduate school in New York City, among them that I am not a mathematician and that I really am a Southerner. In their different ways, those discoveries changed my life.

Autobiography strikes me as an act of presumption in the young, but the importance for my subsequent work of where I went to school was so obvious to me that, at the ripe old age of thirty-nine, I wrote an essay about it. Maybe cognizant at some level of the norms Berger mentioned, I put it in a rather coy third person, but it's me, all right. In Cambridge, my "young Tennessean" learned that

> however unimportant his origins seemed to him, they were an important datum for others, a marker that they used to orient themselves to him, at least at first. The more ill-mannered of his Northern acquaintances made it clear that they saw him as a curious specimen of some sort; a few, at least, saw his Southernness as the salient fact about him, overriding all others.

This account goes on at almost Wolfean length, and I won't quote myself anymore (the essay was reprinted in my book, *One South*). The point is just that "the result of all this was that Southerners in Cambridge at that time almost had to think about the South." Certainly I did, and I began to read about it, too, although this reading had to be on the side, since (so far as I know) MIT didn't offer any courses in Southern history or literature. Anyway, it never occurred to me that I could do my Southern studies for credit, much less as a career.

After I moved on to graduate school at Columbia, I continued to think and read about the South, and to return to it when I could. I was prompted by my Northern friends' curiosity about it and increasingly by my own. But it was not until I took a course on evaluation research that I finally wrote something about it. Our assignment in that course was to assess the effectiveness of some social-action program, and I undertook to evaluate a group from the 1930s that I had read about (in *The Mind of the South*, I think) called the Association of Southern Women for the Prevention of Lynching. Somehow I learned that the Association's records were in the library of Atlanta University, so

I drove to Atlanta from Kingsport one Christmas vacation and immersed myself in those papers (and, insofar as a Southern white boy could in three days, in the life of that remarkable institution). The resulting term paper became my first professional publication, an article in the journal *Social Problems*.

But that paper was a sport. I still thought of myself as an aspiring methodologist, and only an incidental and amateur student of the South—witness the fact that when I ventured out of the sociology department for courses I went only as far as social psychology, not to Columbia's excellent department of history. My next venture in writing about the South, my dissertation, started out as a methodological exercise.

One of my teachers at Columbia was the great methodologist and mathematical sociologist, Paul Felix Lazarsfeld. My math background gave me a considerable advantage with Lazarsfeld, and I soon found myself working as both a teaching and research assistant for this remarkable man. Lazarsfeld was a Viennese Jew, a refugee from the Nazis. His mother had been an early psychoanalyst, a student and analysand of Freud himself; young Paul and Anna Freud had been playmates. As a teenage socialist, Lazarsfeld reputedly took over the Vienna radio station at gunpoint in the revolution of 1919. Trained in mathematics and psychology, he wrote well in three languages and spoke some others, played viola in a string quartet, and was, in short, a splendid example of Mittel Europa at its finest. He could not have been a more exotic figure to an east Tennessee boy like me if he had come from the moon.

My relation with Lazarsfeld, incidentally, is one reason I am skeptical about the claim that students need "role models" from backgrounds like their own. My own education was almost entirely at the hands of teachers who extended my experience and challenged my ignorance in fundamental ways. Lazarsfeld found my growing interest in the South amusing (from his perspective American regional differences were trivial), and I remember his telling me about his son's visit to Texas. Asked what was different from New York, young Robbie had reported that the license plates were a different color.

Anyway, both Lazarsfeld and my other principal teacher, the distinguished survey researcher Herbert Hyman, were enthusiastic about the potential for "secondary analysis," taking old public opinion surveys and reanalyzing them to answer questions other than those they were designed to address. When it came time for me to write a dissertation,

I undertook to produce an example of this sort of work, by using thirty years' worth of Gallup Polls to document the decrease in regional differences in attitudes and values as the South had become an urban, industrial region increasingly like the rest of the United States.

To make a long story short: that was not what I found. Again and again, the differences I was looking at turned out to be as large in the 1960s as they had been twenty or thirty years earlier, and they couldn't be made to go away by statistical controls for the demographic differences between the South and the rest of the country. I came to know the despair of the graduate student whose dissertation is falling apart in his hands, until I lit upon not so much an explanation as a category of similar, puzzling phenomena: the idea that Southerners were behaving like the immigrant ethnic groups that I had come to know in Boston and New York, groups whose own resistance to assimilation was just then being discovered and chronicled in books with titles like *Beyond the Melting Pot* and *The Rise of the Unmeltable Ethnics*. The quite unexpected result was a dissertation later published with the title *The Enduring South: Subcultural Persistence in Mass Society.*

Once Lazarsfeld had set me the task of compiling his bibliography, comprising hundreds of articles, in several languages, published over a forty-year period. When I marveled at his prolixity, he remarked that all of these publications were merely working out the implications of four original ideas. Not a modest man, he quickly added that this is four more than most people have, and three more than it takes to make a career. The idea that Southerners can be viewed as an ethnic group has been my career-making idea. As I learned later, it was not even original with me, but it has turned out to be a powerful metaphor. With that in place, the outlines of almost everything I have done since were pretty well set. Since then, I have used the tools of my trade and any others I could lay hands on to explore the ethnic analogy I hit on back there in graduate school, to sort out as best I could what Southerness is all about—which is to say, in this respect, who I am. I was lucky to stumble into a line of work where I can actually make a living from this sort of self-examination: most people have to pay for psychotherapy. But it is sobering to realize that if I had gone to the University of Tennessee, or Vanderbilt, or Chapel Hill, or Georgia Tech, I would almost certainly be doing something else today. Probably not mathematics, though.

Sources

"The Three Souths." From *Centennial Olympic Games Official Souvenir Program: Games of the XXVI Olympiad*, Atlanta, Georgia, 1996. © 1996 Atlanta Committee for the Olympic Games.

"*The Mind of the South* and Southern Distinctiveness." From Charles W. Eagles (ed.), The Mind of the South: *Fifty Years Later* (Jackson: University Press of Mississippi, 1992).

"The *Times* Looks at Dixie" (review of Peter Applebome, *Dixie Rising: How the South Is Shaping American Values, Politics, and Culture*, 1996). Originally published as "South of the Times," *The Oxford American*, January/February 1997.

"Among the Believers" (review of V. S Naipaul, *A Turn in the South*, 1989). From *Journal of Southern History* 56 (August 1990).

"The Secret History of Civil Rights" (review of Hunter James, *They Didn't Put That on the Huntley-Brinkley!: A Vagabond Reporter Encounters the New South*, 1993; originally published as "Southern Discomfort"). Reprinted, with permission, from the January 1994 issue of *Reason* magazine. Copyright 2003 by Reason Foundation, 3415 S. Sepulveda Blvd., Suite 400, Los Angeles, CA 90034. Website: www.reason.com

"The Smoke Never Clears" (talk on Tony Horwitz, *Confederates in the Attic: Dispatches from the Unfinished Civil War*, 1998). Not previously published.

"One Tough Lady" (review of Florence King, *Lump It or Leave It*, 1992). From *News and Observer* (Raleigh, NC), 8 July 1990.

"A South That Never Was" (review of B. C. Hall and C. T. Wood, *The South*, 1995). Originally published as "The South, Believe It or Not," *Washington Post*, 20 June 1995.

"American Weed" (review of T. H. Breen, *Tobacco Culture: The Mentality of the Great Tidewater Planters on the Eve of the Revolution*, 1985). From *Tobacco Observer*, August 1986.

"Slaves View Slavery" (review of Norman Yetman, ed., *Life under the "Peculiar Institution": Selections from the Slave Narrative Collection*, 1970). From *The Alternative*, January 1973. Courtesy of *The American Spectator* magazine.

"Slipshod Totalitarianism" (review of John Hope Franklin and Loren Schweninger, *Runaway Slaves: Rebels on the Plantation, 1790–1860*, 1999, and William L. Andrews and Henry Louis Gates Jr., eds., *The Civitas Anthology of African American Slave Narratives*, 1999). From *Times Literary Supplement*, 30 June 1999.

"Southern Intellect" (review of Michael O'Brien, ed., *All Clever Men, Who Make Their Way: Critical Discourse in the Old South*, 1982; Fred Hobson, ed.,

"The Southern Elvis." Originally published as "Elvis as Southerner," in Vernon Chadwick (ed.), *In Search of Elvis* (Boulder: Westview Press, 1997).

"The End of Elvis" (review of Peter Guralnick, *Careless Love: The Unmaking of Elvis Presley*, 1999). From *The Oxford American*, Summer 1999.

"Southern Laughter." Portions originally published in *Southern Cultures* 1 (Summer 1995).

"A Cokelorist at Work" (review of Mark Pendergrast, *For God, Country, and Coca-Cola*, 1993). From *Washington Monthly*, June 1993. Reprinted with permission from *The Washington Monthly*. Copyright by Washington Monthly Publishing, LLC, 733 15th St. NW, Suite 1000, Washington, DC 20005. (202) 393–5155. Website: www.washingtonmonthly.com.

"The National Magazine of the South" (review of John Logue and Gary McCalla, *Life at Southern Living: A Sort of Memoir*, 2000). From *Journal of Southern History* 68 (May 2002).

"Carolina Couch Crime" (originally published as "Carolina Couch Controversy"). Reprinted, with permission, from the March 1998 issue of *Reason* magazine. Copyright 2003 by Reason Foundation, 3415 S. Sepulveda Blvd., Suite 400, Los Angeles, CA 90034. Website: www.reason.com

"Taking a Stand." Originally published as "On the Agrarians' *I'll Take My Stand*," in David Perkins, ed., *Books of Passage: 27 North Carolina Writers on Books That Changed Their Lives* (Asheboro, N.C.: Down Home Press, 1996).

"Portrait of Atlanta" (review of Tom Wolfe, *A Man in Full*, 1998). Originally published as "On Being a Man, in Fulton County," *Oxford American*, January/February 1999.

"Nebbish from Mississippi" (review of Richard Ford, *Independence Day*, 1995). From *National Review*, 25 September 1995. © 1995 by National Review, Inc., 215 Lexington Avenue, New York, NY 10016. Reprinted by permission.

"Hollywood Chain Gangs." Originally published as "Southern Discomfort: A Southerner Revisits *Cool Hand Luke*," *AMC: American Movie Classics Magazine*, November 2000.

"The Banner That Won't Stay Furled." From *Southern Cultures* 8 (Spring 2002).

"The Most Southern State?" Originally published as "Florida: The Most Southern State?" In *Forum: The Magazine of the Florida Humanities Council*, Spring 2003.

"Brits and Grits." From *Brightleaf*, September/October 1997.

"Missing." From *Brightleaf*, Fall 1998.

"He's Baaack" (with Merle Black). Not previously published.

"If at First You Don't Secede . . ." Originally published as "The Decline (and Return?) of Localism," *The American Enterprise*, January 2000.

"Party Down" (interview by Van Denton). Originally published as "The South Is Distinctive, but Most Southerners Aren't Ready to Secede," *News and Observer* (Raleigh, NC), 20 June 1999.

"Our Kind of Yankee." Originally published as "A View from the South," *The American Enterprise*, June 2002.

"Choosing the South," not previously published.

"Mixing in the Mountains." From *Southern Cultures* 3, no. 4 (Winter 1997).

"Among the Baptists." Originally published as "Among the Baptists: Reflections of an East Tennessee Episcopalian," in John B. Boles, ed., *Autobiographical Reflections on Southern Religious History* (Athens: University of Georgia Press, 2001). Reprinted by permission of Bill Berry.